KISSING THE TRAIL
NORTHWEST & CENTRAL OREGON

KISSING THE TRAIL
NORTHWEST & CENTRAL OREGON

MOUNTAIN BIKE TRAILS

JOHN ZILLY

SASQUATCH BOOKS
SEATTLE

Printed in the United States of America
Distributed in Canada by Raincoast Books, Ltd.
04 03 02 01 00   5 4 3 2 1

Research assistance: Spencer Harris
Cover and interior design and composition: Kate Basart
Cover photograph: Colin Meagher/In-Motion Photography
Interior photographs: John Zilly, Spencer Harris, Greg Strong
Maps: John Zilly
Copy editor: Kris Fulsaas

Library of Congress Cataloging in Publication Data is available.
Library of Congress Card Number 00-103248
ISBN 1-57061-211-0

Important Disclaimer: Please use common sense. No guidebook can act as a substitute for careful planning and appropriate training. Know your personal limits; it is incumbent upon any user of this guide to assess his or her own skills, experience, fitness, and equipment. There is inherent danger in mountain biking and in the trails described in this book, and readers must assume responsibility for their own actions and safety. Changing or unfavorable conditions in weather, roads, trails, waterways, etc. cannot be anticipated by the author or publisher, but should be considered by any outdoor participants, as trails may become dangerous or unrideable due to such altered conditions. Likewise, be aware of any changes in public jurisdiction. Do not ride on private property without permission. The author and the publisher will not be responsible or liable for your safety or the consequences of using this guide.

The information in this edition is based on facts available at press time and is subject to change. The author and publisher welcome information or updates conveyed by users of this book.

SASQUATCH BOOKS
615 Second Avenue
Seattle, Washington 98104
(206) 467-4300
books@SasquatchBooks.com
www.SasquatchBooks.com

For Dova Isabel
Let your heart choose the trail

Thank you Spencer Harris. Your work and companionship were essential, and the book is better because of your help. Thanks also to Alan Bennett, Marea Castañeda, Jim Emery, Mark Flint, David Graves, Greg Strong, and, of course, Cinda, Dave, Eric, Holly, and Riz.

Northwest & Central Oregon

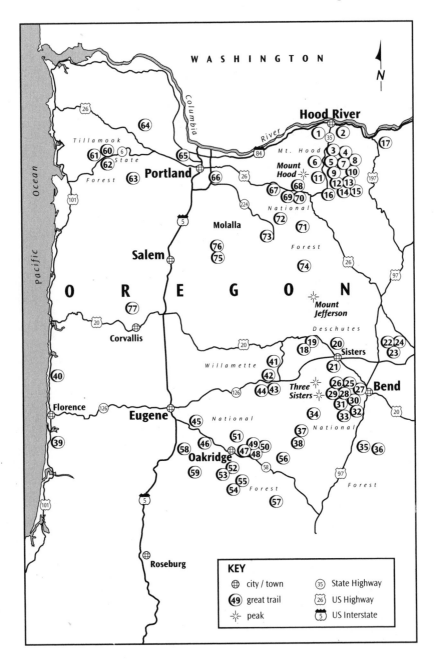

Contents

Rides by Difficulty, Season, Views

Ride №	Ride Name	Spring	Summer	Fall	Winter	Views
2	Historic Highway 30	●	●	●	●	●
27	First Street Rapids	●	●	●	●	
58	Row River	●	●	●	●	

Ride №	Ride Name	Spring	Summer	Fall	Winter	Views
6	East Fork Hood River		●	●		
17	Lower Deschutes Rail-Trail	●	●	●	●	●
22	Smith Rock	◐	●	●		●
40	Siltcoos Lake	●	●	●		
42	McKenzie River Short	◐	●	●		
45	Elijah Bristow State Park	●	●	●		
48	Salmon Creek Warrior Trail	●	●	●		
64	Banks-Vernonia Trail	●	●	●	●	
65	Forest Park	●	●	●	●	
68	Crosstown Trail		●	●		
71	Timothy Lake		●	●		●

Ride №	Ride Name	Spring	Summer	Fall	Winter	Views
1	Post Canyon	●	●	●	◐	
5	Dog River		●	●		
7	Eightmile Creek		●	●		●
8	Knebal Springs		●	●		
11	Umbrella Falls		●	●		
15	Boulder Lakes		◐	●		●
16	Mineral Creek		●	●		
19	Suttle Lake	◐	●	●		●
20	Black Butte	◐	●	●		●
21	Peterson Ridge	◐	●	●		●
23	Burma Road	◐	●	●		●
25	Shevlin Park	◐	●	●		

Ride №	Ride Name	Spring	Summer	Fall	Winter	Views
26	Mrazek		●	●		
28	Tumalo Falls		●	●		●
29	Swampy Lakes		●	●		●
30	Phil's Trail 24.5	◐	●	●		
32	Deschutes River	◐	●	●		
37	Cultus Lake		◐	●		●
38	Lemish Lake		◐	●		●
39	Cummins Creek	●	●	●	●	●
43	Olallie Mountain		●	●		●
47	Salmon Creek Loop	●	●	●		
49	Aubrey Mountain	◐	●	●		
50	Dead Mountain	◐	●	●		
52	Larison Rock		●	●		
54	Middle Fork Willamette	◐	●	●		
59	Brice Creek	◐	●	●		
60	Gales Creek	●	●	●		
61	Tillamook Burn	●	●	●		
63	Hagg Lake	●	●	●		
66	Powell Butte	●	●	●	●	
70	Ski Bowl		●	●		●
73	Clackamas Riverside		●	●		
75	Molalla Rim	●	●	●		
76	Molalla North	●	●	●		
77	Dimple Hill	●	●	●		

Ride №	Ride Name	Spring	Summer	Fall	Winter	Views
3	Surveyors Ridge		●	●		●
9	High Prairie		●	●		●
10	Fifteenmile Creek		●	●		
12	Gunsight Ridge		●	●		●
14	Badger Lake		●	●		●
18	Cache Mountain		●	●		●
24	Gray Butte	◐	●	●		●
31	Phil's Helipad		●	●		
33	Storm King		●	●		

Ride Nº	Ride Name	Spring	Summer	Fall	Winter	Views
34	Lava Lake		●	●		●
35	Paulina Creek		●	●		●
36	Newberry Caldera		◐	●		●
41	McKenzie River		●	●		●
44	King Castle		●	●		●
46	Hardesty Mountain		●	●		
51	Buckhead Mountain		●	●		
53	Larison Creek		●	●		●
55	Moon Point		●	●		●
56	Waldo Lake		◐	●		●
57	Windy Lakes		◐	●		●
62	Standard Grade	●	●	●		
67	Flag Mountain		●	●		
69	Still Creek		●	●		
72	Dry Ridge		●	●		
74	Red Lake		●	●		●

Ride Nº	Ride Name	Spring	Summer	Fall	Winter	Views
4	Surveyors Epic		●	●		●
13	East Mount Hood Epic		◐	●		●

Choosing a Ride

You ought to be able to select an appropriate ride, find the trailhead without getting lost, and then easily negotiate the route (okay, for epic rides all bets are off). This is the guiding principle, as it were, of *Kissing the Trail: Northwest & Central Oregon*. The following describes the book's rating system, explains how the information is presented, and provides an annotated look at some of the wording conventions I use to detail each ride.

Difficulty Rating

The difficulty rating is measured in wheels, ranging from one to five, with one wheel being easiest and five wheels being hardest. The difficulty rating is based on the length of the trip, the steepness of the hills and elevation gain, and the level of bike-handling skill required. This quick reference is located near the title of each ride.

⊕ *(easy):* Just about anyone can make it through a ride rated as one wheel. These rides are short and flat, have well-packed (sometimes paved) riding surfaces, and are perfect for families.

⊕⊕ *(intermediate):* Two-wheel rides primarily traverse dirt roads and rail-trails, although they occasionally venture onto easily negotiated doubletrack and singletrack. These rides are somewhat longer and may have more elevation gain than those rated one wheel. However, they never demand a high skill level, and riders will rarely need to hike-a-bike.

⊕⊕⊕ *(difficult):* More rides in this book receive this rating than any other. These routes—all of which contain some singletrack—travel less than 18 miles and have moderate elevation gains, generally less than 1,600 feet. Typically, a ride rated three wheels combines a dirt-road climb with a singletrack descent. Be prepared for at least a few steep climbs as well as a few rough, technical sections of trail that may require hike-a-biking.

⊕⊕⊕⊕ *(most difficult):* If a ride is long, hilly, and chock-full of challenging singletrack, I have rated it four wheels. Some riders may have to push or carry their bikes for long distances. You'll gain big chunks of elevation and have your bike-handling skills tested on every four wheeler. Remember: If you're not hiking, you're not mountain biking.

⊕⊕⊕⊕⊕ *(extreme epic):* Only two rides in this book are sufficiently difficult to warrant an extreme, epic rating of five wheels. These rides are very long, technical, hilly, and may require miles of walking or hike-a-biking as well as complex route-finding. Do not attempt them unless you are an expert mountain bicyclist, in great physical condition, and enjoy pushing yourself to the limit.

Ride Statistics

Distance
This information is given in miles, along with the ride's format, either loop, out-and-back, one-way, figure eight, or lollipop.

Terrain
Here I note, in synopsis form, the riding surface, the type of trail, the difficulty of the climbs, and the elevation gain. If the word "views" appears on this line, then on clear days you should expect to see a snow-capped volcano, a spectacular mountain lake, a panoramic vista, or all of the above.

Duration
The duration of a ride depends on your skill, stamina, and map-reading abilities, as well as what you did the previous night. Trail conditions and weather can also drastically alter the time it takes to complete a ride. Before you leave, call to find out about current trail and weather conditions.

Travel
The driving distance from nearby towns or cities is listed.

Skill level
Rides are rated for beginner, intermediate, advanced, or expert, depending on the minimum bike-handling ability a rider should have before attempting a particular trail. This rating has nothing to do with fitness; you may be a fine athlete, but I wouldn't recommend an expert trail if you have never mountain biked before.

Season
This entry lists the best time of year to be out on this trail.

Maps
Supplementary maps are extremely helpful, unless you enjoy bivouacking. I typically recommend United States Geological Survey (USGS) topographical maps, United States Forest Service (USFS) ranger district maps, or Green Trails maps.

Restrictions
Here I note which trailheads require parking and trail-use passes. Seasonal trail closures are also noted. Call the managing agency for current trail conditions and restrictions.

More info
The agency that manages the trail is named, and a phone number and Web site are provided. For current trail conditions, maintenance schedule, snow level, permit information, and other restrictions, call ahead.

The Scoop

Each ride begins with a descriptive overview, with trail notes and other anecdotes.

Driving Directions

This paragraph provides detailed instructions for driving to the trailhead. In most cases, I have indicated a point at which you should set the trip odometer in your car to zero.

The Ride

In addition to notes about the terrain, and an occasional quip, the ride section contains a detailed description of the route—up or down, left or right. These paragraphs note the mileage—in bold—for most intersections, hills, tricky sections of trail, vistas, and other significant landmarks. Riding with an odometer is highly recommended.

What follows is an annotated listing of some of the conventions I use in describing the trails in *Kissing the Trail: Northwest & Central Oregon*. **WHOA!** signifies a dangerous section of trail or a turn easily missed, and warns the rider to pay close attention. **WOOF!** identifies the top of a particularly difficult climb. **Stay on the main trail/road** means that other trails or roads exit from the main route—use good judgment to continue on the primary trail or road. When the trail dead-ends at another trail, forcing a 90-degree turn either right or left, the resulting three-way intersection is described as a **T**. Other three-way intersections are usually described as **forks**, though sometimes I write that the **trail divides**. If a faint trail or lesser trail forks off the main trail, I will sometimes tell you to **ignore**, **pass**, or **bypass** rather than describe it as a fork. When two trails or roads cross, the result is usually referred to as a **four-way** intersection. On many trails you'll have to **walk** or **push** your bike up a steep hill. If, however, a long stretch of trail requires an awkward combination of walking and riding, I describe it as a **hike-a-bike**. A **technical** section of trail—typically a narrow tread or steep slope populated by roots, rocks, or other obstacles—demands good bike-handling skills. An especially technical section of trail may be referred to as an **expert** or **trials** section. On unmaintained or faint trails, on trails transformed by clearcutting and road building, and in areas that have mazes of trails, it's sometimes difficult to figure out which way to go. In these instances, I'll likely mention the problematic **route-finding**.

A number of different types of trails and roads are described in this book. A dirt or gravel **road** could be used by a car. Roads in national forests are usually identified by a number preceded by **FR** for Forest Road. **Doubletracks,** also know as **old roads**, refer to narrow, rough roads and may be either motorized or nonmotorized. Sometimes these old roads are **gated** to keep out motor vehicles. Old railroad grades, or **rail-trails**, are abandoned railroad lines that have no tracks or ties. Typically, rail-trails have the look and feel of dirt roads, although rail-trails are almost always flat and nonmotorized. **Trail** and **singletrack**, terms that are used interchangeably, generally refer to soft-surface trails less than 36 inches wide. A **wide trail** refers to a path 3 to 8 feet wide. Sometimes, however, "trail" is used in a generic sense to mean any part of a route, whether paved or soft-surface, between 12 inches and 12 feet wide.

Option

For some rides, I have provided directions to modify the route, to bail out early, bag a peak, catch a nice view, or just noodle along an extra stretch of singletrack.

Gazetteer

Each ride concludes with information on nearby campgrounds and services. The information on the nearest town helps you pinpoint the ride's location, identify the nearest gas station, and lets you know which direction to head to satisfy that Ben & Jerry's craving. Use the information under Gazetteer to plan weekend trips and extended excursions.

Maps and GPS Features

I recorded the route, mileage, and elevation data using a Global Positioning System (GPS) receiver, a cycle computer, two altimeters, and a whole bunch of Sharpies. Using these tools, I wrote the text and created the maps for *Kissing the Trail: Northwest & Central Oregon*. The unique feature of these maps is certainly the GPS data. Using a network of space-based satellites, GPS receivers monitor and track latitude and longitude.

I recorded the twists and turns of every route, then used that track data to create the maps. In some cases, the maps in *Kissing the Trail* are more accurate than any other existing map. (Keep in mind, though, that recreational GPS receivers have a small error factor.) In addition to recording the track data, I used the receiver to make a series of waypoints (GPS lingo for an exact location) for each ride, which I call Ridepoints. Individual Ridepoints are marked on the maps by numbered triangles at key junctures along the ride; you'll also find a complete list of Ridepoints—a route—for each ride in a small box on the map.

The Ridepoint numbers are latitude and longitude coordinates (WGS 84 map datum; dd°mm.mmm format). Ridepoint 1 is the trailhead. To use the Ridepoints, punch the coordinates into your GPS receiver the night before a ride. The following day, your receiver will point toward each successive Ridepoint for the entire loop and tell you where you are in relationship to the other Ridepoints.

Additional map features: The start and finish of each ride are clearly visible, and the highlighted route prevents map face—squinted eyes and a furrowed brow. Arrows indicate the direction of travel, and intermediary trail mileages are noted between the triangular Ridepoints. Key elevations are highlighted, and elevation profiles show all of the ups and downs.

Safety: Keep the Rubber Side Down

At the top of an epic descent, a friend turned to me and said, "Have fun and keep the rubber side down." As he pedaled away his smile indicated he was having fun, but he didn't heed his second piece of advice. And at the bottom he didn't say, "You should try that skin-side-down technique sometime."

Though it's probably more dangerous to drive to the trailhead, bicycling injuries such as cracked collarbones, dislocated shoulders, and fractured wrists are all too common. If, after a crash, you're lucky, you'll hop up and shake it off. If you've sustained serious injuries, extra clothes and a first-aid kit could save your life. But the danger of mountain biking isn't just the spectacular crash. A simple mechanical failure, a sore knee, a wrong turn, or exhaustion can strand you miles from the trailhead and force an unplanned night in the woods. If you don't have the proper supplies and a friend to plan strategy with, you could be in trouble. Often, the worst trouble is self-inflicted: panic and hysteria. If you stay calm, if you have enough to eat and drink, and if you have an extra layer of clothing to put on, you will probably be fine.

Before You Leave
- How's the trail? Is it hunting season? Call the managing agency.
- Check out the mountain weather.
- Let someone know where you plan to ride.

During the Ride
- Never ride alone.
- Always wear a helmet and eye protection.
- Avoid excessive speed. Ride as if a small child is around every corner.
- Carry a first-aid kit.
- Carry extra clothes and a hat, no matter how nice the weather seems.
- Pack sunscreen, a lighter, a pocket knife, extra food, and a flashlight.
- Drink at least two quarts of water per day. Don't count on finding water.
- Carry a map of the area and bring a compass.
- Use a cycle computer.

Recommended Tools
- pump
- patch kit
- extra tube
- tire irons
- spoke wrench
- chain tool
- Allen wrenches
- needle-nose pliers
- crescent wrench
- screwdriver
- spare brake cable

The Trail-Use Debate

Other trail users, sometimes even other mountain bikers, will tell you to get off the trail—you shouldn't be there, it's bad for the trail, there are too many conflicts. That attitude closes a lot of trails, and mountain bikers have borne the brunt of those closures. But if bicyclists ride smart, they don't hurt the environment and they don't cause conflicts. With the number of trail users growing, expectations need to adjust: If you choose a trail that's convenient and popular, then it's absurd to have expect a solitary meditation. The good news is that if you are willing to drive a little farther to a lesser-known trailhead, you'll probably find that solitude, even on an August weekend.

It's Not Our Fault

Some mountain bikers try to say that it's not their problem, but we all need to take responsibility for the way we behave out on the trail. If we adversely affect the environment or frighten other trail users, then we shouldn't be there. Go to Ski Bowl instead.

Most bicyclists search out the magic tucked around the trail's next bend—an old growth cedar, a gurgling creek. We can't deny that mountain biking is great fun. Why should we? Being out in nature is a joyous, not solemn, occasion. But you can be joyous without abusing the trail or any other users.

Cyclists have been a central part of the conservation movement for years—commuting, vacationing, and doing errands on bicycles. Bicyclists have been building and sharing soft-surface trails in the West for more than 100 years. In fact, bicyclists helped invent the idea of outdoor recreation. For that good tradition to continue, we need to keep searching for that magic, yielding the path to others, riding gently, and helping to maintain trails.

The Rules

- Don't leave any trace.
- Don't skid—ever. Take it easy on poorly constructed trails, and avoid wet trails or trails liable to be marred by tires. Walk around all delicate areas.
- Respect all other trail users. Yield the right-of-way to everyone, including hikers, runners, other bicyclists, motorcyclists, and equestrians.
- Stop and dismount when you encounter horses. Stand on the downhill side of the trail, and talk to the horse and rider as they pass.
- Always ride in control.
- Respect wildlife (you are in their home!) and livestock.
- Turn around if you reach a "No Trespassing" sign.

Out Riding: Tips and Techniques

Eating

Eat constantly to avoid the dreaded double-headed bonk. Eating is more important than training and way more effective at holding that bonk at bay than all the titanium components your bank account can afford. I usually start out with at least 1,000 calories of food in my pack: candy bars, energy bars, peanuts, Fig Newtons, and at least one piece of fruit to avoid energy-bar stomach, from which no amount of Tums can save you.

Drinking

Always bring plenty of water and drink constantly. Two quarts a day is the minimum. I've quaffed five quarts of water on really long, hot days. Eating and drinking enough can get you up a lot of hills and get you home before dark.

Walking

Most riders will push their bikes during some part of every ride included in *Kissing the Trail: Northwest & Central Oregon* that is rated three, four, or five wheels. Walking your bike is nothing to be ashamed of—it's part of the sport. Walk to avoid getting hurt, walk to save your legs for the rest of the ride, and walk around muddy areas to save delicate sections of the trail.

Cadence

As a rule, it's best to pedal 70 to 100 rotations per minute while riding a bike. This can seem awkwardly fast if you're not used to "spinning." But a healthy cadence is the easiest way to keep your legs fresh for the longest time possible. Slow, laborious pedal strokes strain muscles, tiring them for the miles ahead. On rough trails, the cadence rule doesn't always apply, but it's good to keep in mind in order to stay smooth and loose.

Descents

The header, digger, cartwheel, auger, and flip are bad. Riding sideways toward small children is also bad. Riding upside down? Again bad. Either ride in control or walk down the steep sections. Sit back to lower your center of gravity, and keep your arms and legs slightly bent. Keep your hands firmly and consistently on the brakes; you'll get nowhere waving one arm around like a cowboy. Don't use your front brake suddenly or erratically. The conundrum of braking: The front brake does most of the real braking, but you have more precise steering and you're less likely to take a header if less pressure is applied to the front brake. Remember that speed is the most hazardous bicycling condition. It's difficult to get hurt at 1 mile per hour; at 20 miles per hour, it's all too easy.

Climbs

The idea is to get to the top without hurling. Ride at a pace you can sustain for the length of the climb, concentrating on deep, relaxed breathing. Avoid locomotive breathing. Generally, it's best to stay seated so your rear wheel doesn't spin out. If traction is not a problem, try pedaling in a standing position occasionally to save your butt and utilize different muscles. Remember: It's okay to take a rest break.

Training

Do some. Of course, if you're already out riding, then it's too late for me to do much sermonizing, but you'll have a better time if you've put some miles in before a tough ride. More importantly, carefully select the ride and your riding partner. Don't ride an epic with an über-biker if you'd rather be following First-gear Freddy on a three-wheeler.

Maintenance

You'll have more fun out on the trail if your bike rolls smoothly, doesn't skip gears, and doesn't screech when you hit the brakes. Think about it: All week long you have to deal with copy machines that don't copy, computers that crash, and co-workers who skip gears and screech—so doesn't it make sense that when you are spending your own free time, you use something that works the way it's supposed to? Keep your bike in good working order.

Insects

During the summer, mosquitoes can be a lot more than a nuisance in the central Oregon Cascades. Don't forget to carry repellant. But on bad years, aggressive mosquitoes can ruin a trip, even with repellant. Immediately after the snow melts and then again after the first hard freeze are good times to go. Call the ranger station and ask about the bug status report.

Hood River and East Mount Hood

For Portlanders, the seventeen rides covered in this section are all within Saturday striking distance and don't require getting up at o'dark-thirty to make it a day trip. With a few exceptions, these are singletrack loops with dirt-road segments. Typically, they pass through fir forests and meadows, and sport exceptional views of Mount Hood. Expect fast, fun, switchbacking descents and technical ridgeline trails. The territory east of Mount Hood is a great place for mountain bikers.

Surveyors Ridge (rides 3 and 4) is perhaps the most talked about and traveled ride in this area, but if you want a great ride—beautiful and challenging but without all the people—try Gunsight Ridge (ride 12), High Prairie (ride 9), a combination of Knebal Springs (ride 8) and Eightmile Creek (ride 7), or Fifteenmile Creek (ride 10) for the descent. Mineral Creek (ride 16) is fun too, although be prepared for the feeling of a journey to the center of the earth. Two of the rides described in this section (rides 4 and 13) are epics—extra long and challenging. Get in shape, load up the extra-fat water pack, and go at it.

Three of the rides—Historic Highway 30 (ride 2), East Fork Hood River (ride 6), and Lower Deschutes Rail-Trail (ride 17)—are quite easy and great for families. Since these are all out-and-back rides, it's easy to tailor the length to fit your experience and fitness by turning around at any time.

The Hood River Ranger District manages many of these trails and has done an admirable job of keeping most of their non–Wilderness Area trails open to bicycles. However, while they generally maintain the trails described here, they have neglected and forgotten other trails in their district. Green Trails maps, the Hood River Ranger District map, and even the district's mountain-bike handout all list trails that have not been maintained in years. North Section Line, Bennett Pass, Crane Creek, Three Mile, and Rocky Butte Trails, to name a few, are either nonexistent or only semipassable, and the same goes for the new loops near Laurance Lake. Asking about the status of trails won't necessarily help. Folks at the ranger station pointed me toward several nonmaintained trails that required lots of walking and bushwhacking. If you want to explore, be prepared for anything. If you check out Fir Mountain, a bewildering maze of trails on private and unmanaged public land near Hood River, be sure to add poison oak to that "anything" list.

1 Post Canyon

⊕⊕⊕

Distance	8.3-mile lollipop
Terrain	Moderate climbing on singletrack and gravel roads with some pushing, singletrack descents; **950-foot gain**
Duration	1 to 2 hours
Travel	Hood River—4 miles; Portland—60 miles
Skill level	Intermediate
Season	Year-round
Maps	USGS 7.5 minute: Hood River
Restrictions	None
More info	Hood River County

The Scoop

Hood River locals like to head out to the Post Canyon/Mitchell Hill area after work; it's fun, and if you ride from town and explore a little, you can spin out more than the eight miles described here. This route climbs up lovely Post

Riding the chrome rooster at Post Canyon

Canyon on singletrack, then loops and weaves, sometimes gratuitously, before mounting Mitchell Hill. At times the route-finding is awkward, as numerous trails and roads crisscross the area, some through clearcuts. Hood River County, the current land manager, and Mount Hood National Forest have a land exchange in the works. If the exchange is consummated (likely in 2000), the Columbia River Gorge National Scenic Area—an agency that manages national forest lands along both the Oregon and Washington sides of the river—will oversee these trails.

Driving Directions

From the intersection of Oak Street and Third Avenue in Hood River, set your odometer to zero and proceed west on Oak Street. Oak Street soon becomes Cascade Avenue. At 1.8 miles, turn left on County Club Road. At 3.4 miles, turn right on Post Canyon Road. When the road turns to gravel at 4 miles, pull over and park.

From Portland, drive east on Interstate 84. Take exit 62, just before Hood River. Turn right at the end of the ramp and then right again on Country Club

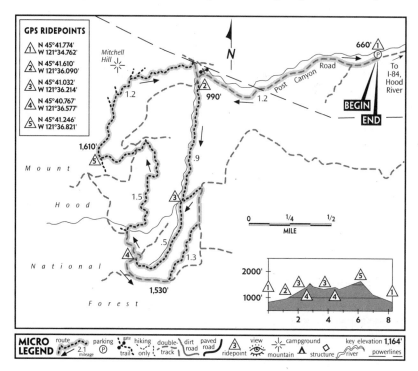

GPS RIDEPOINTS

1. N 45°41.774'
   W 121°34.762'
2. N 45°41.610'
   W 121°36.090'
3. N 45°41.032'
   W 121°36.214'
4. N 45°40.767'
   W 121°36.577'
5. N 45°41.246'
   W 121°36.821'

MICRO LEGEND — route · 2.1 mileage · parking ℗ · gate · hiking trail only · double-track · dirt road · paved road · △ ridepoint · view · mountain · campground · structure ▲ · river · key elevation **1,164'** · powerlines

Road and zero your odometer. At 1.6 miles, turn right on Post Canyon Road. When the road turns to gravel at 2.2 miles, pull over and park at a wide spot in the road.

The Ride

From the start of the gravel road, spin up Post Canyon Road, climbing. Stay on the main road as you pass numerous trails and doubletracks to the right and left. At **1.1** miles, reach a fork and bear left. **WHOA!** Just around the corner, **1.2** miles, find an unmarked trail on the left. Turn left here and follow the upward draw of the creek. The trail braids in places, splitting off into forks and then returning together. Don't freak. But when the trail forks at **2.1** miles, stay to the right and continue climbing. After a steep section, the trail ends at a gravel road, **2.6** miles. Turn left and ride up the road.

Climb to a fork in the road, bear left, and gradually descend. At **3** miles, find a singletrack on the left and take it. The trail zips and swings, then ends at a dirt road at **3.4** miles—turn left. **WHOA!** At **3.6** miles, take the easily missed singletrack on the left. After a quick descent, reach a familiar fork (the one at 2.1 miles) and turn left. Reach the gravel road again at **4.4** miles, and this time turn right. Just around the bend, **4.6** miles, turn left on an old, bermed-out dirt road. Descend a series of whoops and pushes, then turn right onto a narrow trail at **4.8** miles. Ignore a trenched-out trail on the left.

From here, the trail—sometimes hard-packed, sometimes loose, dusty, and rocky—climbs and descends through an exposed clearcut, possibly forcing some walking. Back into the fir forest, reach a fork at **5.6** miles and turn left, away from the dirt road. Cross a dirt road a few pedal rotations farther. At **5.9** miles, reach a T at a wide trail and turn right. The trail forks four times over the next mile: Each time bear right, following the new trail route. At **7** miles, the trail dumps out into a wide dirt open space under power lines where four dirt roads exit. Take a sharp right turn onto a rocky road and then immediately bear right again onto a lesser dirt road. At **7.1** miles, reach a T at Post Canyon Road. Turn left and ride back down to the parking pulloff, **8.3** miles, to complete the ride.

Gazetteer

Nearby camping: Toll Bridge, Sherwood (primitive)
Nearest food, drink, services: Hood River

2 Historic Highway 30

Distance	9-mile out-and-back
Terrain	Easily rolling paved road; 250-foot gain; views
Duration	1 to 2 hours
Travel	Hood River—2 miles; Portland—65 miles
Skill level	Beginner
Season	Year-round
Maps	USGS 7.5 minute: White Salmon
Restrictions	Oregon State Parks Day-use Permit required
More info	Oregon State Parks, 800-551-6949, www.prd.state.or.us

The Scoop

The Historic Columbia River Highway (Historic Highway 30), once the main thoroughfare for vehicles traversing the Columbia River Gorge, is now a state trail and closed to motorized travel. Oregon State Parks gated the old road between Hood River and Mosier, repaired two tunnels along the route, and

Columbia River from the historic trail

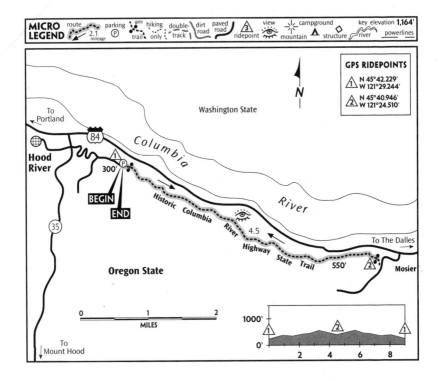

reopened it to hikers and bikers. This easy trail runs along the bluffs and basalt cliffs that form the southern wall of the gorge, affording outstanding views of the river.

Driving Directions

From Portland, drive east on Interstate 84. Take exit 64, just past Hood River. Zero out your odometer at the end of the interstate ramp and turn right. Immediately turn right again and wind up the hill. At 0.3 mile, reach a four-way intersection and turn left, following signs for the Historic Columbia River Highway. Stay on the main road. At 1.5 miles, reach the parking area and trailhead.

The Ride

From the western trailhead, ride east on the old paved road. The route climbs easily through pine, oak, and bigleaf maple, affording views north of the wide Columbia River Gorge and the browned hills of southern Washington. The way climbs, then rolls along the old chiseled roadway. At around the

3-mile mark, pass through two tunnels and then descend to a white gate, the eastern end of the trail, at **4.5** miles. Turn around here and pedal back to the western trailhead to complete the ride, **9** miles.

Gazetteer

Nearby camping: Toll Bridge, Sherwood (primitive)
Nearest food, drink, services: Hood River

3 Surveyors Ridge

⊕⊕⊕⊕

Distance	24.3-mile loop
Terrain	Moderate climb on paved and gravel road, rugged ridgeline singletrack; 890-foot gain; views
Duration	4 to 6 hours
Travel	Hood River—17 miles; Portland—81 miles
Skill level	Advanced
Season	Summer, fall
Maps	Green Trails: Hood River, Mount Hood
Restrictions	None
More info	Mount Hood National Forest, Hood River District, 541-352-6002, www.fs.fed.us/r6/mthood/

The Scoop

For good reason, Surveyors Ridge is one of the most well-known mountain bike trails in Oregon—*wow* views of Mount Hood are found around nearly every corner, lovely wildflowers cavort in the meadows and clearcuts, and it's a fun, challenging trail. The route winds up forest roads to start, then scampers down the trail, over root and rock and across meadowed hillsides. As with most ridge trails, the constant and unpredictable ups and downs can be both exhilarating and draining. The cumulative elevation gain logs in at more than 4,000 feet. Be careful not to bonk.

Driving Directions

From Portland, drive east on Interstate 84 and take exit 64, just past Hood River. Zero out your odometer at the end of the interstate ramp. Turn right and then immediately right again, following signs for State Highway 35. Proceed straight through the intersection at 0.3 mile, now heading south on Hwy 35. At 10.9 miles, turn left on Pine Mont Drive (Forest Road 17). Stay on the main road. At 17.3 miles, just after passing under some power lines, turn right and follow the sign for Surveyors Ridge Trail. Park at the trailhead on your left at 17.7 miles.

More Surveyors Ridge twisties

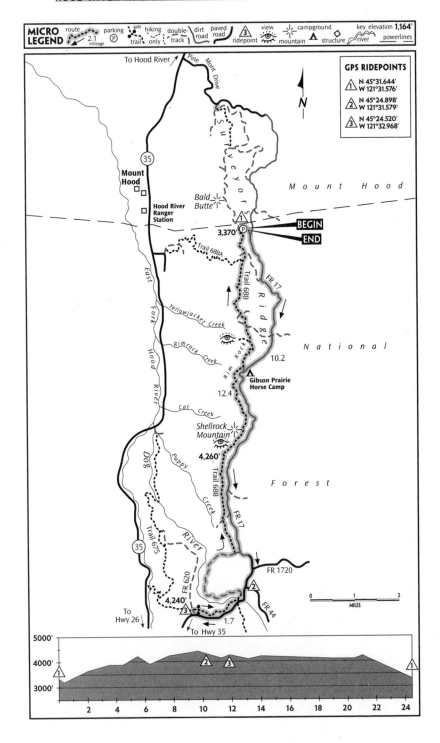

MICRO LEGEND — route 2.1 mileage · parking Ⓟ · gate hiking trail · hiking only · double-track · dirt road · paved road · ③ ridepoint · view mountain · campground · structure · powerlines · key elevation **1,164'** · river

To Hood River

Pine Mount Drive

Surveyors Ridge

N

GPS RIDEPOINTS
△1 N 45°31.644' W 121°31.576'
△2 N 45°24.898' W 121°31.579'
△3 N 45°24.520' W 121°32.968'

35

Mount Hood

Bald Butte

Mount Hood

Hood River Ranger Station

△1
3,370' Ⓟ

BEGIN
END

Trail 688A

Trail 688

FR 17

Ridge

National

East Fork Hood River

Yellowjacket Creek

Rimrock Creek

Rim Rock

10.2

12.4

△ **Gibson Prairie Horse Camp**

Cat Creek

Dog

Shellrock Mountain

4,260'

Puppy Creek

Trail 688

FR 17

Forest

River

35

Trail 675

FR 620

FR 1720

△2

4,240'
△3

To Hwy 26

1.7

FR 44

To Hwy 35

0   1   2
MILES

5000'
4000'
3000'

△1
△2 △3
△1

2   4   6   8   10 12 14 16 18 20 22 24

The Ride

From the small parking area at the trailhead, ride back down the dirt road to FR 17 and turn right. Stay on the main road, sometimes paved, sometimes gravel, as it climbs gently. At **2** miles, pass through Long Prairie. At **3.2** miles, ride straight through a four-way intersection. Crest a high point around **5.5** miles. Reach a fork at **8.9** miles and bear right. Crest another high point, and then reach a T at **9.7** miles. From the T, turn right, following the sign for FR 44. At **10.2** miles, FR 17 ends—bear right on FR 44. The road descends, then climbs. At **11.9** miles, turn right onto FR 620. Immediately find Surveyors Ridge Trail 688 on the right.

Ride around the white gate and head east. The trail, hard-packed and fast, descends slightly to a fork, **13.3** miles. Bear left, cross Dog River, and then climb through Cooks Meadow. At **13.9** miles, stay to the left (ignoring a doubletrack on the right) and cross a small creek. From here, follow the doubletrack around a clearcut hillside. In June and July, fireweed, paintbrush, lupine, and shooting star line the route. The doubletrack is dusty and rocky in sections. **WHOA!** At **15.8** miles, leave the doubletrack by turning left onto Trail 688. This turn is easily missed. Cross a dirt road at **16.6** miles. Pass through stands of fir that alternate with clearcuts filled with fireweed. Starting at about **17.9** miles, there's a tough climb to the top of an open knoll, which affords awesome views of Mount Hood.

From the knoll, the trail descends, churning through the forest, to a fork at **18.7** miles—turn right and continue down before climbing again. At **19.3** miles, when the trail kisses a dirt road on the right, bear to the left. After a few more pedal strokes, bear left again onto the singletrack. From here, the trail winds around some interesting rock outcrops and traverses a series of hillside meadows that afford more Mount Hood views. The trail is at times technical due to embedded rocks and the tricky side slope. At a fork, **20.6** miles, bear to the left and climb. At **21.2** miles, pass a short trail to a lookout on the left. Cross gravel roads at **21.3** and **21.7** miles. When the trail forks at **22.4** miles, bear right and descend the rocky trail. Reach a fork at **23.3** miles, go right, then cross another gravel road. At **24.3** miles, the trail dumps out at the trailhead under the power lines to complete the loop.

Gazetteer

Nearby camping: Eightmile Crossing (primitive), Sherwood (primitive)
Nearest food, drink, services: Parkdale, Hood River

4 Surveyors Epic

Distance	33.2-mile loop
Terrain	Steep, technical singletrack climb, tough ridgeline trail, paved start and finish; 2,810-foot gain; views
Duration	5 to 8 hours
Travel	Hood River—15 miles; Portland—78 miles
Skill level	Advanced
Season	Summer, fall
Maps	Green Trails: Hood River, Mount Hood
Restrictions	None
More info	Mount Hood National Forest, Hood River District, 541-352-6002, www.fs.fed.us/r6/mthood/

The Scoop

Here's a way to ride the fabled Dog River descent without succumbing to a two-car shuttle, which, let's face it, is weak. And besides, isn't riding thirty-three miles better than riding six? With ten miles of paved road and less than 3,000 feet of elevation to gain, this loop straddles the epic fence, but the southbound route up Surveyors Ridge is challenging, and the climb up Bald Butte strenuous. Surveyors Epic serves up a sampling of the best riding in the Hood River Ranger District, with a tough ridgeline singletrack, incredible views of Mount Hood, and, of course, the romping Dog River descent. If you are up for an epic and have never ridden east of Mount Hood, this is a great place to start.

Driving Directions

From Portland, drive east on Interstate 84 and take exit 64, just past Hood River. Zero out your odometer at the end of the interstate ramp. Turn right and then immediately right again, following signs for State Highway 35. At 0.3 mile, proceed straight through the intersection, now heading south on Hwy 35. At 14.4 miles, turn right and park at the Hood River Ranger Station.

The Ride

From the dirt parking area at the ranger station, ride out to the highway and turn left, riding north. Pass the Hood River General Store, then descend to the ride's low point around **3** miles. Climb gently to Pine Mont Drive (Forest Road 17), **3.5** miles, and turn right. The road, still paved but rising more steadily now, winds up the open, north end of Surveyors Ridge, bearing southeast. At **5.4** miles, turn right on a gravel road. Just after a bend, **5.6** miles, the road forks. This is gut-check time; the route gains 1,600 feet over the next two and one-half miles. Take the unmarked trail that begins between the two prongs of the fork. The trail is smooth and hard-packed but very steep.

At **6.6** miles, the trail ends at a T—turn right onto the dirt road. Reach another T at **6.9** miles, and again turn right. When the road forks at **7.1** miles, bear left, climbing, then descending, then climbing steeply—perhaps walking—toward the summit of Bald Butte. **WOOF!** Take a break at the top, **8.2** miles, and wait until your hyperventilating becomes run-of-the-mill gasping so you can appreciate the views of Mount Hood. Mount Adams and Mount St. Helens are also visible to the north. From the top, continue north, descending a steep, ragged dirt road covered with death-cookies. At **9.1** miles, ride under a set of power lines. As the road bends to the left, find the singletrack on the right and take it: Surveyors Ridge Trail 688.

Cross a gravel road at **9.9** miles. When the trail forks at **10.1** miles, stay to the left on Trail 688 toward Clinger Springs. From here, through stands of fir

Perfect Surveyors day near Rim Rock

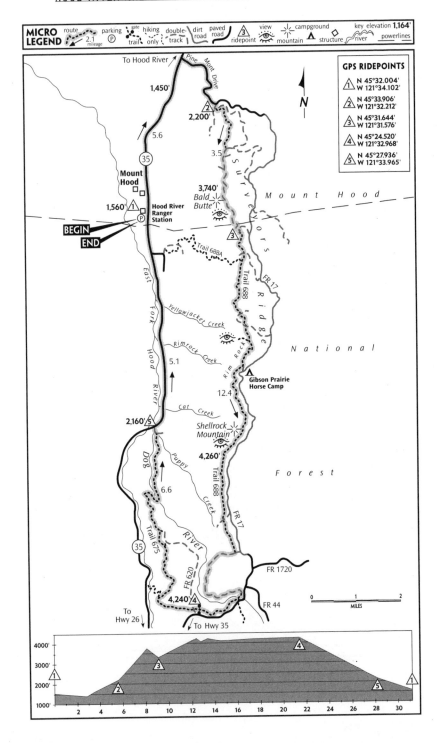

MICRO LEGEND
route — parking (P) — gate — hiking trail only — double-track — dirt road — paved road — (3) ridepoint — view mountain — campground — structure — river — key elevation **1,164'** — powerlines
2.1 mileage

GPS RIDEPOINTS

1. N 45°32.004' W 121°34.102'
2. N 45°33.906' W 121°32.212'
3. N 45°31.644' W 121°31.576'
4. N 45°24.520' W 121°32.968'
5. N 45°27.936' W 121°33.965'

To Hood River
Pine Mont Drive
1,450'
2,200' — 2
N
3.5
5.6
35
Mount Hood
3,740' Bald Butte — Mount Hood
1,560' — 1
Hood River Ranger Station (P)
BEGIN
END
Trail 688A
3
Surveyors Ridge
FR 17
East Fork Hood River
Yellowjacket Creek
Trail 688
National
Rimrock Creek
5.1
Rim Rock
Gibson Prairie Horse Camp
12.4
Cat Creek
Shellrock Mountain
2,160' — 5
4,260'
Forest
Dog
Puppy Creek
Trail 688
6.6
35
Trail 675
River
FR 17
FR 620
FR 1720
4,240' — 4
FR 44
To Hwy 26
To Hwy 35

0 1 2 MILES

4000'
3000'
2000'
1000'
2 4 6 8 10 12 14 16 18 20 22 24 26 28 30

and brushy clearcuts, the trail climbs, its tread embedded with rocks and roots. Cross gravel roads at **11.7** and **12.1** miles. Reach a fork at **12.3** miles and stay to the left. (The right prong leads to an old fire lookout along Rim Rock—a great spot for a break.) The way descends quickly—a rocky, open, west-facing traverse—to a fork at **12.8** miles. Bear right, continuing toward Clinger Springs on Trail 688.

After passing across the top of some cliffs, the trail kisses a road on the left: Bear right. Several trail undulations farther, cross a gravel road, **16.7** miles. At **17.6** miles, the trail ends at a T with a doubletrack—turn right. Follow the doubletrack, rocky and steep in spots, around a long bend through lily and lupine, columbine and shooting star, to a creek crossing at **19.8** miles. After crossing the creek, bear right, riding singletrack again through Cooks Meadow. At **20** miles, cross Dog River and immediately reach a fork—go right. From here, the trail is smooth, hard-packed, and fast. At **21.5** miles, ride around a white gate. This is the end of Surveyors Ridge Trail. Pedal across the dirt spur that acts as an ad hoc trailhead and head down Dog River Trail 675.

Let the fast descent begin. Reach a fork at **22.4** miles and bear right, continuing down Dog River Trail. *Wheee!* Traversing north across a steep slope, the trail occasionally skirts the edge of a cliff. **WHOA!** At an unmarked fork, **24** miles, take a sharp, switchbacking left (if you reach a dirt road, you've gone too far). At **24.5** miles, ignore the trail back on the right. After a long switchback to the southeast, cross Dog River and continue north again along the east side of the river. At **27.7** miles, the trail ends at a dirt road—turn left. At **28.1** miles, reach the trailhead along Hwy 35. Turn right and pedal down the highway. At **33.2** miles, reach Hood River Ranger Station on the left to complete the loop.

Gazetteer

Nearby camping: Eightmile Crossing (primitive), Sherwood (primitive)
Nearest food, drink, services: Parkdale, Hood River

5 Dog River

⊕⊕⊕

Distance	6.6-mile one-way shuttle
Terrain	Bomber singletrack descent; 2,085-foot loss
Duration	1 hour
Travel	Hood River—31 miles; Portland—73 miles
Skill level	Advanced
Season	Summer, fall
Maps	Green Trails: Mount Hood
Restrictions	None
More info	Mount Hood National Forest, Hood River District, 541-352-6002, www.fs.fed.us/r6/mthood/

The Scoop

Better than sex, say some when describing the thrilling Dog River descent. Despite the hyperbole (or need of a new bike seat), this description is on the right track. Advanced riders love the tight switchbacks and hair-raising,

A slow section on Dog River Trail

open-it-up traverses. This trail gets hammered in the summer from riders skidding around each switchback and blind corner; the tread gradually transforms from dirt to dust to a fine powder that's oh-so-good for your bike's moving parts (not to mention your nasal passages). Take it easy out there and watch for other trail users.

Driving Directions

From Portland, take US Highway 26 eastbound about 56 miles, past Ski Bowl and Government Camp, to its junction with State Highway 35. Set your odometer to zero, and turn north onto Hwy 35. At 6.2 miles, cross Bennett Pass. At 13.4 miles, pass Forest Road 44 on the right. At 20.9 miles, drop a car off at the Dog River trailhead on the right. Then turn around and drive south

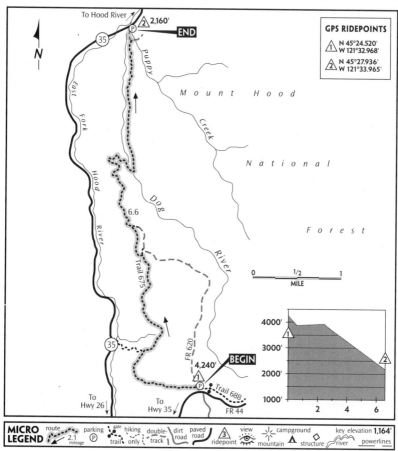

on Hwy 35, back to FR 44. Turn left onto FR 44, and again set your odometer to zero. At 3.8 miles, turn left onto FR 620 and immediately park.

From Hood River (exit 64 off Interstate 84), set your odometer to zero and drive south on Hwy 35. At 19.5 miles, drop a car off at the Dog River trailhead on the left, then continue south on Hwy 35. At 27 miles, turn left onto FR 44. At 30.8 miles, turn left onto FR 620 and immediately park.

The Ride

Facing away from FR 44, you'll find Dog River Trail 675 on the left. Let the fast descent begin. Reach a fork at **0.9** mile and bear right, continuing down Dog River Trail. *Wheee!* Traversing north along a steep slope, the trail occasionally skirts the edge of a cliff. **WHOA!** At an unmarked fork, **2.5** miles, take a sharp, switchbacking left (if you reach a dirt road, you've gone too far). At **3** miles, ignore the trail back on the right. After a long switchback to the southeast, cross Dog River and continue north again along the east side of the river. At **6.2** miles, the trail ends at a dirt road—turn left. At **6.6** miles, reach the trailhead along Hwy 35 to complete the ride.

Gazetteer

Nearby camping: Eightmile Crossing (primitive), Sherwood (primitive)
Nearest food, drink, services: Parkdale, Hood River

East Fork Hood River
⊕⊕

Distance	10.8-mile out-and-back
Terrain	Wide, fast singletrack with a few short, tough climbs; 500-foot gain
Duration	1 to 2 hours
Travel	Hood River—25 miles; Portland—71 miles
Skill level	Intermediate
Season	Summer, fall
Maps	Green Trails: Mount Hood
Restrictions	None
More info	Mount Hood National Forest, Hood River District, 541-352-6002, www.fs.fed.us/r6/mthood/

The Scoop

This trail, wide and smooth, travels along the East Fork of Hood River. While it's not listed as a *views* ride, the trail often runs right next to the river, and it's

Zipping along East Fork's buff trail

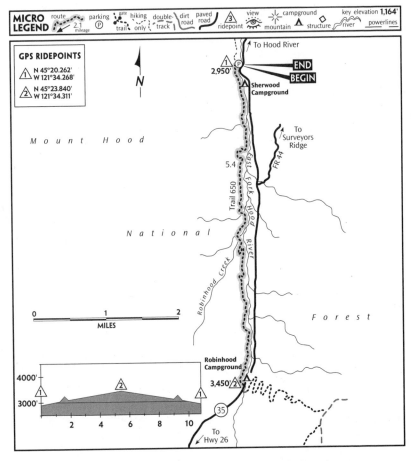

MICRO LEGEND: route, 2.1 mileage, parking ℗, gate, hiking trail only, double-track, dirt road, paved road, ③ ridepoint, view, mountain, campground, structure, river, key elevation **1,164'**, powerlines

GPS RIDEPOINTS
△1 N 45°20.262'
   W 121°34.268'
△2 N 45°23.840'
   W 121°34.311'

N

To Hood River
△1 ℗
2,950'
END
BEGIN
△ Sherwood Campground

To Surveyors Ridge

East Fork Hood River

FR 44

5.4

Trail 650

M o u n t   H o o d

N a t i o n a l

Robinhood Creek

F o r e s t

0   1   2
MILES

Robinhood Campground
3,450' △2

4000'
3000'
△1   △2   △1
2   4   6   8   10

35

To Hwy 26

very picturesque. East Fork Hood River Trail is a fence sitter between a two- and three-wheel rating. Most of the trail is quite easy—a wide singletrack—however, several climbs and a few sandy sections may pose a challenge for less adventurous mountain bikers. Just turn around early if you have trouble.

Driving Directions

From Portland, take US Highway 26 eastbound about 56 miles, past Ski Bowl and Government Camp, to its junction with State Highway 35. Set your odometer to zero, and turn north onto Hwy 35. At 6.2 miles, cross Bennett Pass. At 15.1 miles, just past Sherwood Campground, turn left into the gravel parking area and trailhead alongside the highway.

From Hood River (exit 64 off Interstate 84), set your odometer to zero and drive south on Hwy 35. At 14.4 miles, pass the Hood River Ranger Station on the right. At 25.3 miles, turn right into the gravel parking area and trailhead alongside the highway (just before Sherwood Campground).

The Ride

From the highway, the trail immediately drops down to the river. Just across a bridge, the trail forks—turn left. Heading upriver now, the trail climbs through a dark fir forest. At **1.3** miles, the trail switchbacks up the bank, then drops back to the river again one-half mile farther. The forest opens up as you proceed upriver. After a few more ups and downs, the grade of the trail evens out and follows close to the river all the way up to Robinhood Campground, **5.4** miles. Turn around here and ride back to the trailhead parking, **10.8** miles.

Gazetteer

Nearby camping: Sherwood (primitive), Robinhood (primitive)
Nearest food, drink, services: Parkdale, Hood River

7 Eightmile Creek

✿✿✿

Distance	6.3-mile loop
Terrain	Moderate singletrack climb, singletrack descent; 860-foot gain; views
Duration	1 to 2 hours
Travel	Hood River—35 miles; Portland—77 miles
Skill level	Intermediate
Season	Summer, fall
Maps	Green Trails: Flag Point
Restrictions	USFS Trail Park Pass required
More info	Mount Hood National Forest, Hood River District, 541-352-6002, www.fs.fed.us/r6/mthood/

The Scoop

This singletrack loop begins with a rolling climb to Fivemile Lookout, then descends a furious set of switchbacks before finishing with a lovely, meander-

Trail 459 follows Eightmile Creek in a quiet forest

ing climb along Eightmile Creek. It's a fun but short ride, perfect for the second ride of the day, an easy day, or a friend-with-suspect-fitness-level day. When it's clear, views from the lookout are outstanding. The trail, open only to hikers and mountain bikers, is in good shape, although it can get dusty later in the summer.

Driving Directions

From Portland, take US Highway 26 eastbound about 56 miles, past Ski Bowl and Government Camp, to its junction with State Highway 35. Set your odometer to zero, and turn north onto Hwy 35. At 6.2 miles, cross Bennett Pass. At 13.4 miles, turn right onto Forest Road 44. At 18.9 miles, turn right to stay on FR 44 (to the left is FR 17). At 21.3 miles, turn left on FR 120 and park immediately.

From Hood River (exit 64 off Interstate 84), drive south on Hwy 35. After about 27 miles, turn left onto FR 44 and set your odometer to zero. At 5.5 miles, turn right to remain on FR 44 (to the left is FR 17). At 7.9 miles, turn left on FR 120 and park immediately.

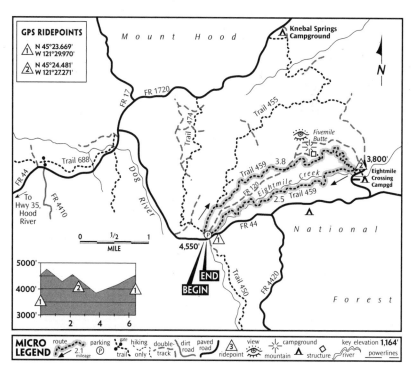

Four volcano view from
Fivemile Butte Lookout

The Ride

On a wide, rough trail, ride away from FR 44 and FR 120. After about fifty yards, reach a fork and turn right, following the sign to Trail 459. The trail narrows and climbs. At **0.5** mile, the trail forks: Go right on Eightmile Loop Trail 459. The trail traverses to a high point and then cruises down the pine- and fir-covered hillside to the saddle between Eightmile Creek and the headwaters of Fivemile Creek where, at **1.5** miles, it crosses a dirt road and begins climbing Fivemile Butte. After ascending a healthy traverse, through fireweed and pine, reach a fork at **2.2** miles. The trail on the left leads to Fivemile Butte Lookout, less than one-quarter mile away; it's a must-do side trip, with views of Mount Hood, Mount Adams, Mount St. Helens, and, on especially clear days, Mount Rainier.

To continue the loop, bear right at the fork at **2.2** miles. After a short sputter, the trail switchbacks steeply down the dusty east edge of the butte. It's a fun descent. At **3.8** miles, arrive at a four-way and turn right. From here, the trail winds gently upstream along Eightmile Creek, which gurgles among grand fir, spruce, Canadian dogwood, and fern. At **6.3** miles, reach FR 120 to complete the loop.

Gazetteer

Nearby camping: Eightmile Crossing (primitive)
Nearest food, drink, services: Parkdale, Hood River

8 Knebal Springs

☼☼☼

Distance	9.2-mile loop
Terrain	Difficult climbing on singletrack and paved road, some pushing; 1,340-foot gain
Duration	2 to 3 hours
Travel	Hood River—35 miles; Portland—77 miles
Skill level	Advanced
Season	Summer, fall
Maps	Green Trails: Flag Point
Restrictions	USFS Trail Park Pass required
More info	Mount Hood National Forest, Hood River District, 541-352-6002, www.fs.fed.us/r6/mthood/

The Scoop

I like the Knebal Springs loop a lot. It makes a great 15.5-mile ride when combined with Eightmile Creek (ride 7). Not much for views (unless you take the

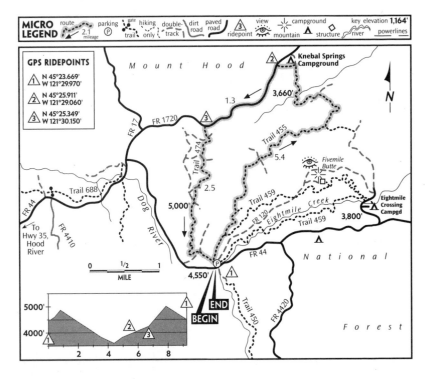

short spur out to Perry Point for an expansive look out into the rolling, hazy brown void of eastern Oregon), this loop provides a tour of sorts though fir and pine forests, clearcuts, thickets of manzanita, and high meadows on a variety of trails from fast slalom to loose technical to pine-needle grinder. Stretches of the trail become quite dusty as summer progresses, and the fine powder functions as an attractive eyeliner on riders who follow too close. Horses add to the dusty conditions—with more than just churned-up dirt. At a rest stop on this ride, my riding partner's pack tipped off of his handlebars and made a direct hit in a pile of horse pucky. Score one for the trail gremlins.

Driving Directions

From Portland, take US Highway 26 eastbound about 56 miles, past Ski Bowl and Government Camp, to its junction with State Highway 35. Set your odometer to zero, and turn north onto Hwy 35. At 6.2 miles, cross Bennett Pass. At 13.4 miles, turn right onto Forest Road 44. At 18.9 miles, turn right to stay on FR 44 (to the left is FR 17). At 20.9 miles, ignore a dirt road and the

Knebal Springs Trail sign on the left. At 21.3 miles, turn left on FR 120 and park immediately.

From Hood River (exit 64 off Interstate 84), drive south on Hwy 35. After about 27 miles, turn left onto FR 44, and set your odometer to zero. At 5.5 miles, turn right to remain on FR 44 (to the left is FR 17). At 7.5 miles, ignore a dirt road and the Knebal Springs Trail sign on the left. At 7.9 miles, turn left on FR 120 and park immediately.

The Ride

On a wide, rough trail, ride away from FR 44 and FR 120. After about fifty yards, reach a fork and turn right, following the sign to Trail 455. The trail narrows and climbs. At **0.5** mile, the trail forks—bear left on Bottle Prairie Trail 455. Continue ascending to a fork at **0.8** mile—bear left again (one-quarter mile to the right you'll find Perry Point). From here, whiz down a twisting, frolicking, dusty descent. Cross a dirt road at **2.5** miles. Reach a fork in the trail at **3.5** miles, and bear left on Knebal Springs Trail 474.

At **3.8** miles, reach a dirt road and turn left. After a few pedal rotations, regain the trail on the right. From here, the trail becomes rocky and loose as it descends to cross Middle Fork Fivemile Creek. Beyond the creek, the trail, still dusty and shifting, climbs straight up through a hallway of manzanita. Most riders will likely hike-a-bike this stretch. As the hillside levels, bear left to remain on the trail. Reach Knebal Springs Campground at **5** miles. Ride along the campground road, staying to the left. At **5.1** miles, take the single-track on the left. When the trail ends at a paved road, **5.4** miles, turn left on the road and continue climbing.

At **6.7** miles, find Knebal Springs Trail 474 on the left. Take the trail, pushing your bike to begin. The trail crosses a dirt road on a jog to the right, climbs relentlessly, then crosses another dirt road on a jog to the left, **7.2** miles. WOOF! At **7.6** miles, reach a T at a dirt road and turn right. At **7.7** miles, bear left to return to the singletrack. Cross another dirt road, then noodle across a high meadow. At **8.4** miles, back into the woods now, begin a fast descent. Cross a dirt road at **8.9** miles. Pass by a trail on the left, and reach the trailhead at **9.2** miles to complete the ride.

Gazetteer

Nearby camping: Eightmile Crossing (primitive), Pebble Ford (primitive)
Nearest food, drink, services: Parkdale, Hood River

9 High Prairie

✿✿✿✿

Distance	16.1-mile loop
Terrain	Tough singletrack climbs, some walking, gravel and paved roads; 1,800-foot gain; views
Duration	3 to 5 hours
Travel	Hood River—31 miles; Portland—73 miles
Skill level	Advanced
Season	Summer, fall
Maps	Green Trails: Mount Hood, Flag Point
Restrictions	None
More info	Mount Hood National Forest, Hood River District, 541-352-6002, www.fs.fed.us/r6/mthood/

The Scoop

The singletrack climbs and descents are challenging, though not murderous, and the views of Mount Hood from High Prairie are hard to beat. The ride begins with a short stretch of singletrack followed by several miles of paved forest road. After the warm-up, a demanding trail climbs most of the way to High Prairie. A gravel road links High Prairie with Cooks Meadow Trail, a raucous descent.

Driving Directions

From Portland, take US Highway 26 eastbound about 56 miles, past Ski Bowl and Government Camp, to its junction with State Highway 35. Set your odometer to zero, and turn north onto Hwy 35. At 6.2 miles, cross Bennett Pass. At 13.4 miles, turn right onto Forest Road 44. At 17.2 miles, turn left onto FR 620 and immediately park.

From Hood River (exit 64 off Interstate 84), drive south on Hwy 35. After about 27 miles, turn left onto FR 44 and set your odometer to zero. At 3.8 miles, turn left onto FR 620 and immediately park.

The Ride

Facing away from FR 44, take the trail on the right, Surveyors Ridge Trail 688. The smooth, hard-packed trail roller-coasters, rising slightly. At **1.4** miles, reach a fork and turn right on Cooks Meadow Trail 639. Almost immediately,

Mount Hood from High Prairie

the trail hits FR 44: Turn left on this paved road and begin climbing. At **1.7** miles, bear right to remain on FR 44. At **4.1** miles, reach FR 120 on the left and an unmarked doubletrack on the right. Turn right and ride south on the doubletrack, gently climbing along Eightmile Creek. The way quickly narrows to singletrack. At **5.4** miles, the trail levels somewhat and meanders through a forest of grand fir, lodgepole pine, and larch. Ignore an unmaintained trail on the left at **5.9** miles, and continue toward Upper Eightmile Meadow on Trail 450. From here, the trail noodles through a thick stand of fir, finally emerging into Eightmile Meadow at a fork, **6.8** miles. Take the right fork.

From Eightmile Meadow, the trail ascends at a hectic rate, crossing dirt roads at **7** and **7.2** miles. WOOF! The worst of the climbing is over at **8** miles. Reach FR 4420 at **8.1** miles and turn right (the trail across the road enters Badger Creek Wilderness). The climb continues up FR 4420 but at an easier grade. At **8.9** miles, the road, which designates the border of the wilderness area, levels out and cuts through High Prairie, a lovely, wildflowered meadow just north of Lookout Mountain. Reach a fork in the road at **9.6** miles and turn right on FR 4410. Before bombing down the road, check out the four-volcano view from this intersection.

FR 4410, gravelly and at times washboarded, winds down the top of the ridge that connects Gunsight Ridge to the south with Surveyors Ridge to the north. Watch out for vehicles on the road during this fast descent. At **12.1** miles, turn right onto Cooks Meadow Trail 639 and immediately begin climbing again. Through a light fir forest accented by small meadows, the trail soon bends left and rounds the west side of the hill, **12.6** miles. From here,

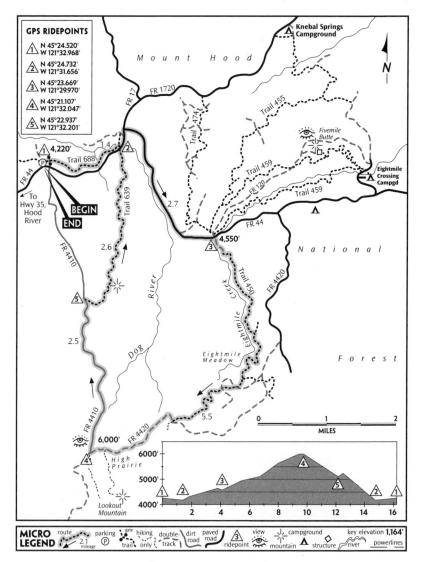

the trail, twisted and root-strewn, hardscrabble in spots, launches furiously down the hillside toward Cooks Meadow. Cross a dirt road at **13.7** miles and continue the fast, sometimes technical descent. The trail crosses FR 44 at **14.7** miles. Immediately after crossing the paved road, the trail forks—turn left onto Trail 688. Ride the fast hard-pack to the trailhead at **16.1** miles to compass the route.

Gazetteer

Nearby camping: Eightmile Crossing (primitive), Pebble Ford (primitive)
Nearest food, drink, services: Parkdale, Hood River

10 Fifteenmile Creek

❀❀❀❀

Distance	10.8-mile lollipop (17.8-mile option)
Terrain	Awesome singletrack descent followed by nasty singletrack climb, some pushing; **1,800-foot gain**
Duration	2 to 4 hours
Travel	Hood River—39 miles; Portland—82 miles
Skill level	Advanced
Season	Summer, fall
Maps	Green Trails: Flag Point
Restrictions	None
More info	Mount Hood National Forest, Hood River District, 541-352-6002, www.fs.fed.us/r6/mthood/

The Scoop

Short for a four-wheel ride, this loop makes up for it with a half-mile hair-ball drop and a grueling singletrack climb. The descent is one of the best. First through a mixed fir forest, then—lower on the ridge between Cedar and Fifteenmile Creeks—through ponderosa pine meadows punctuated with goblinlike rock formations, the spirited trail drops and weaves and drops some more. It's fun and exciting. The final drop is rocky and loose, a walk for less skilled riders. As for direction of travel, counterclockwise (as described here) is potentially ridable the entire loop for very strong riders, whereas riding clockwise forces a three-quarter-mile hike but is an easier ride for the rest of the loop. Either way, this is one of those gee-whiz descents that you'll dream about for a long time.

Driving Directions

From Portland, take US Highway 26 eastbound about 56 miles, past Ski Bowl and Government Camp, to its junction with State Highway 35. Turn north onto Hwy 35, and proceed about 13 miles to Forest Road 44. Turn right onto FR 44, and zero out your odometer. At 5.5 miles, bear right to remain on FR 44. At 8.9 miles, turn right onto FR 4420. Stay on the paved road. At 11.2 miles, stay left onto FR 2730. At 13.2 miles, reach Fifteenmile Creek Campground on the left and park.

At the top of Trail 456—another Clif Shot, please

From Hood River (exit 64 off Interstate 84), drive south on Hwy 35. After about 27 miles, turn left onto FR 44 and set your odometer to zero. At 5.5 miles, bear right to remain on FR 44. At 8.9 miles, turn right onto FR 4420. Stay on the paved road. At 11.2 miles, stay left to FR 2730. At 13.2 miles, reach Fifteenmile Creek Campground on the left and park.

The Ride

The trail exits the small campground next to the toilet. Bear right at the immediate fork and descend on Fifteenmile Trail 456. When the trail forks at **0.5** mile, take a sharp right, drop to the creek, and cross the bridge on Cedar Creek Trail 457. After a short climb away from the creek, follow the bouncing singletrack, tricky in spots, as it descends from a mixed stand of fir and pine down through an open forest of scattered ponderosa pine, winding across dry, yellow-meadowed knolls and past variously shaped rock hoodoos.

At **3.7** miles, the trail crosses a doubletrack and continues down. From the **4.5**-mile point, the trail is gnarled—loose, rocky, and steep—and may require a walk. At **5.2** miles, reach the ride's low point when you cross Fifteenmile Creek. Immediately reach a T and turn left (for a longer ride, see "Option" below). The trail is good and gradually climbs. After **7** miles, though, the trail

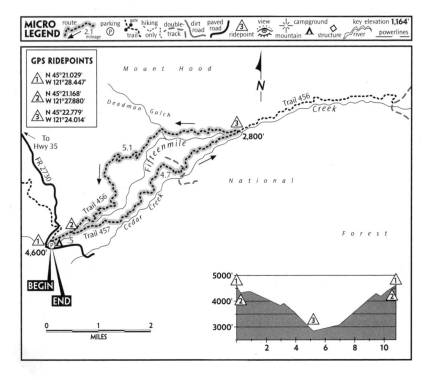

seems to head straight up, gaining huge chunks of elevation. It's a probable hike-a-bike. **WOOF!** By **9.6** miles, the torture is largely over, as the trail winds across an open, rocky hillside. Reach a fork in the trail at **10.3** miles and stay to the right. At **10.8** miles, arrive back at the campground and trailhead to complete the ride.

Option

At the T at 5.2 miles, turn right and ride 3.5 miles, gradually descending, to the end of Trail 456. Turn around and ride back. This 7-mile addition creates the rare upside-down lollipop ride format. Reason to take this spur: It extends the descent and drops into a pure stand of oak. Reason not to take it: It doesn't go anywhere, and it just ensures that you will bonk at the end.

Gazetteer

Nearby camping: Fifteenmile Creek (primitive), Pebble Ford (primitive)
Nearest food, drink, services: Parkdale, Hood River

11 Umbrella Falls

☼☼☼

Distance	4.4-mile figure eight
Terrain	Singletrack climb and descent, some sections steep and technical; 800-foot gain
Duration	1 to 2 hours
Travel	Hood River—33 miles; Portland—64 miles
Skill level	Intermediate
Season	Summer, fall
Maps	Green Trails: Mount Hood
Restrictions	None
More info	Mount Hood National Forest, Hood River District, 541-352-6002, www.fs.fed.us/r6/mthood/

The Scoop

The falls are the thing here. Umbrella Falls, wide and rippling, highlight this short loop. Sections of the loop are quite steep, so plan on a hike-a-bike climb unless you are a great climber. In summer, this area is heavily traversed by hikers, so ride with caution.

Driving Directions

From Portland, take US Highway 26 eastbound about 56 miles, past Ski Bowl and Government Camp, to its junction with State Highway 35. Set your odometer to zero, and turn north onto Hwy 35. At 6.2 miles, cross Bennett Pass. At 7.5 miles, turn left on Forest Road 3545 toward Sahalie Falls Loop. At 7.9 miles, park at the trailhead on the right.

From Hood River (exit 64 off Interstate 84), drive south on Hwy 35. After about 33 miles, turn right on FR 3545, toward Sahalie Falls Loop, and set your odometer to zero. At 0.4 mile, park at the trailhead on the right.

The Ride

Take the trail that exits from the right side of the road. At **0.3** mile, ignore a faint trail back on the left. Reach a fork at **0.4** mile and turn left on Umbrella Falls Trail 667. The trail begins a steady ascent. After crossing a ski run, **0.6** mile, the way becomes quite steep. Hit a doubletrack at **1.2** miles and bear left. Cross under a ski lift and continue the thigh-burning climb, past the ski

Umbrella Falls

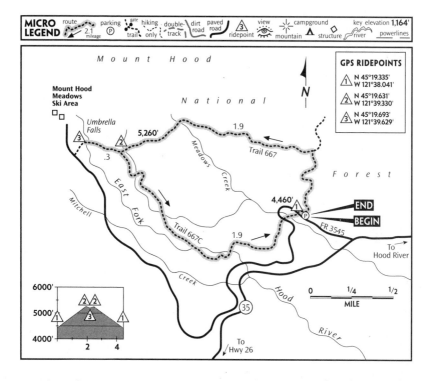

area boundary, to a crest at **1.7** miles. At **1.9** miles, reach a fork and stay to the right, continuing on Umbrella Falls Trail.

At **2.2** miles, reach a bridge at Umbrella Falls. (For a great view of Mount Hood, continue down the trail to a paved road, turn right, and ride a short distance up to the ski area parking lot.) For this loop, turn around at Umbrella Falls and ride back to the previous fork. Turn right on Sahalie Falls Trail 667C at **2.5** miles. The trail, smooth and hard-packed, with enough roots to keep it interesting, descends now, crossing several broken bridges before snaking along the top of a ravine. At **4.2** miles, cross a paved road, following the sign toward Umbrella Falls Trail. Return to FR 3545 and the trailhead at **4.4** miles to finish.

Gazetteer

Nearby camping: Robinhood (primitive)
Nearest food, drink, services: Government Camp

12 Gunsight Ridge

✿✿✿✿

Distance	16.5-mile loop
Terrain	Paved and dirt road climb, tough ridgeline trail, steep singletrack descent; **2,320-foot gain**; views
Duration	3 to 5 hours
Travel	Hood River—30 miles; Portland—67 miles
Skill level	Advanced
Season	Summer, fall
Maps	Green Trails: Mount Hood
Restrictions	None
More info	Mount Hood National Forest, Hood River District, 541-352-6002, www.fs.fed.us/r6/mthood/

The Scoop

On Gunsight Ridge some summers, stubborn snow patches, tucked in the ridge's coves and swales, refuse to melt until August. Be prepared. In the six weeks or so after melt-out, though, the ridge lights up in a riot of wildflowers

Switchie practice on Gumjuwac Trail

that swirl around the sparse mountain hemlock and noble fir forest. And the views of Mount Hood are epic. While the loop gains most of its elevation on State Highway 35 and Forest Road 3550, the real challenge comes along Gunsight Ridge, a typical ridge trail that rises and drops with steep, jagged unpredictability. The descent from Gumjuwac Saddle is a switchback clinic.

Driving Directions

From Portland, take US Highway 26 eastbound about 56 miles, past Ski Bowl and Government Camp, to its junction with Hwy 35. Set your odometer to zero, and turn north onto Hwy 35. At 6.2 miles, cross Bennett Pass. At 10.8 miles, park at Gumjuwac trailhead on the right, across the highway from Robinhood Campground.

From Hood River (exit 64 off Interstate 84), drive south on Hwy 35. After about 27 miles, pass FR 44 on the left and set your odometer to zero. At 2.6 miles, park on the left at Gumjuwac trailhead, across the highway from Robinhood Campground.

The Ride

From the trailhead, ride south on Hwy 35. At **4.6** miles (a good warm-up spin and 1,000-foot climb), reach Bennett Pass. At the top of the pass, turn left on Bennett Pass Road (FR 3550), which is dirt, and continue climbing. When the road forks at **5.7** miles, bear left. At **5.9** miles, the road divides again—bear right and continue up. (Note: Maps show Trail 684 paralleling the road from this point on, but Trail 684 has not been maintained in years and doesn't exist. Don't spend any time searching for it.) Rougher, steeper, and narrower now, the road forks at **6.4** miles—go left, continuing up the ridgeline. The narrow ridge affords excellent views of Mount Hood and the Hood River Valley. Pass around the dramatic rocky crown of the ridge, descend for a short distance, then climb again.

At **8.7** miles, just before the road reaches a T, turn left on Gunsight Ridge Trail 685. The trail, rocky and technical at times, follows the ridgeline up. The trail parallels FR 3550, which runs just to the east of the ridge top, but most of the time you aren't aware of the dirt road. WOOF! Crest a high point, then at **11.4** miles pass a rocky viewpoint on the left. At **11.7** miles, the trail kisses the road, then climbs to another high point and noodles across a small, lovely subalpine meadow. Views: Mount Hood to the west, Mount Jefferson to the east. At **12.1** miles, when the trail drops to FR 3550, bear left and ride along the road. The singletrack begins again on the left at **12.3** miles.

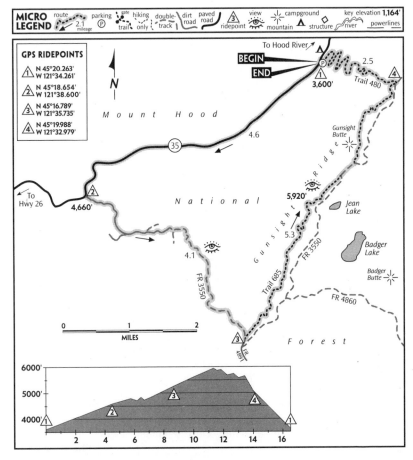

From here, the trail climbs around the east side of Gunsight Butte, another high point, before heading down the blade of the ridge to Gumjuwac Saddle, **14** miles. At the saddle, the trail kisses the road and then bears left on Gumjuwac Trail 480. The trail gains more momentum here, losing more than 1,600 feet in just over two miles. After the **14.5**-mile mark, the switchies come fast and furious. **WHOA!** Watch for hikers, who use this trail to access Badger Creek Wilderness. At **16.4** miles, the trail ends at a dirt road—turn right. At **16.5** miles, reach Hwy 35 and the trailhead parking area to complete the loop.

Gazetteer

Nearby camping: Robinhood (primitive)
Nearest food, drink, services: Government Camp, Hood River

13 East Mount Hood Epic

❀❀❀❀❀

Distance	31.6-mile one-way shuttle
Terrain	Dirt-road climbs, rigorous ridge trails, some pushing, fast descents; 4,000-foot loss; views
Duration	6 to 9 hours
Travel	Hood River—34 miles; Portland—98 miles
Skill level	Advanced
Season	Late summer, fall
Maps	Green Trails: Mount Hood, Hood River
Restrictions	None
More info	Mount Hood National Forest, Hood River District, 541-352-6002, www.fs.fed.us/r6/mthood/

The Scoop

Don't let the mammoth elevation loss fool you—the cumulative gain on this ride logs in at more than 5,000 feet. The East Mount Hood Epic begins with a 1,500-foot dirt-road and singletrack climb, and tosses in another 1,000-foot climb after ten miles. Most of the rest of the ride consists of the jagged ups and downs of difficult ridge-trail riding. Is this the top? Not yet. After thirty-one miles, you'll find yourself walking up a minefield of death-cookies toward the top of Bald Butte. Who signed me up for this? The ridgeline trail affords almost continuous views, so along the way you'll become familiar with the cracks and cirques, cliffs and coves of east Mount Hood. Bring plenty of food and water. In case of the unexpected bonk, four bailout points are noted in the ride description. The bailouts don't significantly reduce the mileage, but they do offer easier road routes back to the car.

Driving Directions

From Portland, drive east on Interstate 84 and take exit 64, just past Hood River. Zero out your odometer at the end of the interstate ramp. Turn right and then immediately right again, following signs for State Highway 35. Proceed straight through the intersection at 0.3 mile, now heading south on Hwy 35. At 10.9 miles, turn left on Pine Mont Drive (Forest Road 17). At 12.3 miles, drop off a car at the gravel pullout on the right. Return to Hwy 35, turn left,

Mount Hood from Gunsight Ridge

reset your odometer to zero, and continue south. At 23.3 miles, turn left on Bennett Pass Road (FR 3550) and park immediately.

The Ride

From Bennett Pass, ride up FR 3550, climbing moderately. When the road forks at **1.1** miles, bear left. At **1.3** miles, the road divides again—bear right and continue up. (Note: Maps show Trail 684 paralleling the road from this point on, but Trail 684 has not been maintained in years and doesn't exist. Don't spend any time searching for it.) Rougher, steeper, and narrower now, the road forks at **1.8** miles—go left, continuing directly up the ridgeline. On a clear day, Mount Hood is so close it seems you can reach out and grab a handful of snow off Newton Clark Glacier. Pass around the dramatic rocky crown of the ridge, descend for a short distance, then climb again.

At **4.1** miles, just before the road reaches a T, turn left on Gunsight Ridge Trail 685. The trail, rocky, technical, and steep at times, follows the ridgeline. WOOF! Crest a high point, then at **6.8** miles pass a rocky viewpoint on the left. At **7.1** miles, the trail kisses the road. From here, climb to another high point and noodle across a small subalpine meadow, where you'll see views of Mount Hood to the west and Mount Jefferson to the east. At **7.5** miles, when the trail drops to FR 3550, bear left and ride along the road. The singletrack begins again on the left at **7.7** miles.

The trail climbs around the east side of Gunsight Butte, another high point, before heading down the steep edge of the ridge to Gumjuwac Saddle, **9.4** miles. (Bailout: Turn left on Gumjuwac Trail 480 and ride down to Hwy 35. Turn right on Hwy 35 and ride to Pine Mont Drive.) From the saddle, continue north on FR 3550. Stay on the main road. The serious climbing begins at **9.6** miles as you grind up the open, west-facing bowl of Lookout Mountain. WOOF! At **11.3** miles, reach a fork—the ride's crest—at High Prairie. Turn left on FR 4410. Before bombing down FR 4410, though, check out the four-volcano view from this intersection.

FR 4410, gravelly and washboarded, winds down the ridge that connects Gunsight Ridge to the south with Surveyors Ridge to the north. Watch out for vehicles on the road during this fast descent. At **13.8** miles, turn right onto Cooks Meadow Trail 639 and immediately begin climbing. The trail soon bends left and rounds the west side of the hill, **14.3** miles. From here, the trail, twisted and root-strewn, hardscrabble in spots, launches down the hillside toward Cooks Meadow. Cross a dirt road at **15.4** miles and continue down. The trail crosses FR 44 at **16.4** miles. (Bailout: Either turn left and take

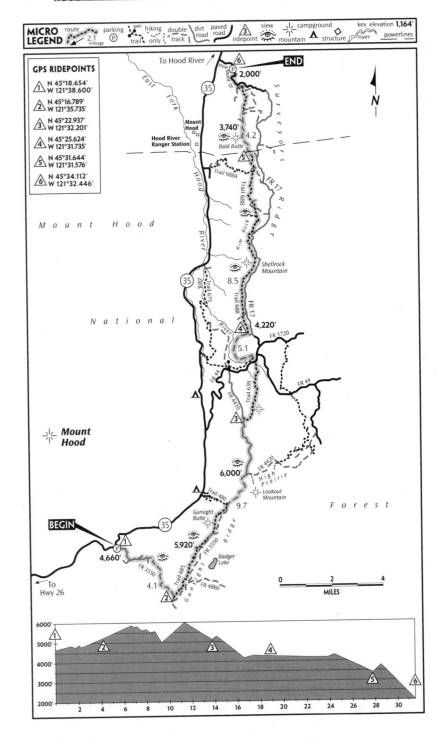

FR 44 to Hwy 35; or turn right and take FR 44 to FR 17, then take Hwy 35 or FR 17 north to the end of the ride.) Immediately after crossing the paved road, the trail forks—turn right onto Surveyors Ridge Trail 688, cross Dog River, and climb through Cooks Meadow.

At **17** miles, stay to the left (ignoring a doubletrack on the right) and cross a small creek. From here, follow the doubletrack through a cleared area. The doubletrack is dusty and rocky in sections. **WHOA!** At **18.9** miles, turn left onto Trail 688—it's easily missed. Cross a dirt road at **19.7** miles. Pass through stands of fir alternated with clearcuts and fireweed. Starting around **21** miles, there's a tough climb to the top of an open knoll, which affords awesome views of Mount Hood.

The trail descends, churning through the forest, to a fork at **21.8** miles—turn right and continue down before climbing again. At **22.4** miles, when the trail kisses a doubletrack, bear to the left. After a few more pedal strokes, bear left again onto the singletrack. (Bailout: Take the doubletrack 50 yards to FR 17, turn left, and ride north to the end of the ride.) From here, the trail traverses a series of hillside meadows. Past rock outcrops, the trail is technical and tricky in places, with embedded rocks and a side slope. At a fork, **23.7** miles, bear to the left and climb. At **24.2** miles, pass a trail on the left that leads to the site of an old lookout. After a short traverse, descend. Cross gravel roads at **24.4** and **24.8** miles. When the road forks at **25.5** miles, bear right and descend the rocky trail. Reach a fork at **26.4** miles and go right. Cross another gravel road.

At **27.4** miles, the trail dumps out at the trailhead under the power lines. (Bailout: Turn right at the power lines and take the dirt road one-half mile to FR 17. Turn left on FR 17 and ride north to the end of the ride.) From here, cross under the power lines, veering left, and climb the horrible, ogreish road to the top of Bald Butte. At **28.3** miles, reach the top. Do you care about views any more? Descend northward down the doubletrack. At **29.4** miles, stay to the right. When the doubletrack forks again, **29.6** miles, bear left. **WHOA!** At **29.9** miles, turn left to find an easily missed singletrack. The trail rips down the north slope of Surveyors Ridge, a nice ride through fir forest. At **30.9** miles, the trail dumps out at an intersection of three roads: Go straight, downhill. At **31.1** miles, reach Pine Mont Drive, which is paved, and turn left. At **31.6** miles, reach the gravel pullout on the left to complete the ride.

Gazetteer

Nearby camping: Robinhood (primitive)
Nearest food, drink, services: Government Camp, Hood River

HOOD RIVER AND EAST MOUNT HOOD
Badger Lake

Distance	22.4-mile out-and-back
Terrain	Moderate to difficult climbing on rough dirt roads; 1,030-foot gain; views
Duration	3 to 6 hours
Travel	Hood River—34 miles; Portland—62 miles
Skill level	Intermediate
Season	Summer, fall
Maps	Green Trails: Mount Hood
Restrictions	None
More info	Mount Hood National Forest, Hood River District, 541-352-6002, www.fs.fed.us/r6/mthood/

The Scoop

Tucked in a deep pocket between Badger Butte and Gunsight Ridge, Badger Lake is packed with fish (and scoured by mosquitoes). Don't have an SUV but

Badger Lake

you still want to fish for the lake's fatties? Ride your bike. This is a basic out-and-back ride on rough ridgeline roads. However, the dirt road–only route and moderate elevation gain belie this ride's difficulty. The cumulative elevation gain adds up to more than 3,000 feet, and sections of the road are quite steep. Forest Road 140 in to the lake is a cherry stem into the Badger Creek Wilderness.

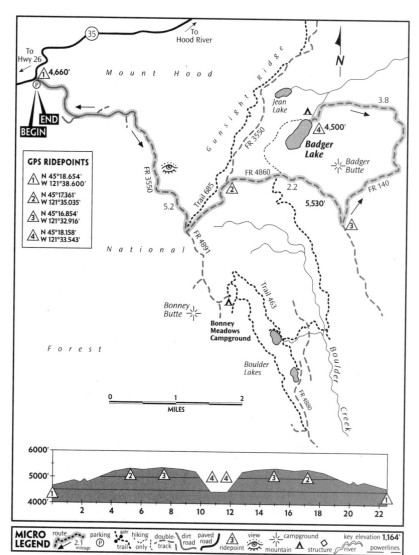

GPS RIDEPOINTS

1. N 45°18.654'
   W 121°38.600'
2. N 45°17.361'
   W 121°35.035'
3. N 45°16.854'
   W 121°32.916'
4. N 45°18.158'
   W 121°33.543'

MICRO LEGEND — route, 2.1 mileage, parking (P), gate, hiking trail only, double-track, dirt road, paved road, ridepoint, view, mountain, campground, structure, river, key elevation 1,164', powerlines

Driving Directions

From Portland, take US Highway 26 eastbound about 56 miles, past Ski Bowl and Government Camp, to its junction with State Highway 35. Set your odometer to zero, and turn north onto Hwy 35. At 6.2 miles, turn right onto Bennett Pass Road (FR 3550) and park immediately.

From Hood River (exit 64 off Interstate 84), set your odometer to zero at the end of the interstate ramp and drive south on Hwy 35. At 34.2 miles, turn left onto Bennett Pass Road (FR 3550) and park immediately.

The Ride

From Bennett Pass, ride up FR 3550, climbing moderately. When the road forks at **1.1** miles, bear left. At **1.3** miles, the road divides again—bear right and continue up. Rougher, steeper, and narrower now, the road forks at **1.8** miles—go left, continuing up the ridgeline. Pass around the dramatic rocky crown of the ridge, descend for a short distance, then climb again. At **4.1** miles, pass Gunsight Ridge Trail on the left and immediately reach a T in the road. Turn left, continuing on FR 3550 toward Badger Lake. At **5.2** miles, reach a fork and bear right onto FR 4860.

From here, the rock-strewn road descends quickly on the narrow ridge between Boulder Creek and Badger Lake. At a low point on the ridge, trails exit on the right and left—continue on FR 4860, climbing again. At **7.4** miles, reach a fork and turn left onto FR 140. Pass Valley View Cabin on the left and cruise a comfortable descent. Around **9.5** miles, the road becomes rougher as it drops precipitously toward Badger Lake. You'll wish you had that 40-pound, full-suspension downhill bike about now (and that 18-pound, tin-can cross-country model on the climb back out). At **10.9** miles, after you've burned through a set of brake pads, the road levels. Stay to the left and at **11.2** miles reach the lake. When you're done casting for fatties, turn your bike around and retrace your route to Bennett Pass, **22.4** miles.

Gazetteer

Nearby camping: Robinhood (primitive)
Nearest food, drink, services: Government Camp, Hood River

Boulder Lakes

◍◍◍

Distance	**17.6-mile** lollipop (**6.4-mile** option)
Terrain	Climbing and descending, some steep and technical, on dirt roads and singletrack; **900-foot gain**; views
Duration	3 to 5 hours
Travel	Hood River—34 miles; Portland—62 miles
Skill level	Advanced
Season	Late summer, fall
Maps	Green Trails: Mount Hood, Mount Wilson
Restrictions	USFS Trail Park Pass required
More info	Mount Hood National Forest, Hood River District, 541-352-6002, www.fs.fed.us/r6/mthood/

The Scoop

The simple elevation gain listed for this ride, 900 feet, is deceptive. Since you reach the route's high point around the middle of the ride and then drop

Boulder Creek

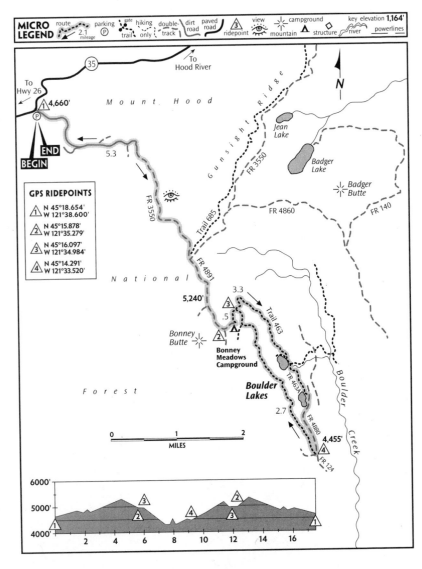

MICRO LEGEND — route, 2.1 mileage, P parking, gate, hiking trail only, double-track, dirt road, paved road, △3 ridepoint, view, mountain, campground, structure, river, key elevation 1,164', powerlines

GPS RIDEPOINTS

△1 N 45°18.654'
W 121°38.600'

△2 N 45°15.878'
W 121°35.279'

△3 N 45°16.097'
W 121°34.984'

△4 N 45°14.291'
W 121°33.520'

again, the cumulative gain on this route tops 3,000 feet. Still, it's more exploratory than difficult, with more than two-thirds on various dirt roads. The trail down to the lake is a technical challenge; it's also used extensively by hikers. Boulder Lake, plunked into a large, rocky cirque east of Bonney Butte, makes for a great picnic stop. The views of Mount Hood from the road climb are icing.

Driving Directions

From Portland, take US Highway 26 eastbound about 56 miles, past Ski Bowl and Government Camp, to its junction with State Highway 35. Set your odometer to zero, and turn north onto Hwy 35. At 6.2 miles, turn right onto Bennett Pass Road (Forest Road 3550) and park immediately.

From Hood River (exit 64 off Interstate 84), set your odometer to zero at the end of the interstate ramp and drive south on Hwy 35. At 34.2 miles, turn left onto Bennett Pass Road (FR 3550) and park immediately.

The Ride

From Bennett Pass, ride up FR 3550, climbing moderately. When the road forks at **1.1** miles, bear left. At **1.3** miles, the road divides again—bear right and continue up. Rougher, steeper, and narrower now, the road forks at **1.8** miles—go left, continuing up the ridgeline. On a clear day, Mount Hood is so close it seems you can reach out and grab a handful of snow off Newton Clark Glacier. Pass over the rocky crest of the ridge, descend for a short distance, then climb again.

Pass Gunsight Ridge Trail on the left, **4.1** miles, and immediately reach a T. Turn right on FR 4891 toward Bonney Meadows and continue ascending. After a crest, reach a fork and bear left at **5.1** miles. At **5.3** miles, turn left on FR 120 toward Bonney Meadows Campground. Just after entering the campground at **5.6** miles, stay left and find an unmarked trail on the left next to a campsite. A sign soon assures you that you're on Boulder Lake Trail 463. At **5.8** miles, reach a fork and bear left toward Boulder Lake. After a short noodle, the trail switchbacks down a steep hillside and then traverses south across several rockfalls.

After a short cannonball, reach Boulder Lake and a fork at **7.4** miles. Stay to the left and begin circling the lake clockwise. Pass through several campsites, then reach a fork at **7.5** miles. Turn right on Little Boulder Lake Trail 463A. The narrow trail climbs a ridge, tops out, and then drops to Little Boulder Lake, **8.1** miles. Turn left, away from the lake. Almost immediately the trail ends at FR 4880—turn right and pedal south. On sunny days, FR 4880 affords hazy views south of the low hills and plains, bare and mottled, of eastern Oregon. **WHOA!** Immediately after passing FR 124 on the left, **9.1** miles, find a faint trail on the right, marked by a small cairn and an ancient sign: Loop.

The trail, which may need brushing, climbs north at a moderate grade, skirting close to the edge of the ridge on occasion and offering views down to

Boulder Lakes and into the Boulder Creek valley. Reach a T at **11.6** miles and turn right toward Bonney Meadow Campground. At **11.8** miles, arrive at another T and turn left. When the trail ends at the campground road, **12** miles, turn right and retrace your path to Bennett Pass. Reach a T at **12.3** miles and turn right on FR 4891. Stay on the main road, climbing and then descending to a fork at **13.5** miles. Turn left onto FR 3550, following the sign toward Hwy 35. Reach Bennett Pass at **17.6** miles to complete the ride.

Option

With a four-wheel-drive vehicle, you can drive to Bonney Meadows Campground and begin riding from there. This slashes 11.2 miles of dirt-road riding from the ride, but now it may not be long enough given the effort it takes to get there.

Gazetteer

Nearby camping: Bonney Meadows (primitive), Robinhood (primitive)
Nearest food, drink, services: Government Camp, Hood River

Boulder Lake from Forest Road 4860

16 Mineral Creek

⊕⊕⊕

Distance	13.3-mile lollipop
Terrain	Sandy singletrack descent, dirt road and singletrack climb; 1,060-foot gain
Duration	3 to 4 hours
Travel	Hood River—36 miles; Portland—60 miles
Skill level	Advanced
Season	Summer, fall
Maps	Green Trails: Mount Hood, Mount Wilson
Restrictions	None
More info	Mount Hood National Forest, Hood River District, 541-352-6002, www.fs.fed.us/r6/mthood/

The Scoop

This is not a popular mountain-bike route, partly because of the faint, sandy trail, but primarily because no one talks about it. It's a good one, though. The

Mount Hood from White River Sno-Park

descent follows a singletrack, sandy at times, along bright orange Mineral Creek. In a few sections, the trail seems to disappear altogether in the disorienting sandy plain of the creek, not unlike a journey to the center of the earth. Stick with it, however, and the fast traverse along the White River Trail will make you smile. The Barlow Road climb out, through a dark, rich forest, is gradual and only lightly traveled by vehicles.

Driving Directions

From Portland, take US Highway 26 eastbound about 56 miles, past Ski Bowl and Government Camp, to its junction with State Highway 35. Set your odometer to zero, and turn north onto Hwy 35. At 4.2 miles, turn left into White River West Sno-Park.

From Hood River (exit 64 off Interstate 84), drive south on Hwy 35. After about 34 miles, cross Bennett Pass and set your odometer to zero. At 2 miles, turn right into White River West Sno-Park.

The Ride

To begin, cross Hwy 35. Just across the highway from the paved Sno-Park, find a trail into the woods. Pass through an ad hoc campsite and follow the Mineral Jane Ski Trail signs and blue diamonds that mark the route. The trail, somewhat sandy and not so defined, gradually descends, crisscrossing the creek over several low cross-country ski bridges. At **1** mile, reach a fork and bear left on the lesser trail. The trail becomes even less defined. Follow the wide corridors through the woods and watch for blue diamonds and low log bridges.

At **2** miles, the trail spills out onto a sandy wash populated by pines, and some walking is necessary despite the downhill grade. Follow the occasional blue diamonds and tall wood posts that flag the route. The trail here, winding in and out of the pines, paralleling the bright orange channel of Mineral Creek, is defined only by the hoof and wheel tracks in the sand and is easy to lose in the wide, gray, sloping wash. With some surfing, some walking, the hike-a-bike continues. **WHOA!** At **2.7** miles, the posts and diamonds seem to end, and the way must be Zenned for a short distance—continue downhill slightly to the left.

A pine-needle tread begins at **3** miles as the trail, pursuing an ancient road, winds into a mixed forest. Wood posts appear again. At **3.6** miles, bear right and cross a short bridge. From here, enter a darker forest, highlighted by huge cedar and Douglas fir. This is a fast descent on a good trail. Cross a bridge at **4.8** miles. Ten yards farther, the trail dumps out at the end of a dirt road—bear right and cruise down this road. At **6** miles, reach a four-way intersection: Turn right onto Barlow Road (FR 3530) and ride gradually up toward Barlow Pass. Stay on the main road. At **7.8** miles, pass Grindstone Campground on the left.

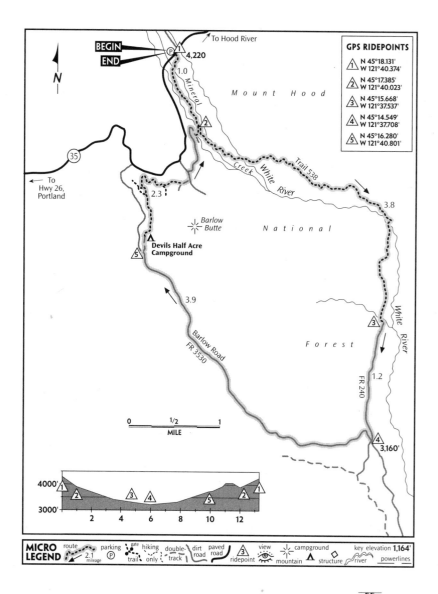

GPS RIDEPOINTS

1	N 45°18.131' W 121°40.374'
2	N 45°17.385' W 121°40.023'
3	N 45°15.668' W 121°37.537'
4	N 45°14.549' W 121°37.708'
5	N 45°16.280' W 121°40.801'

MICRO LEGEND
route 2.1 mileage • parking P • gate • hiking trail only • double-track • dirt road • paved road • ridepoint • view • campground • mountain • structure • river • key elevation **1,164'** powerlines

Ignore a road on the left at **8.5** miles. At **9.9** miles, reach a fork and turn right on FR 220 toward Devils Half Acre Campground. At the campground, **10.1** miles, turn right and climb the steep, grassy hillside, a likely push. This is Barlow Creek Trail. After one hundred yards, the trail levels as it enters the woods. When the trail forks at **10.8** miles, bear right on Mineral Jane Ski Trail. Pass Trail 670 on the right one-quarter mile farther.

The trail ends at a road, **11.1** miles—bear left on the road. Ignore a lesser road on the right. Reach a T at **11.4** miles and turn left. Ignore a road back on the right. Then at a fork at **11.5** miles, bear right, following the blue diamonds. When the road ends, **12** miles, turn right onto an old dirt road. At **12.1** miles, turn left onto a singletrack. At **12.2** miles, cross a bridge and immediately reach a T—turn left. From here, ride back up the slightly sandy trail to Hwy 35 at **13.3** miles.

Gazetteer

Nearby camping: Still Creek, Robinhood (primitive), Devils Half Acre (primitive)
Nearest food, drink, services: Government Camp

17 Lower Deschutes Rail-Trail

⊕⊕

Distance	22.2-mile out-and-back
Terrain	Nearly flat with two short hills; 115-foot gain; views
Duration	2 to 4 hours
Travel	Hood River—36 miles; Portland—100 miles
Skill level	Beginner
Season	Year-round
Maps	USGS 30x60 minute: Goldendale
Restrictions	None
More info	Oregon State Parks, 800-551-6949, www.prd.state.or.us

The Scoop

This ride follows the grand views of the winding Deschutes River canyon, green in spring, golden in summer and fall. If you do go in summer, try this ride at dawn or be prepared for a scorching, 100-degree day. Like most rail-trails,

Sunrise in the lower Deschutes River canyon

57

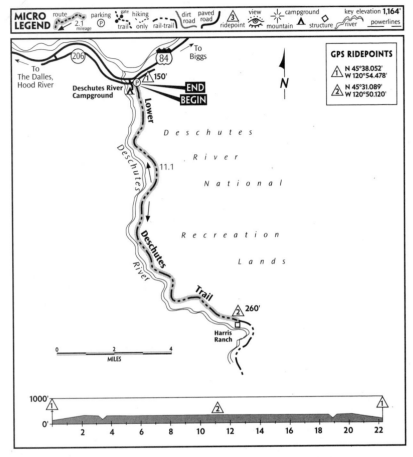

this one is wide and level. Sections of the trail can be sandy. Be sure to turn around well before you get tired or run low on water. Most of the time there are more folks fishing on the river below the trail than biking on it. While most of the trail is on BLM land, Oregon State Parks offers the most up-to-date information.

Driving Directions

From Portland, drive east on Interstate 84 past The Dalles and take exit 97 at Celilo. Set your odometer to zero at the end of the interstate ramp. Turn right, then immediately turn left onto State Highway 206, following the signs toward Deschutes Park. At 3.1 miles, turn right and park in the dirt parking area on the left next to Deschutes River State Park Campground.

Derelict Harris Ranch

The Ride

From the trailhead parking, take the trail next to the campground's entrance road. The trail starts out steep and sandy, but after less than one-quarter mile it flattens out and begins meandering along the river. Lined with sage and low brush, dominated by expansive golden-brown hillsides and high, rocky escarps, the wide trail winds above the Deschutes River. Ignore the numerous trails on the right that lead down to the river. Pass occasional thickets of blackberry. At **3.1** miles, the trail drops steeply to a low point and then climbs back up to the level grade. WHOA! Take care on this rocky section of trail.

From here the trail is sandy in sections, rough and bumpy in others, as it matches the river's long, languorous turns. At **11.1** miles, reach the weathered-gray derelicts that comprised Harris Ranch. Though the trail continues much farther south, turn around here and ride back to the trailhead, **22.2** miles, to complete the ride.

Gazetteer

Nearby camping: Deschutes River State Park
Nearest food, drink, services: The Dalles, Biggs

Bend and Central Oregon

Tired of the rain, mud, and overcastness of western Oregon? Bend, one of the West's best mountain-bike destinations, combines dry weather with terrific trails. Just two hours from Eugene and three hours from Portland, these 22 Bend-area rides provide great fodder for winter bike dreams and easy weekend tripping for most Oregonians. The riding is best early in the summer when the trails aren't too dusty and the thermostat isn't too high.

Bend's lower-elevation trails wind through pure stands of ponderosa pine—huge, orange-barked trees (or was it the orange lenses?). Upper-elevation trails rise through stands of grand fir into the subalpine zone of noble fir and mountain hemlock. The typical Bend ride hits lots of well-graded singletrack, and offers up amazing views of the central Oregon Cascades. The descents are giant slaloms—smooth and fast and dreamlike.

For a great introduction to the area's zippy trails, try Peterson Ridge (ride 21), Swampy Lakes (ride 29), Phil's Trail 24.5 (ride 30), or Lava Lake (ride 34). But Bend is famous for its numerous renegade trails, unofficial trails that appear without permission, like game trails (heck, we're all animals). These trails, controversial and of uncertain status, are almost always a blast to ride. I've included two: Mrazek (ride 26) and Storm King (ride 33). While some would prefer that I not document these trails, I'm including them because you'll hear about them as soon as you arrive in Bend, they are well worn by mountain bikes, and they haven't been closed by the Forest Service. Indeed, the Forest Service may soon add these trails to the official trail system, and they are currently building official links to some of these unofficial trails. Some locals are sensitive—they built the trails for, well, themselves—so ride smart: no out-of-control riding, no riding off trail, and no skidding. Buy your bike gear in Bend and the shop guys will probably give you the skinny about other unmarked trails (buy them a few pints after work and they'll probably show you the trails themselves).

For my gas money, the most outstanding trail near Bend is the circuit around Newberry Caldera (ride 36)—one of the best trails in the West. It's tough, exciting, and spectacular. There are shabby trails even in Bend. Forget about Lower Black Butte Trail, and while Trails 61 and 62 near Skeleton Cave look interesting on the map, manzanita-shredded arms and unstable, horse-trodden trails are what you have to look forward to.

18 BEND AND CENTRAL OREGON
Cache Mountain
❀❀❀❀

Distance	14.5-mile figure eight
Terrain	Long tough dirt-road climb, steep singletrack descent; 1,890-foot gain; views
Duration	2 to 4 hours
Travel	Bend—38 miles; Eugene—89 miles
Skill level	Advanced
Season	Summer, fall
Maps	U.S. Forest Service: Sisters Ranger District
Restrictions	None
More info	Deschutes National Forest, Sisters District, 541-549-2111, www.fs.fed.us/r6/deschutes/

The Scoop

Not particularly high or distinctive, Cache Mountain rises above a pocket of lakes to the west and north. The dirt-road climb to the top, through pine and

Mount Washington from the west flank of Cache Mountain

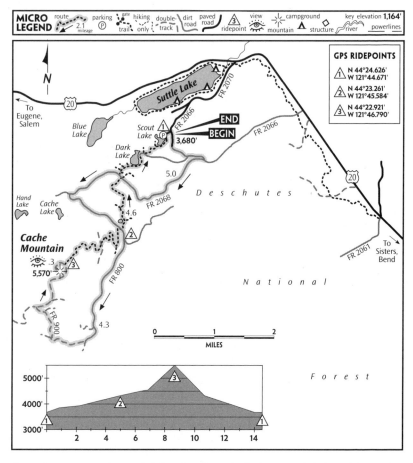

MICRO LEGEND — route · 2.1 mileage · parking Ⓟ · gate · hiking trail only · double-track · dirt road · paved road · ▲ 3 ridepoint · view · campground · mountain · structure · river · key elevation 1,164' · powerlines

fir and, on upper slopes, brick-colored earth, isn't too painful, and from the summit the eastern slopes of Oregon's central Cascades, sublime and oddly ordered, span out in a remarkable panorama. The singletrack down is live— twisting and ragged in sections—and unmarked, and this can make compassing the route problematic; carefully follow the directions below. Several stretches of the trail pass through a tree kill that is the result of beetle infestation, causing a lot of blowdown, and this makes for cumbersome riding when the trail hasn't been cleared—and even sometimes when it has. Try calling ahead for current conditions; however, since this trail is not in the official Sisters Ranger District system, take the information with a grain of salt.

Driving Directions

From Bend, drive northwest on US Highway 20 to Sisters. At the west end of Sisters, set your odometer to zero as you pass the Sisters Ranger Station on the right and continue northwest on US 20. At 13.7 miles, turn left on Suttle Lake Road. At 14.8 miles, pass South Shore Campground on the right. At 15 miles, turn left on Forest Road 2066. At 15.5 miles, turn right on FR 700, toward Scout Lake. At 15.6 miles, turn left and then park on the right.

The Ride

From the parking area, ride back to FR 2066. Turn right and pedal up the paved road. Bear left at the fork at **0.7** mile. The road turns to gravel and heads up. Reach a T at **0.9** mile and take a sharp right on FR 2068. From here, stay on the main road, ignoring numerous spurs, as you gradually climb. At **3.8** miles, reach a fork and bear left. Reach a fork at **5** miles and turn right on FR 800. The gradual climb continues through ponderosa pine and grand fir along the east flank of Cache Mountain. When the road forks at **6.7** miles, stay on the main road to the left. Reach a fork at **6.9** miles and go right. The road climbs more steeply now, past lesser spur roads, up into noble fir elevations.

At **7.6** miles, reach a fork and bear right onto FR 900. Views of Three Sisters and Mount Washington emerge. At **8.1** miles, pass by a road on the right, continuing up FR 900. Reach a T at **8.3** miles and turn right, remaining on FR 900. When the road forks at **8.6** miles, stay to the left. At **9.3** miles, note the unmarked singletrack on the right. You'll take this, but first continue up the road to the top of Cache Mountain. Reach the summit at **9.6** miles. On a clear day, all the area's mountains are visible: Three Sisters, Broken Top, Mount Washington, Three Finger Jack, Mount Jefferson, and even the top of Mount Hood far to the north.

When you are done gawking, ride back down the road to the unmarked singletrack, now on your left at **9.9** miles, and take it. The trail, which is not signed at all, is ragged and steep in places as it corkscrews down the northeast slope of Cache Mountain. Fire and beetle infestation have devastated the forest here, and rampikes stand like lifeless gray ghosts. The relentless blowdown of dead trees has made it difficult for the Forest Service to stay current with the maintenance that this section of trail needs. Call ahead if you don't like getting off and on your bike a lot. When it's buffed out, though, this is a nice descent.

At **11** miles, cross a doubletrack. Reach a fork at **11.5** miles and turn left. Cross a dirt road at **11.8** miles, then pass by a small pond on the left. The trail divides just after the pond—bear left. At **12.3** miles, reach a fork and bear right, still descending. The trail, wide and fast here, reaches a road at **13** miles. WHOA! Turn left onto the road, pedal about 15 yards, and then turn right onto a singletrack. (Don't take the trail immediately across the road.) The trail forks and then immediately forks again: Turn left and then right in quick succession. At **13.2** miles, reach a fork and go right, descending again. Ignore a trail back to the left on **13.4** miles.

The trail drops to Dark Lake, then winds around the lake counterclockwise, finally ending at a dirt road, **13.7** miles. Turn right onto the dirt road, then after a few rotations turn onto the second trail on the left, signed Scout Lake. Ignore a faint trail on the right, and then at **13.9** miles, bear right at the fork. From here, the trail switchbacks down to the lake. Bear right and pedal counterclockwise around the lake. At **14.5** miles, turn right to the parking area to complete the circuit.

Gazetteer

Nearby camping: Scout Lake, South Shore
Nearest food, drink, services: Sisters

19 Suttle Lake

✪✪✪

Distance	13.2-mile lollipop
Terrain	Rolling singletrack, wide in spots; 200-foot gain; views
Duration	2 to 3 hours
Travel	Bend—33 miles; Eugene—93 miles
Skill level	Intermediate
Season	Late spring, summer, fall
Maps	U.S. Forest Service: Sisters Ranger District
Restrictions	USFS Trail Park Pass required
More info	Deschutes National Forest, Sisters District, 541-549-2111, www.fs.fed.us/r6/deschutes/

The Scoop

From the trailhead on a roads-to-trails conversion, this route noodles and winds—it's not quite zippy—across the flats between Cache Mountain and Black Butte, following the northwestern slant of US Highway 20. Although you can't see the highway from the trail, you can hear the occasional traffic noise. The trail around Suttle Lake is fun and popular with families, fishermen, and campers out for a walk, so ride with care. Not the place to ride fast and impress your friends with that new crossover move, this is a nice intermediate ride with no tough climbing and lots of fine views of the lake.

Driving Directions

From Bend, drive northwest on US 20 through Sisters. At the west end of Sisters, set your odometer to zero as you pass the Sisters Ranger Station on the right, continuing northwest on US 20. At 9.9 miles, turn left onto Forest Road 2060, and immediately park at the small trailhead on the right. (Note: There is additional parking directly across US 20.)

The Ride

From the trailhead, ride north, following the Roads to Trails signs. The trail, which fumbles between doubletrack and singletrack, crosses a dirt road at **0.9** mile. When the trail forks at **2.2** miles, bear right on FR 700. But at **2.3** miles, bear left onto a singletrack, again following the Roads to Trails sign. Cross a dirt road at **2.6** miles. The way ascends moderately from here. Cross a

dirt road again at **4.3** miles, then cross over a paved road a short distance farther. From here, stay on the main trail, first ignoring a trail on the left and
then bearing left at a fork. Reach a five-way intersection at **4.7** miles and go
straight on the main trail that wraps clockwise around Suttle Lake.

WHOA! Since the trail around the lake is popular with families, ride con-
servatively. As you ride, stay to the right, ignoring the spur trails on the left.
The trail, which is mostly wide with a few roots and tight corners thrown in

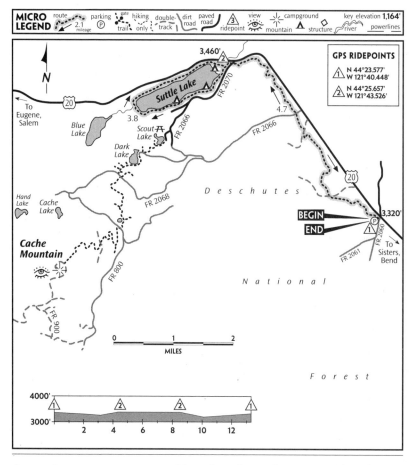

for good measure, passes several boat launches and campgrounds as it traverses the south side of the lake. At the west end of the lake, the trail crosses several bridges. As you reach a campground on the northeast end of the lake, **8.2** miles, follow the trail signs up to the left onto a paved road. Follow the paved road to an intersection at **8.4** miles and cross this intersection, veering right, to the singletrack that continues on the far side. Cross a bridge. At an intersection of trails, **8.5** miles, bear left and ride back toward the trailhead following the Roads to Trails signs. Reach the trailhead at **13.2** miles.

Gazetteer

Nearby camping: Indian Ford, South Shore
Nearest food, drink, services: Sisters

20 BEND AND CENTRAL OREGON
Black Butte

Distance	16-mile lollipop
Terrain	Constant ups and downs, some steep, on rocky roads, wide and narrow trails; 750-foot gain; views
Duration	2 to 4 hours
Travel	Bend—29 miles; Eugene—97 miles
Skill level	Intermediate
Season	Late spring, summer, fall
Maps	U.S. Forest Service: Sisters Ranger District
Restrictions	None
More info	Deschutes National Forest, Sisters District, 541-549-2111, www.fs.fed.us/r6/deschutes/

The Scoop

With none of the irregular crags and ridges and late-summer snow that characterize most other mountains near Bend, Black Butte looms out of the ponderosa pine distance like a foreboding shadow. And this looming, along with a perfect cone-shaped symmetry, makes this is the best-formed lollipop route in *Kissing the Trail,* drawing as many pointing fingers out of car windows as those other mountains. The cool thing is that you can point at it and then go ride around it. Of course, without any of the zippy singletrack and only a few of the snowcapped views that this area is known for, the mountain-bike routes on Black Butte—both upper and lower—don't rate among my top choices in the Bend-Sisters area. The tread is sometimes ragged and horse-torn, sometimes steep and scattered with loose rocks, and there's very little real singletrack. But if you pass Sisters with any frequency, your mountain bike latched to the top, your finger pointing, you may at last give in so you can say you've circled Black Butte, the most perfect lollipop route in Oregon.

Driving Directions

From Bend, drive northwest on US Highway 20 to Sisters. At the west end of Sisters, set your odometer to zero as you pass the Sisters Ranger Station on the right, and continue northwest on US 20. At 9.9 miles, turn left onto Indian Creek Road (Forest Road 2060), and immediately park at the trailhead on the right.

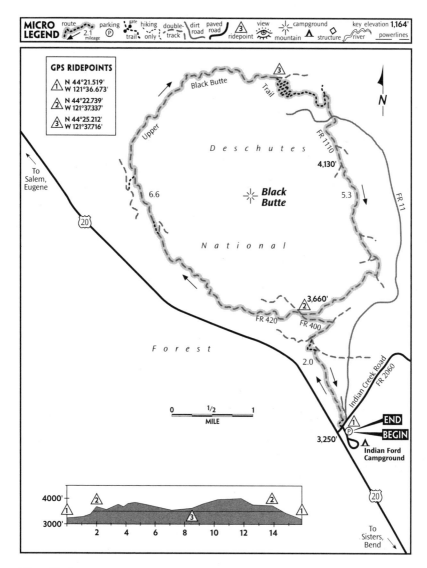

GPS RIDEPOINTS

⚠️1 N 44°21.519'
W 121°36.673'

⚠️2 N 44°22.739'
W 121°37.337'

⚠️3 N 44°25.212'
W 121°37.716'

The Ride

From the trailhead parking area next to the entrance to Indian Ford Campground, cross Indian Creek Road to a narrow trail. Descend slightly, then bear left on a doubletrack, following wood posts marked Roads to Trails. Stay left. The doubletrack, sandy and horse-worn, ascends slightly, through old-growth ponderosa pine. At **1** mile, bear left onto a narrow trail. At **1.3** miles, the trail

Following the manzanita corridors

ends at a dirt road: Turn left, then immediately right, following the sign toward Upper Black Butte Trail. When you reach a fork in the road at **1.6** miles, turn up to the left on FR 400. The climb is short but can be brutal: hot, loose, rocky, and steep.

Reach a four-way at **2** miles and turn left on FR 420. The route, alternating between doubletrack and wide singletrack, through open pine forests and tight corridors of manzanita, rounds the southwestern slope of Black Butte, climbing and falling and, at times, affording glimpses of the Three Sisters and Mount Washington. WHOA! At **4.7** miles, turn left on an unmarked single-track; it's easily missed. At **4.8** miles, when the trail ends, continue straight on the doubletrack. At **5.6** miles, ignore a singletrack back on the left that connects with Lower Black Butte Trail. Continue straight on Upper Black Butte Trail.

At **6** miles, the doubletrack begins rounding the north slope of the butte, descending slightly. Through the fir and pine, you can occasionally see Three Finger Jack and Mount Jefferson. WHOA! At **8.6** miles, turn right onto a sin-gletrack; it's an easy turn to miss. The trail climbs steadily, switchbacking up the hillside. At **9.3** miles, the trail bends left, alternating between singletrack and doubletrack. Reach a fork at **10** miles and go right, following the Roads to Trails sign. After a tough climb, cross a gravel road. The route follows FR 1110 now, and it's doubletrack the rest of the way. At **10.5** miles, reach a fork and bear right. When the road divides at **10.9** miles, bear left. To the south-east, you'll see long views into the mottled expanse of eastern Oregon.

At **11.8** miles, stay to the right on FR 190. At **12.1** miles, reach a fork and bear left, twice. At **12.5** miles, reach a fork and go right, following the Roads to Trails sign. Reach a four-way at **13.9** miles and turn left. The road descends steeply; the surface is loose and rocky. Reach a T at **14.4** miles—turn right. At **14.7** miles, reach a four-way: Turn left and then immediately right onto a sin-gletrack, following the trail sign. Bear right at **14.9** miles and also at **15.8** miles. Turn right at **15.9** miles and climb slightly. At **16** miles, reach the end of the trail across the road from the trailhead to complete the ride.

Gazetteer

Nearby camping: Indian Ford, South Shore
Nearest food, drink, services: Sisters

21 BEND AND CENTRAL OREGON
Peterson Ridge

✪✪✪

Distance	14.8-mile loop
Terrain	Moderate paved-road climb, zippy doubletrack and singletrack descent; **640-foot gain**; views
Duration	2 to 4 hours
Travel	Bend—23 miles; Eugene—103 miles
Skill level	Intermediate
Season	Late spring, summer, fall
Maps	U.S. Forest Service: Sisters Ranger District
Restrictions	None
More info	Deschutes National Forest, Sisters District, 541-549-2111, www.fs.fed.us/r6/deschutes/

The Scoop

A favorite of Sisters locals, this is the kind of riding that makes Bend-area mountain biking famous—fast, winding, hard-packed trails with banked corners, through an open pine forest. It's such a fun loop, in fact, that when

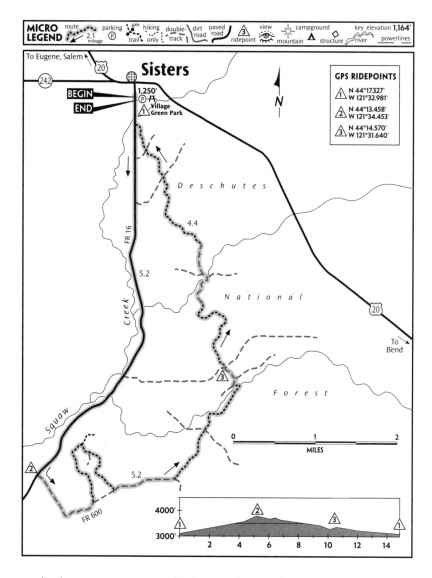

you're done you may want to ride it a couple more times. To this end, you can make it longer and more difficult by riding out and back on the trail rather than using the paved forest road to loop it. Equestrians are discouraged from using this trail, so it stays smooth and fast.

Driving Directions

From Bend, drive northwest on US Highway 20 to Sisters. In Sisters, turn left (south) on Elm Street. After a couple of blocks, find the Village Green—a town park—on the left, opposite the town's fire station. Park here on the left.

The Ride

From the Village Green, pedal south on Elm Street. At **0.4** mile, pass the Sisters Mountain Bike Loop/Peterson Ridge trailhead on the left and continue south. Elm Street becomes Forest Road 16. After a gentle climb, the paved forest road rises more steeply beginning around the **4.1**-mile point. WHOA! Just past the crest of the hill and just before a narrow pullout on the left, turn left onto an unmarked doubletrack, **5.2** miles.

The doubletrack descends to a T at **5.7** miles. Turn left onto FR 600. Ride over a berm and continue straight on the road. WHOA! At **6.1** miles, turn left onto the unmarked singletrack. The smooth, hard-packed trail zips through and around ponderosa pine, juniper, and manzanita. At **6.7** miles, bear right at the fork, following the bike signs. At **6.9** miles, bear left. Stay on the main trail and follow the bike signs. Reach a T with a doubletrack, FR 600, at **7.7** miles and turn left. WHOA! At **8.5** miles, turn left to return to singletrack riding with the added banked-corner feature. *Wheee!* Cross a dirt road, then descend sharply.

Cross a creek at **10.1** miles, and turn right onto the doubletrack. After a few pedal rotations, reach a fork and turn left, continuing on doubletrack. At **10.4** miles, reach a four-way—ride straight across the dirt road to the wide trail opposite. The trail alternates between single- and doubletrack. Bear to the left at **11.1** miles. Near a campsite, **11.8** miles, bear right onto a doubletrack. WHOA! At **12.1** miles, turn left onto a narrow trail, and immediately cross over the canal. From here, turn left on the dirt road, then bear right at the fork. At **12.5** miles, follow the bike signs as the route crosses a dirt road to a singletrack.

Continue to follow the bike signs as the trail, which crosses a series of doubletracks, snakes frenetically through the pine forest. At **14.4** miles, reach the end of the trail. Turn right onto FR 16 (Elm Street) and spin back to the Village Green to complete the ride, **14.8** miles.

Gazetteer

Nearby camping: Indian Ford
Nearest food, drink, services: Sisters

22 Smith Rock

⊕⊕

Distance	4.2-mile out-and-back
Terrain	Short dirt-road descent then easy, nearly flat trail; 190-foot gain; views
Duration	1 hour
Travel	Bend—25 miles; Eugene—131 miles
Skill level	Intermediate
Season	Late spring, summer, fall
Maps	USGS 7.5 minute: Redmond
Restrictions	Oregon State Parks Day-use Permit required
More info	Oregon State Parks, 800-551-6949, www.prd.state.or.us

The Scoop

Out on the edge of Eastern Oregon's high desert just northeast of Terrebonne, the Crooked River snakes around a humongous prow of rock known as Smith

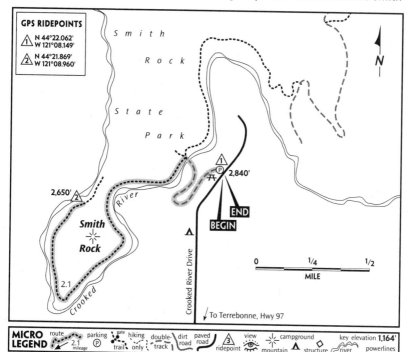

The Crooked River at Smith Rock State Park

Rock. Carabiners, harnesses, and climbing rope fill the old Subaru wagons and air-cooled Westfalias that haul in underfinanced pilgrim climbers from all over the world. The mountain-bike trails that begin from Smith Rock State Park are less well known but offer an exciting range of experience and scenery. This route sticks to the short, easy trail that cuts around the base of Smith Rock alongside the Crooked River. There's lots of additional trail to explore, or you can lay your bike down and take off on some of the park's foot trails. Looking for a more difficult ride? Check out ride 23 (Burma Road) or 24 (Gray Butte).

Driving Directions

From Bend, drive about 22 miles north on US Highway 97. In Terrebonne, turn right on B Avenue toward Smith Rock State Park, and set your odometer to zero. B Avenue becomes Northeast Smith Rock Way. At 0.6 mile, turn left on First Street Northeast, which soon becomes Wilcox Avenue. At 2.7 miles, turn left on Crooked River Drive. At 3.2 miles, reach the day-use parking area for Smith Rock State Park.

The Ride

From the day-use parking area, take the paved trail toward Smith Rock. At the edge of the bluff, the trail becomes a ragged, gravelly road as it descends toward the river, possibly requiring a short walk. Ignore the trail on the right as you descend; stay on the road. At the bottom of the road, cross a wood bridge over Crooked River. At the four-way just across the bridge, turn left onto the wide dirt trail, and pedal along the base of the towering rocks. Stay along the river, ignoring numerous climbers' trails on the right. At the **1**-mile point, walk up a set of stairs. From here the trail traverses the hillside above the river.

Cross between some big rocks on the left and Smith Rock on the right. The sandy trail winds through low brush. At **1.7** miles, traverse a difficult, loose scree slope. The trail soon widens and zips again, running for a short distance right along the river. At **2.1** miles, the trail becomes quite technical, loose and rocky. Turn around here and retrace your route along Crooked River and then up to the parking area, **4.2** miles.

Gazetteer

Nearby camping: Smith Rock State Park (primitive)
Nearest food, drink, services: Terrebonne, Redmond

23 Burma Road

✺✺✺

Distance	11-mile lollipop
Terrain	Dirt-road climbs and descents, singletrack descent; 1,120-foot gain; views
Duration	2 to 4 hours
Travel	Bend—25 miles; Eugene—131 miles
Skill level	Intermediate
Season	Late spring, summer, fall
Maps	USGS 30x60 minute: Bend
Restrictions	Oregon State Parks Day-use Permit required
More info	Oregon State Parks, 800-551-6949, www.prd.state.or.us

The Scoop

Let's face it: Burma Road sounds like it might be a cool ride, kind of exotic, off into who-knows-where land. Well, this ride isn't that extraordinary, but it does include two sections of nice singletrack and starts out from Smith Rock

Smith Rock

State Park, which is awesome. The zippy singletrack along the Crooked River that begins the ride is terrific but over altogether too soon. That's where Burma Road begins, a First-gear Freddie climb that, on hot summer days, will sauté your brain in olive oil and garlic if you don't drink enough water. After a descent and another dirt-road climb, the route takes a fast singletrack back to Burma Road and then returns to the state park. It's a fun, not overly strenuous ride.

Driving Directions

From Bend, drive about 22 miles north on US Highway 97. In Terrebonne, turn right on B Avenue toward Smith Rock State Park, and set your odometer to zero. B Avenue becomes Northeast Smith Rock Way. At 0.6 mile, turn left

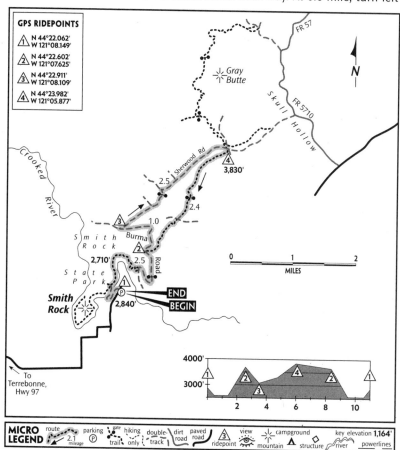

on First Street Northeast, which soon becomes Wilcox Avenue. At 2.7 miles, turn left on Crooked River Drive. At 3.2 miles, reach the day-use parking area for Smith Rock State Park.

The Ride

From the day-use parking area, take the paved trail toward Smith Rock. At the edge of the bluff, the trail becomes a ragged, gravelly road as it descends toward the river. Ignore the trail on the right as you descend. At the bottom of the road, cross a wood bridge over Crooked River. At the four-way intersection immediately across the bridge, turn right onto a dirt trail that spins along the river through pine and sage and rocky crags.

When the trail forks at **1.4** miles, turn left and walk up the steep, loose trail. At **1.6** miles, the trail ends at the Burma Road: Turn left and climb. The road, steep and exposed to the sun, cuts a switchback at **2** miles and continues up. WOOF! Crest the ridge at **2.5** miles, ignoring the singletrack on the right, and click in to a bigger gear for the fast descent. Views: the Three Sisters, Broken Top, and Mount Jefferson. WHOA! At **3.5** miles, just as your speed has peaked, reach a fork and take a sharp right onto Sherwood Road, which is unmarked (if you haven't turned and you start climbing, you've gone too far).

Sherwood Road climbs gently at first. At **4.5** miles, ignore a lesser doubletrack on the right, then pass through a gate and bear right. When the road forks at **4.8** miles, turn right and continue up. After a steep quarter-mile climb, reach Gray Butte Trail on the left and right (immediately before a four-way intersection), **6** miles. Turn right onto the trail. From here, stay on the main trail, ignoring numerous lesser trails. The way zips down a long traverse across a steep, sage-covered hillside toward the Three Sisters.

Pass through a gate at **7** miles. At **7.5** miles, pass straight through a four-way, then immediately turn left to return to the singletrack. After another full-throttle descent, the trail ends at the crest of Burma Road, **8.4** miles. Turn left and cruise down the steep road back toward Smith Rock State Park. At **9.3** miles, turn right onto the unmarked singletrack that drops precipitously down to Crooked River. At the bottom of the hill, bear right and noodle along the riverside trail to the wood bridge on the left, **10.4** miles. Cross the river and climb back to the day-use parking area to complete the ride, **11** miles.

Gazetteer

Nearby camping: Smith Rock State Park (primitive)
Nearest food, drink, services: Terrebonne, Redmond

24 BEND AND CENTRAL OREGON
Gray Butte
⊕⊕⊕⊕

Distance	18.6-mile figure eight
Terrain	Dirt- and gravel-road climbs, singletrack climbs and descents; 1,540-foot gain; views
Duration	3 to 5 hours
Travel	Bend—25 miles; Eugene—131 miles
Skill level	Advanced
Season	Late spring, summer, fall
Maps	USGS 30x60 minute: Bend
Restrictions	Oregon State Parks Day-use Permit required
More info	Oregon State Parks, 800-551-6949, www.prd.state.or.us

The Scoop

This figure-eight route travels over the same dirt roads and singletrack as Burma Road (ride 23), but then adds a big loop around Gray Butte. It's a more

Traversing the ridge toward Burma Road

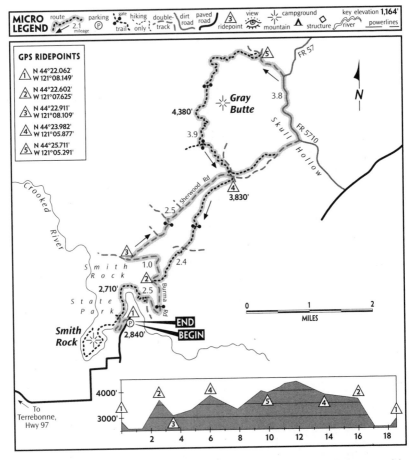

MICRO LEGEND — route, 2.1 mileage, P parking, gate, hiking trail only, double-track, dirt road, paved road, 3 ridepoint, view, mountain, campground, structure, river, key elevation **1,164'**, powerlines

GPS RIDEPOINTS

1. N 44°22.062' W 121°08.149'
2. N 44°22.602' W 121°07.625'
3. N 44°22.911' W 121°08.109'
4. N 44°23.982' W 121°05.877'
5. N 44°25.711' W 121°05.291'

FR 57

Gray Butte
4,380'
3.8
3.9
Skull Hollow
FR 5710

Crooked River

Sherwood Rd
2.5
4 3,830'

3
1.0
2.4

Smith Rock
2,710'
State Park
2.5
Burma Rd

0   1   2
MILES

Smith Rock
1
P
2,840'
END
BEGIN

To Terrebonne, Hwy 97

4000'
3000'
2 4 6 8 10 12 14 16 18

challenging ride than Burma Road, and the singletrack's much better, with some sections that dance and fly and others that trip and stumble. Whatever: If it's singletrack, it's all good. The ride begins at Smith Rock State Park and, during the course of three separate climbs, ascends into the Crooked River National Grasslands, which is managed by the BLM. It can be hot out there, so drink plenty of water.

Driving Directions

From Bend, drive about 22 miles north on US Highway 97. In Terrebonne, turn right on B Avenue toward Smith Rock State Park, and set your odometer to zero. B Avenue becomes Northeast Smith Rock Way. At 0.6 mile, turn left on First Street Northeast, which soon becomes Wilcox Avenue. At 2.7 miles, turn left on Crooked River Drive. At 3.2 miles, reach the day-use parking area for Smith Rock State Park.

The Ride

From the day-use parking area, take the paved trail toward Smith Rock. At the edge of the bluff, the trail becomes a gravelly road as it descends toward the river. Ignore a trail on the right as you descend. At the bottom of the road, cross a wood bridge over Crooked River. At the four-way just across the bridge, turn right onto a dirt trail that runs along the river.

When the trail forks at **1.4** miles, turn left and walk up the steep, loose trail. At **1.6** miles, the trail ends at the Burma Road: Turn left and climb. The road, steep and exposed to the sun, switchbacks at **2** miles and continues up. WOOF! Crest the ridge at **2.5** miles, ignoring the singletrack on the right, and gear up for a fast descent. Views: Three Sisters, Broken Top, and Mount Jefferson. WHOA! At **3.5** miles, just as you've attained top speed, reach a fork and take a sharp right onto Sherwood Road, which is unmarked (if you haven't turned and you start climbing, you've gone too far).

Sherwood Road climbs gently at first. At **4.5** miles, ignore a lesser double-track on the right, then pass through a gate and bear right. When the road forks at **4.8** miles, turn right and continue up. After a steep quarter-mile climb, reach Gray Butte Trail at **6** miles (just before a four-way). Turn left onto the trail. At **6.3** miles, turn right at the fork. The trail immediately crosses a dirt road and descends, past a corral and down into a narrow drainage. When the trail dumps out to a road, **7.7** miles, bear left and continue down, passing through Skull Hollow. When the road ends at a T, turn left on Forest Road 5710.

The road is covered with large rocks, and this makes the otherwise moderate climb more difficult. Reach a fork at **9.2** miles and go left on FR 57, following the sign to Gray Butte trailhead. The road plateaus a quarter-mile farther, crosses a cattle grate, and descends. At **9.8** miles, reach a fork in the road. WHOA! Turn left onto the unmarked singletrack here and climb gently. At **10** miles, ignore a trail back on the right. From here the trail rounds the back side of Gray Butte, ascending in fits and starts. Ignore another trail on the right, then cross an old doubletrack.

At **10.8** miles, pass through a gate—be certain to close it. Top out a quarter-mile farther to spectacular views to the right; Gray Butte is high to the left. The trail rolls across the west flank of the butte. The descent begins at **11.9** miles, fast and sometimes rough. Reach a T at **12.6** miles. Turn left, pass through a gate, and continue descending. As the trail approaches a dirt road,

13.3 miles, stay to the right on the trail. At **13.5** miles, bear right at the fork. At **13.7** miles, the trail crosses the road at the top of Sherwood Canyon. From here, stay on the main trail, ignoring numerous lesser trails. Zip down a long traverse on a steep, sage-covered hillside toward Three Sisters.

Pass through a gate at **14.7** miles. At **15.2** miles, pass straight through a four-way, then immediately turn left to return to the singletrack. After another fast descent, the trail ends at the crest of Burma Road, **16.1** miles. Turn left and cruise down the steep road toward Smith Rock State Park. At **17** miles, turn right onto the unmarked singletrack that drops precipitously down to Crooked River. At the bottom of the hill, turn right and meander back to the wood bridge, **18.1** miles. Cross the river and climb back to the day-use parking area to complete the ride, **18.6** miles.

Gazetteer

Nearby camping: Smith Rock State Park (primitive)
Nearest food, drink, services: Terrebonne, Redmond

25 Shevlin Park

☉☉☉

Distance	4.8-mile loop
Terrain	Easy, wide and narrow trails, a couple technical spots; 250-foot gain
Duration	1 hour
Travel	Bend—5 miles; Eugene—120 miles
Skill level	Intermediate
Season	Late spring, summer, fall
Maps	U.S. Forest Service: Bend Ranger District
Restrictions	None
More info	Bend Metro Park and Recreation District, 541-389-7275

The Scoop

Up Tumalo Creek and down the opposite side, this short loop at Shevlin Park is intended for beginners. However, a couple of sections of the trail aren't ridable, so be prepared to carry your bike for short distances (this is why it's

Crossing Tumalo Creek

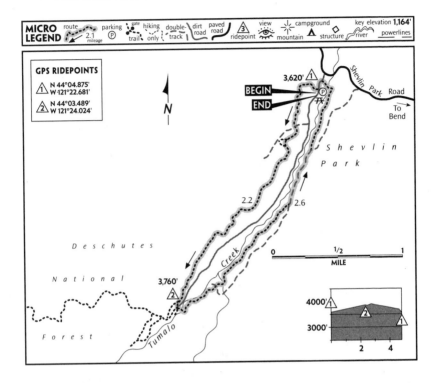

rated intermediate). Also, this loop is heavily used by walkers and trail runners, so pedal accordingly. Many intermediate and advanced riders begin from Bend—for the added workout—and use this loop as a jumping-off point to explore the numerous trails beyond Shevlin's borders, including the Mrazek Trail (ride 26).

Driving Directions

From the junction of US Highway 97 and Northeast Greenwood Avenue in Bend, zero out your odometer and head west on Greenwood. Stay on the arterial as Greenwood becomes Northwest Newport Avenue and then Shevlin Park Road. At 4.7 miles, turn left into the parking area for Shevlin Park. Park in the gravel area on the right, past the work shed.

The Ride

Take the trail that exits from the gravel parking area on the right. At **0.5** mile, proceed straight through the four-way intersection. Reach a fork at **0.7** mile and bear left. After a few pedal strokes, ignore the trail back on the right. The trail rises slightly, traversing the hillside above a dirt road, through ponderosa pine, juniper, and manzanita. At **2.2** miles, bear left at the fork and drop to a five-way intersection. Ride straight through the intersection down to Tumalo Creek.

Cross over the narrow bridge and walk up the short but steep hill. At **2.6** miles, cross a doubletrack. At **2.8** miles, cross a creek and ignore a faint trail back on the right. At **3.6** miles, reach a T and turn left on the dirt road. But at **3.9** miles, turn left to return to the singletrack. The trail descends, through pine and sage, then switchbacks down to Tumalo Creek. When the trail peters out, **4.5** miles, ride across the grassy field toward the creek. Cross over the bridge and bear left. Ride to the gravel parking area to complete the loop, **4.8** miles.

Gazetteer

Nearby camping: Tumalo State Park
Nearest food, drink, services: Bend

26 Mrazek

ⓧ ⓧ ⓧ

Distance	18.2-mile out-and-back
Terrain	Long, moderate singletrack climb, zipster descent; 1,320-foot gain
Duration	3 to 5 hours
Travel	Bend—5 miles; Eugene—120 miles
Skill level	Intermediate
Season	Summer, fall
Maps	U.S. Forest Service: Bend Ranger District
Restrictions	None
More info	Deschutes National Forest, Bend–Fort Rock District, 541-388-5664, www.fs.fed.us/r6/deschutes/

The Scoop

This ride, a hodgepodge of trails that cross private land, Forest Service property, and Bend Recreation District parkland, is a great introduction to the area west of Shevlin Park. Using the Bend Ranger District map to trace out huge, epic loops, ambitious and creative riders might use this trail as simply the start or finish of a Frankenstein trail. Use your imagination. Some Bend locals say they would prefer to keep Mrazek a secret. Of course, when you arrive in town and start asking about cool mountain-bike trails, it's the first one you'll hear about. And there's good reason: It's a blast. While much of this ride isn't on any official trail system, it gets a fair amount of use—primarily by mountain bikers—it has a history of use, and, importantly, it hasn't been signed closed. In fact, the Forest Service is considering making it part of the official system. Since locals are particular about so-called renegade trails like this one, ride smart: no out-of-control riding, no riding off trail, and no skidding.

Driving Directions

From the junction of US Highway 97 and Northeast Greenwood Avenue in Bend, zero out your odometer and head west on Greenwood. Stay on the arterial as Greenwood becomes Northwest Newport Avenue and then Shevlin Park Road. At 4.7 miles, turn left into the parking area for Shevlin Park. Park in the gravel area on the right, past the work shed.

The Ride

Take the trail that exits from the gravel parking area on the right. At **0.5** mile, proceed straight through the four-way intersection. Reach a fork at **0.7** mile and bear left. After a few pedal strokes, ignore the trail back on the right. The trail rises slightly, traversing the hillside above a dirt road. At **2.2** miles, bear right at the fork. At **2.3** miles, reach a fork and turn right, immediately climbing a steep, rocky, loose hill. At **2.5** miles, ignore a trail on the left and continue up through pine and thick manzanita. Stay on the main trail.

The trail seems to end at a doubletrack at **2.9** miles. Turn left on the doubletrack, then cross a dirt road to regain the singletrack. At **3.2** miles, turn

Bike splicing on the Mrazek Trail

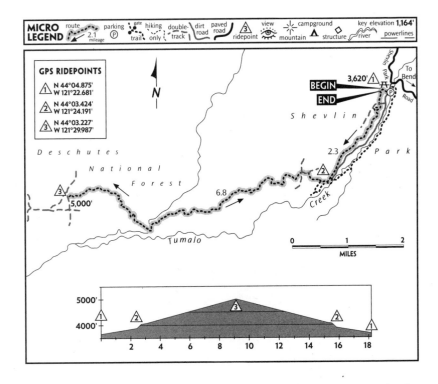

left onto the doubletrack, then immediately right onto the singletrack. The trail, narrower now and dusty in sections, slaloms in and around the pines, with some openings barely wider than a set of handlebars. At around **4.5** miles, the trail crosses a series of doubletracks. At **7** miles, the trail crosses a dry canal, then a doubletrack before climbing steeply. At **7.8** miles, the grade eases and the long ridge ahead provides a perspective from the gradually sloped pine plain.

At **9.1** miles, the trail ends at Forest Road 4602-400. (There are numerous epic loop possibilities from here: Dirt roads connect to trails near Three Creek Lake, Tumalo Falls—ride 28, Swampy Lakes—ride 29, and Phil's Trail 24.5—ride 30.) For this ride, though, turn around and follow the galloping singletrack all the way back to the parking area at Shevlin Park, **18.2** miles.

Gazetteer

Nearby camping: Tumalo State Park
Nearest food, drink, services: Bend

27 BEND AND CENTRAL OREGON
First Street Rapids

Distance	5.4-mile out-and-back
Terrain	Wide wood-chip trail with short ups and downs; 120-foot gain
Duration	1 hour
Travel	Bend—1 mile; Eugene—115 miles
Skill level	Beginner
Season	Year-round
Maps	No useful supplementary map
Restrictions	None
More info	Bend Metro Park and Recreation District, 541-389-7275

The Scoop

This wide trail is popular with walkers, trail runners, dog walkers, and some families. Variously known as the First Street Rapids Trail and the Bend Riverside Trail, the official name is the Deschutes River Trail—the same, unfortunately, as ride 32. One of the easiest rides in this book, this out-and-back route follows the course of the Deschutes River and affords dramatic views into the canyon.

Driving Directions

From the junction of US Highway 97 and Division Street in Bend, set your odometer to zero and head south on Division. At 0.7 mile, turn right on Revere Avenue. At 0.9 mile, turn left on Hill Street. At 1.2 miles, turn right on Northwest Portland Avenue. At 1.4 miles, turn right onto Northwest First Street. At 1.6 miles, First Street dead-ends at the trailhead.

The Ride

From the trailhead, ride around the gate and descend the hill on a road. At **0.6** mile, stay to the left on Deschutes River Trail, climbing a short but steep hill to avoid the golf course on the right. After passing the golf course, stay to the right and parallel the road on a sort of wood-chip sidewalk. **WHOA!** The trail seems to end at **0.9** mile. Cross the road on the left to find the continuation of the trail. From here, stay on the main trail, ignoring spurs on the right.

Deschutes River canyon

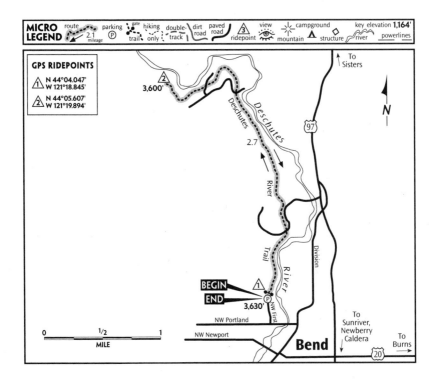

Cross the road twice more at **2.0** and **2.3** miles. The trail follows along the canyon rim. When the wood chips end at a T, **2.7** miles, turn around and retrace your tracks. Arrive back at the trailhead at **5.4** miles.

Gazetteer

Nearby camping: Tumalo State Park
Nearest food, drink, services: Bend

Tumalo Falls
⊕⊕⊕

Distance	7-mile out-and-back
Terrain	Moderate singletrack climbs and descents; **200-foot gain**; views
Duration	1 to 2 hours
Travel	Bend—12 miles; Eugene—127 miles
Skill level	Intermediate
Season	Summer, fall
Maps	U.S. Forest Service: Bend Ranger District
Restrictions	USFS Trail Park Pass required
More info	Deschutes National Forest, Bend–Fort Rock District, 541-388-5664, www.fs.fed.us/r6/deschutes/

The Scoop

You can drive a car to Tumalo Falls, but riding your bike is better. The single-track out to the falls, through pine, then later the thick manzanita of the oddly barren Tumalo Creek canyon, rises and drops in quick bursts, reminding

On top of Tumalo Falls

me of those hot days on the highway when I hold my arm out of the window and use my hand to quickly fly up and down. Tumalo Falls is dramatic and beautiful, and there's a picnic area at the falls for a meditative lunch. Best of all, though, trails head out from the falls (including Swampy Lakes, ride 29) and lead to some of the best riding around Bend. Get in shape and check it out.

Driving Directions

From the junction of US Highway 97 and Northwest Franklin Avenue in Bend, set your odometer to zero and head west on Franklin (which becomes Northwest Riverside Boulevard). At 1.2 miles, turn right onto Northwest Tumalo Avenue. Continue straight ahead as Tumalo becomes Northwest Galveston Avenue and then Skyliners Road. At 4.5 miles, pass Forest Road 220 (to Phil's Trail 24.5, ride 30; Phil's Helipad, ride 31) on the left. At 11.9 miles, turn left into the wide, gravel parking lot for Skyliners Snow Play Area.

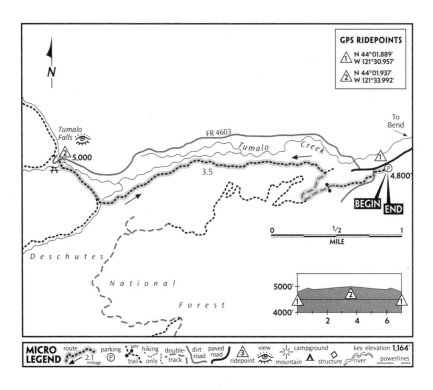

The Ride

From the parking area, take the trail that leads past the bathroom toward Tumalo Falls. The trail, narrow and winding, climbing slightly, crosses a dirt road and then kisses it. At **0.6** mile, pass around an old green gate and climb what used to be FR 434. When you reach a fork at **0.8** mile, turn right and descend, heading toward Tumalo Falls. At **1.1** miles, reach a fork and bear left. From here, the trail gradually ascends along the south bank of Tumalo Creek. Scattered pines and thick manzanita line the trail.

At **3.1** miles, reach a fork and bear right, continuing along the creek toward Tumalo Falls. At **3.5** miles, arrive at the picnic area below the falls. There's a nice view of the falls from the lower picnic area, but a quarter-mile push up North Fork Trail gets you right on top of the falls. Turn around when you're done and ride back the way you came, returning to Skyliners Snow Play Area at **7** miles.

Gazetteer

Nearby camping: Tumalo State Park
Nearest food, drink, services: Bend

29 BEND AND CENTRAL OREGON
Swampy Lakes

Distance	14-mile lollipop
Terrain	Singletrack climb and descent, some doubletrack, some steep climbing; 1,180-foot gain; views
Duration	2 to 4 hours
Travel	Bend—12 miles; Eugene—127 miles
Skill level	Intermediate
Season	Summer, fall
Maps	U.S. Forest Service: Bend Ranger District
Restrictions	USFS Trail Park Pass required
More info	Deschutes National Forest, Bend–Fort Rock District, 541-388-5664, www.fs.fed.us/r6/deschutes/

The Scoop

A series of very ridable switchbacks ascend from a pine forest into fir and hemlock. But because of a persistent snowpack that refused to melt until sometime later in the summer, we got lost at Swampy Lakes and wandered through the snow with our bikes on our shoulders for a while. The GPS, map, compass, altimeter, and Snickers bar saved us from our wandering. After figuring out the twists and turns of a trail under several feet of snow, we rocketed back down the ridge to Tumalo Creek, jonesing to explore the cornucopia of trails that branch out from Tumalo Falls (ride 28) and Swampy Lakes. It's some of the best riding anywhere.

Driving Directions

From the junction of US Highway 97 and Northwest Franklin Avenue in Bend, set your odometer to zero and head west on Franklin (which becomes Northwest Riverside Boulevard). At 1.2 miles, turn right onto Northwest Tumalo Avenue. Continue straight ahead as Tumalo becomes Northwest Galveston Avenue and then Skyliners Road. At 4.5 miles, pass Forest Road 220 (to Phil's Trail 24.5, ride 30; Phil's Helipad, ride 31) on the left. At 11.9 miles, turn left into the wide, gravel parking lot for Skyliners Snow Play Area.

Tumalo Falls

The Ride

From the parking area, take the trail that leads past the bathroom toward Tumalo Falls. The trail, narrow and winding, climbing slightly, crosses a dirt road and then kisses it. At **0.6** mile, pass around an old green gate and climb what used to be FR 434. When you reach a fork at **0.8** mile, turn right and descend, heading toward Tumalo Falls. At **1.1** miles, reach a fork and bear left. From here, the trail gradually ascends, traversing the south bank of Tumalo Creek through thick manzanita. An impressive series of rock escarpments are positioned high above the opposite side of the creek.

At **3.1** miles, reach a fork and take a sharp left (you can bear right and ride less than one-half mile up to Tumalo Falls, then turn around and ride back to this fork). The trail follows the South Fork of Tumalo Creek, climbing. Pass a

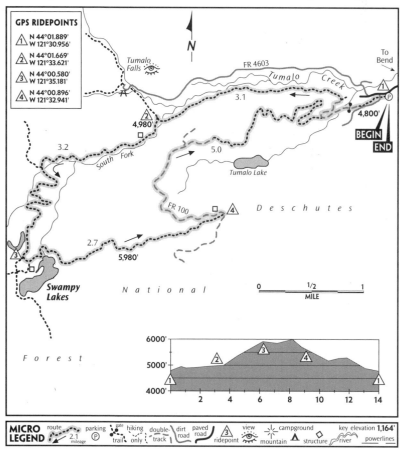

camping shelter on the right at **3.3** miles. Reach a fork at **4.5** miles and turn left, immediately crossing a bridge. From here, the trail leaves the creek and switchbacks up the hillside, through a shaded forest of various pines, firs, and mountain hemlock. Just after passing a shallow lake on the right, reach an unmarked fork at **6.3** miles—turn left. At Swampy Lakes Shelter, **6.4** miles, the trail divides again—bear left.

Pass by the large meadow at Swampy Lakes, then cross a small creek. The trail bends to the right here. A short distance farther, the trail veers back to the left and climbs gently to the ride's high point around **8** miles. A fun descent down Swede Ridge follows. At **9** miles, the trail dumps out at FR 100—turn left toward Swede Ridge Shelter. Pass by the shelter and descend quickly on FR 100, a doubletrack. At **10.6** miles, stay to the right, ignoring a faint doubletrack on the left. At **10.7** miles, the doubletrack narrows, finally becoming singletrack at **10.9** miles. The trail, loose and rocky in sections, weaves across the top of the flat ridge before switchbacking down a steep manzanita-covered slope. Reach a fork at **13.3** miles and bear right. Pass around the old green gate and bear left on the trail. After numerous twists and turns, cross a dirt road and then reach the trailhead parking area at **14** miles to complete the ride.

Gazetteer

Nearby camping: Tumalo State Park
Nearest food, drink, services: Bend

30 Phil's Trail 24.5

⊕⊕⊕

Distance	12.8-mile loop
Terrain	Great trail, smooth, fast, no hard climbing; 620-foot gain
Duration	2 to 3 hours
Travel	Bend—5 miles; Eugene—120 miles
Skill level	Intermediate
Season	Late spring, summer, fall
Maps	U.S. Forest Service: Bend Ranger District
Restrictions	USFS Trail Park Pass required
More info	Deschutes National Forest, Bend–Fort Rock District, 541-388-5664, www.fs.fed.us/r6/deschutes/

The Scoop

Whether after work, between shifts, or just before beer-thirty, many locals begin a ride on Phil's Trail right from town. It's an easy, five-mile spin up Skyliners Road, less if you start in west Bend. The added benefit, of course, is

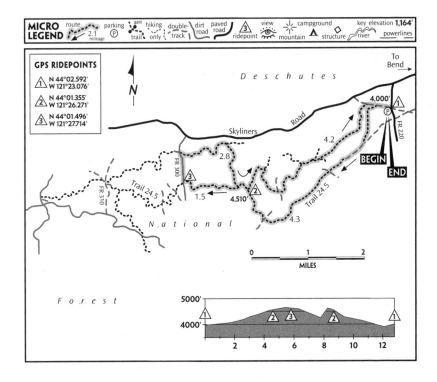

MICRO LEGEND: route — 2.1 mileage, parking Ⓟ, gate, hiking trail, double-track, dirt road, paved road, view ridepoint ⚠3, campground, mountain, key structure, elevation **1,164'**, river, powerlines

GPS RIDEPOINTS

⚠1 N 44°02.592' W 121°23.076'

⚠2 N 44°01.355' W 121°26.271'

⚠3 N 44°01.496' W 121°27.714'

To Bend

Deschutes

Skyliners Road

4,000'

4.2

2.8

FR 300

⚠3

Trail 24.5

1.5

4,510'

⚠2

Trail 24.5

4.3

FR 310

N a t i o n a l

F o r e s t

BEGIN

END

FR 220

0   1   2
MILES

5000'
4000'
2   4   6   8   10   12

that you don't need a Trail Park Pass if you don't park at the trailhead. Ahhh! The area that's known as Phil's Trail is actually a jumble of trails and double-tracks, several days' worth of riding. And it's good riding, the epitome of Bend mountain biking, with zippy, smooth, hard-packed trails that wend through open pine forest and manzanita. This loop, the shortest of two loops that begin from Phil's trailhead, provides a good introduction to the area.

Driving Directions

From the junction of US Highway 97 and Northwest Franklin Avenue in Bend, set your odometer to zero and head west on Franklin. Franklin becomes Northwest Riverside Boulevard. At 1.2 miles, turn right onto Northwest Tumalo Avenue. Continue straight ahead as Tumalo becomes Northwest Galveston Avenue and then Skyliners Road. At 4.5 miles, turn left on Forest Road 220. At 4.9 miles, turn right and then immediately left into a dirt parking area.

The Ride

Ride west down the dirt road away from FR 220. Follow the signs that read Phil's Trail 24.5. At **0.2** mile, turn left onto a wide trail. It rolls up and down quickly. At **0.4** mile, bear left at the fork, following Phil's Connect 24.5. From here, stay on the obvious main route, which flirts between trail and doubletrack. At **1.1** miles, the doubletrack reaches a T at a gravel road—turn right. At **1.7** miles, when the road more or less ends, ride out the singletrack, marked 24.5. The trail winds through the pine forest. Proceed straight through a four-way on Phil's 24.5 at the **2**-mile mark. From here, the singletrack mounts a hillside, climbing steadily to another four-way at **3.6** miles. Continue straight ahead on the singletrack, now fast, spry, and more level.

At **4.3** miles, reach a fork and turn left, continuing out Phil's Trail 24.5 (Kent's Trail bears to the right). The trail, smooth and hard-packed, through ponderosa pine, zips in and around low manzanita. During the second half of the summer the trail can be somewhat dusty but remains solid and fast. At an unmarked fork, **4.6** miles, go left on the main trail. Over the next mile, the trail crosses a series of doubletracks on a slight descent. When the trail ends at FR 300, **5.8** miles, turn right and descend the wide, brick-red cinder road. The road drops, climbs, then drops again to a fork at **6.3** miles. WHOA! Turn right onto an unmarked singletrack here.

The trail cruises through open forest, crossing numerous doubletracks. At **7.6** miles, reach a fork and bear right. The trail dips, then climbs. Reach a T at **8.3** miles and turn left, covering familiar ground. At **8.6** miles, reach another T and turn left onto Kent's Trail. WHOA! At **9.2** miles, take a not-so-intuitive hard right on Trail 24.5 and immediately climb a short hill. Follow the trail across a dirt road at **9.9** miles, and then descend. The trail braids apart and comes back together at **10.3** miles: Left is a steep compression drop, right is a more moderate descending traverse. When the trail forks at **10.6** miles, bear right and continue descending, now out of the trees into a sunny, open area. Back into the pines, the trail widens to doubletrack. At **12.2** miles, bear right to remain on the doubletrack. At **12.4** miles, ignore a trail back on the right. When the doubletrack dumps you out onto a dirt road, bear right and ride up to the parking area, **12.8** miles.

Gazetteer

Nearby camping: Tumalo State Park
Nearest food, drink, services: Bend

31 Phil's Helipad

✹✹✹✹

Distance	21-mile figure eight (17.5-mile option)
Terrain	Superfun singletrack descents, climbs, and noodles, a few doubletracks and dirt roads; **1,480-foot gain**
Duration	3 to 5 hours
Travel	Bend—5 miles; Eugene—120 miles
Skill level	Intermediate
Season	Summer, fall
Maps	U.S. Forest Service: Bend Ranger District
Restrictions	USFS Trail Park Pass required
More info	Deschutes National Forest, Bend–Fort Rock District, 541-388-5664, www.fs.fed.us/r6/deschutes/

The Scoop

This is kid-in-a-candy-store stuff. The big chunk of land between Skyliners Road to the north, State Highway 46 (Century Drive) to the south, and Bend

Helipad bound: noodling through pine and manzanita

and Tumalo Falls to the east and west—more than twenty square miles—is a computer geek's brain's worth of trail and doubletrack connections, switchbacking grunts, Jedi dreams, and zippy memories. Like a mountain biker's brain, this figure-eight loop uses only a small part of the twenty square, and, in turn, Phil's Trail is only a subset of the figure eight. But when Bend locals talk about Phil's Trail, it's usually in an expansive sense, in an overloaded, way-too-many-possibilities sense, and it's all good. Exploring the trails and dirt roads across the greater Phil's system is guaranteed to put a bigger smile on your face than any geek's package of stock options could. Ride on!

Driving Directions

From the junction of US Highway 97 and Northwest Franklin Avenue in Bend, set your odometer to zero and head west on Franklin. Franklin becomes Northwest Riverside Boulevard. At 1.2 miles, turn right onto Northwest Tumalo Avenue. Continue straight ahead as Tumalo becomes Northwest Galveston Avenue and then Skyliners Road. At 4.5 miles, turn left on Forest

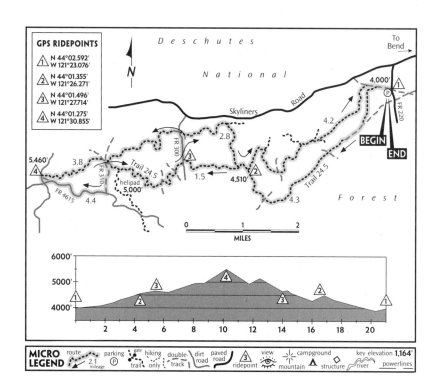

Road 220. At 4.9 miles, turn right and then immediately left into a dirt parking area.

The Ride

Ride west down the dirt road away from FR 220. Follow the signs that read Phil's Trail 24.5. At **0.2** mile, turn left onto a wide trail. It rolls up and down quickly. At **0.4** mile, bear left at the fork, following Phil's Connect 24.5. From here, stay on the obvious main route, which changes from trail to double-track and back. At **1.1** miles, the doubletrack reaches a T at a gravel road— turn right. At **1.7** miles, when the road more or less ends, ride out the singletrack, marked 24.5. The trail winds through the pine forest. At the **2**-mile mark, proceed straight through a four-way on Phil's 24.5. From here, the winding singletrack mounts the hillside, climbing steadily to another four-way at **3.6** miles. Continue straight ahead on the singletrack, now fast, spry, and more level.

At **4.3** miles, reach a fork and turn left, continuing out Phil's Trail 24.5 (Kent's Trail bears to the right). The trail, smooth and hard-packed, through ponderosa pine, zips in and around low manzanita. During the second half of the summer the trail can be somewhat dusty but remains solid and fast. At an unmarked fork, **4.6** miles, go left on the main trail. Over the next mile, the trail crosses a series of doubletracks on a slight descent. When the trail ends at FR 300, **5.8** miles, turn right and descend the wide, brick-red cinder road. The road drops, climbs, then drops again to a fork at **6.3** miles. Turn left on FR 310, an old doubletrack. Stay to the left as you ride up FR 310. At **6.5** miles, when the doubletrack seems to end at a camp spot, find the unmarked singletrack that heads gradually up.

The trail winds and rolls uphill through ponderosa pine. Cross a couple of doubletracks during the ascent. At **8.1** miles, reach a four-way—turn left. You're back on FR 310 now. Pass a doubletrack (and a Trail 24.5 sign) on the left at **8.2** miles. (Note: Turn left here to chop three and one-half miles off the ride; see "Option" below.) At **8.8** miles, reach a T and turn right on FR 4615. Climb steadily up the main road, ignoring lesser spurs—into a mixed forest that includes grand and, farther up, noble fir. Pass a doubletrack on the right, then, at **10.1** miles, reach a four-way and turn right on FR 300. Just up the hill, past a doubletrack, turn right onto an unmarked singletrack, **10.2** miles. This is the ride's high point.

Put on your goggles. From here, the trail romps down the hillside, slaloming in and out of the grand firs. At **11.7** miles, the trail dumps out onto a doubletrack—bear right. Almost immediately the doubletrack ends at a T at FR 310. You've been here before. Turn right onto FR 310, covering the same ground for a short way. This time when you reach the fork, now at **11.8** miles, turn left onto the doubletrack, following the Trail 24.6 sign. The route flirts between doubletrack and wide trail, climbing; stay on the obvious main path. The trail finally narrows to singletrack. At **12.2** miles, ignore an unmarked singletrack on the right. Follow the carbonate signs to the left. At **12.4** miles, reach the helipad, marked by white and orange painted rocks.

Off the top, the trail, reddish, with pumice rocks embedded in the tread, corkscrews down the manzanita-covered hillside. A couple of hair-ball switchbacks and glimpses of Bend later, reach a doubletrack and bear left. The singletrack quickly begins again on the right. The trail climbs and descends, crosses a doubletrack at **13.6** miles, and then Ts at a dirt road at **14** miles. Turn left and immediately pass Phil's Trail 24.5 on the right. Stay on the road. At **14.5** miles, another familiar intersection, turn right on the unmarked singletrack. The trail rips across the open forest, crossing numerous doubletracks along the way. At **15.8** miles, reach a fork and bear right. The trail dips, then climbs.

Reach a T at **16.5** miles and turn left, again covering familiar ground. At **16.8** miles, reach another T and turn left onto Kent's Trail. WHOA! At **17.4** miles, take a not-so-intuitive hard right on Trail 24.5 and immediately climb a short hill. Follow the trail across a dirt road at **18.1** miles, and then descend rapidly. The trail braids apart and comes back together at **18.5** miles: Left is a steep compression drop, right is a more moderate descending traverse. When the trail forks at **18.8** miles, bear right and continue descending, now out of the trees into a sunny, open area. Back into the pines, the trail widens to doubletrack. At **20.4** miles, bear right to remain on the doubletrack. At **20.6** miles, ignore the trail back on the right. When the doubletrack dumps you out onto a dirt road, bear right and ride up to the parking area, **21** miles.

Option

As noted above, turn left at the fork at 8.2 miles and follow the directions from the 11.8-mile mark. Follow the rest of the route, and the total mileage is 17.5.

Gazetteer

Nearby camping: Tumalo State Park
Nearest food, drink, services: Bend

32 Deschutes River Trail

⊕⊕⊕

Distance	16.6-mile out-and-back
Terrain	Rolling riverside singletrack; **360-foot gain**
Duration	2 to 4 hours
Travel	Bend—7 miles; Eugene—122 miles
Skill level	Intermediate
Season	Late spring, summer, fall
Maps	U.S. Forest Service: Bend Ranger District
Restrictions	None
More info	Deschutes National Forest, Bend-Fort Rock District, 541-388-5664, www.fs.fed.us/r6/deschutes/

The Scoop

The Deschutes River Trail is the most heavily used trail in the Bend area—it's a beautiful riverside trail, it's close to town, and there are no long climbs. In late spring and then again in the fall, when there's less daylight and fewer out-of-towners to crowd the trail, Bend locals ride here, often starting out from town (which adds about 15 miles). During the summer, especially on weekends when this trail is abuzz with walkers and bicyclists, locals hide out on the high, remote, nonsystem trails west of town. The Deschutes River Trail is actually a pretty confusing system of three parallel trails—a hiking trail, a

Spinning along the Deschutes

biking trail (Trail 2.3), and an equestrian trail—that join together in places, split apart in others. Bikes are allowed on most of the hiking trail, and this description details that route. It's the most winding and scenic of the trails. (Just don't run anybody down or it will surely be closed to bikes.) Note: Meadow Picnic Area is the only trailhead parking along this trail that doesn't require a Trail Park Pass.

Driving Directions

From the junction of US Highway 97 and Northwest Franklin Avenue in Bend, set your odometer to zero and head west on Franklin. Franklin becomes Northwest Riverside Boulevard. At 1.2 miles, turn right onto Northwest Tumalo Avenue. Continue straight ahead as Tumalo becomes Northwest Galveston Avenue. At 1.6 miles, turn left onto Northwest 14th Street; this soon becomes Century Drive (State Highway 46). At 6.4 miles, turn left at the Meadow Picnic Area sign onto Forest Road 100, which is dirt. At 7.8 miles, reach the trailhead and the end of the road at Meadow Picnic Area

The Ride

The Deschutes River Trail, wide and hard-packed, heads away from the turnaround at Meadow Picnic Area, running just above the bank of the river. Tall ponderosa pines shade the trail. At **0.5** mile, reach a fork and turn left, riding along a sometimes muddy trail that bisects two ponds. Stay on the main trail, ignoring numerous lesser spurs on the right. At **0.7** mile, continue on the trail across the gravel turnaround. At **1.3** miles, pass through a boat launch at Lava Island. Across the river is the sharp, jagged, char-black flow of Lava Butte Geological Area. The trail, rolling and tricky in sections, kisses the equestrian trail several times—stay to the left. Around the **2**-mile mark, the route follows a dirt road. Stay to the left and regain the trail after a short distance.

At **2.2** miles, reach a fork in the trail and bear right, following the bike sign. Reach a four-way at **2.4** miles and proceed straight ahead. At **3.4** miles, pass by another boat launch and stay to the left. Reach a fork at **3.9** miles—turn right and climb a short hill. When the trail forks again at **4.1** miles, bear left. At **4.4** miles, ignore the trail back on the left. At **4.8** miles, reach Dillon Falls Campground. Stay to the left on the campground road. At **4.9** miles, turn left on a narrow trail that passes through a gap in the fence and crosses a wide meadow along the river. Reenter the pine forest at **5.3** miles and wind along the buff trail. When the trail forks at **6.3** miles, bear right. At **6.6** miles, the trail passes through another picnic area next to a flat-water section of the river.

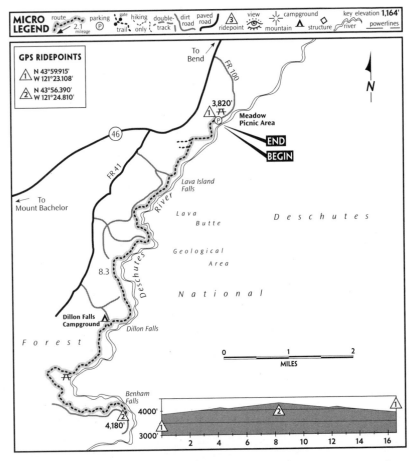

Ride the slight ups and downs as the trail follows the river. At **7.4** miles, ignore a trail on the right. Reach a T at **7.9** miles and turn left. Benham Falls—a rush of water through a narrow rock canyon—appears on the left. The trail, quite wide now, switchbacks up the bank next to the falls. Continue up to the parking area above Benham Falls, **8.3** miles. After you're done checking out the falls, turn around and follow the trail back to Meadow Picnic Area, **16.6** miles.

Gazetteer

Nearby camping: Tumalo State Park
Nearest food, drink, services: Bend

33 Storm King

✿✿✿✿

Distance	**29.7-mile** loop
Terrain	Singletrack climbs and descents, short difficult section near top, 9.5 miles on paved roads; **1,410-foot gain**
Duration	3 to 6 hours
Travel	Bend—1 mile; Eugene—115 miles
Skill level	Advanced
Season	Summer, fall
Maps	U.S. Forest Service: Bend Ranger District
Restrictions	USFS Trail Park Pass required
More info	Deschutes National Forest, Bend-Fort Rock District, 541-388-5664, www.fs.fed.us/r6/deschutes/

The Scoop

Necessity is the mother of invention, and all that. Well, too much time staring at the map and wondering "wouldn't it be cool if . . . " seems to be the mother of many of the new trails in and around Bend. In this case, wouldn't it be cool if you could connect the Phil's Trail system with the Deschutes River Trail? Answer: Yes. Thus and so did Storm King evolve. This is a nonsystem

Divining the Storm King way

trail, and as such it's not marked, it's not sanctioned, and it's a lot of fun. I've included it here because it gets used and it hasn't been signed closed. In fact, the Forest Service is considering making it part of the official system. Since Bend locals are particular about nonsystem trails like this one—"they're ours, dammit"—ride smart: no out-of-control riding, no riding off trail, and no skidding.

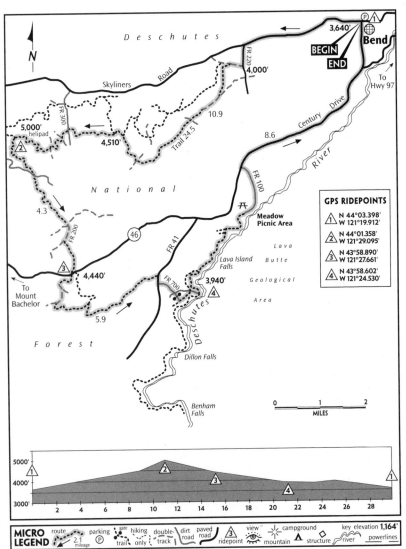

Driving Directions

From the junction of US Highway 97 and Northwest Franklin Avenue in Bend, set your odometer to zero and head west on Franklin. Franklin becomes Northwest Riverside Boulevard. At 1.2 miles, turn right onto Northwest Tumalo Avenue. Continue straight ahead as Tumalo becomes Northwest Galveston Avenue. At 1.6 miles, park near the intersection of Galveston and Northwest 14th Street.

The Ride

From the intersection of Galveston and Northwest 14th Street, pedal east on Galveston, which soon becomes Skyliners Road. At **2.9** miles, turn left on Forest Road 220. At **3.3** miles, turn right onto a dirt road and ride past the trailhead parking area on the left. Ride west down the dirt road away from FR 220. Follow the signs that read Phil's Trail 24.5. At **3.5** miles, turn left onto a wide trail. It rolls up and down quickly. At **3.7** miles, bear left at the fork, following Phil's Connect 24.5. From here, stay on the obvious main trail, which changes from trail to doubletrack and back. At **4.4** miles, the doubletrack reaches a T at a gravel road—turn right. At **5** miles, when the road more or less ends, ride out the singletrack, marked 24.5. The trail winds through the pine forest. Proceed straight through a four-way on Phil's 24.5 at the **5.3**-mile mark. From here, the winding singletrack mounts the hillside, climbing steadily to another four-way at **6.9** miles. Continue straight ahead on the singletrack, now fast, spry, and more level.

At **7.6** miles, reach a fork and turn left, continuing out Phil's Trail 24.5 (Kent's Trail bears to the right). The trail, smooth and hard-packed, through ponderosa pine, zips in and around the low manzanita. During the second half of the summer the trail can be somewhat dusty but remains solid and fast. At an unmarked fork, **7.9** miles, go left on the main trail. Over the next mile, the trail crosses a series of doubletracks on a slight descent. When the trail reaches FR 300, **9.1** miles, it jogs to the left across the wide, brick-red cinder road and continues up. Cross a doubletrack at **9.5** miles. After a set of steep, somewhat rocky switchbacks through a sea of manzanita, reach the so-called helipad, marked by white and orange painted rocks, at **10.9** miles. Pass across the helipad, ignoring a faint doubletrack on the right. At **11.1** miles, reach a fork and bear left onto an unmarked trail.

The trail begins with a few whoops, then snakes through the woods on a gradual decline. Ragged in sections, the trail continues the steady descent, crossing numerous dirt roads and doubletracks. At **13.9** miles, when the trail dumps out at a three-way intersection of dirt roads, bear easily right on FR 200. At **14** miles, turn left onto the singletrack. From here the trail rises and falls through pine and scattered manzanita. Cross a dirt road at **14.4** miles. The trail traverses and drops gradually, reaching State Highway 46 at **15.2** miles. **WHOA!** Be careful crossing the highway to the trail opposite.

At **15.8** miles, bear left onto a doubletrack. When the doubletrack forks at **15.9** miles, bear right and ascend. At **16.4** miles, find a faint, unmarked singletrack on the left and take it. The narrow tread winds through the pine forest. At **17** miles, bear left onto a wide trail. A few spins of the pedals farther, turn right on an unmarked singletrack. **WHOA!** This is an easy trail to miss. At **17.4** miles, bear right on an old doubletrack. Reach a T at **17.8** miles: Go straight, taking the singletrack that begins from this intersection. The trail, which is faint here, crosses a doubletrack at **18.7** miles. At **19.2** miles, the trail crosses another dirt road at an oblique angle.

The faint trail drops into a draw, then climbs the opposite side. Immediately before reaching a dirt parking area, **19.5** miles, bear right on a marginal trail and ride the small ridge to a paved road, FR 41, where the trail ends at **19.6** miles. Turn right on FR 41. At **19.8** miles, turn left onto FR 700 toward Big Eddy. When you reach a four-way at **20** miles, go straight, riding around a gate on FR 752. Stay on the doubletrack as it crosses a trail at **20.2** miles. When the doubletrack forks at **20.3** miles, bear right. At **20.4** miles, reach a four-way and turn left. From here, the trail cruises along, smooth and fast. At **21.1** miles, reach a dirt road, turn right, and ride fifty yards to the parking area at Big Eddy, where you'll find the Deschutes River Trail. Turn left on the trail.

At **22.2** miles, pass through the boat launch area at Lava Island. Stay to the right to continue along the trail. From here, stay on the main trail. Cross a gravel turnaround. At **22.9** miles, take the sometimes muddy trail that cuts between two ponds. Reach a T at **23** miles and turn right. The trail ends at Meadow Picnic Area, **23.5** miles. From Meadow, ride along the dirt road, bearing left and climbing to Century Drive, which is paved, **24.9** miles. Turn right on Century Drive and ride the highway into Bend. When the road divides closer to town, bear left and Century Drive becomes Northwest 14th Street. Ride to the intersection of Northwest 14th Street and Northwest Galveston Avenue to complete the loop, **29.7** miles.

Gazetteer

Nearby camping: Tumalo State Park
Nearest food, drink, services: Bend

BEND AND CENTRAL OREGON
34 Lava Lake
✪✪✪✪

Distance	24.5-mile loop
Terrain	Gradual but zippy singletrack descent, paved road climb; 720-foot gain; views
Duration	3 to 5 hours
Travel	Bend—27 miles; Eugene—120 miles
Skill level	Intermediate
Season	Summer, fall
Maps	U.S. Forest Service: Bend Ranger District
Restrictions	USFS Trail Park Pass required
More info	Deschutes National Forest, Bend–Fort Rock District, 541-388-5664, www.fs.fed.us/r6/deschutes/

The Scoop

Lava Lake is big and deep blue—a great swim on those dry, 90-degree summer days around Bend. From the trailhead near Sparks Lake, the pumice-

September on the zippy Lave Lake Trail

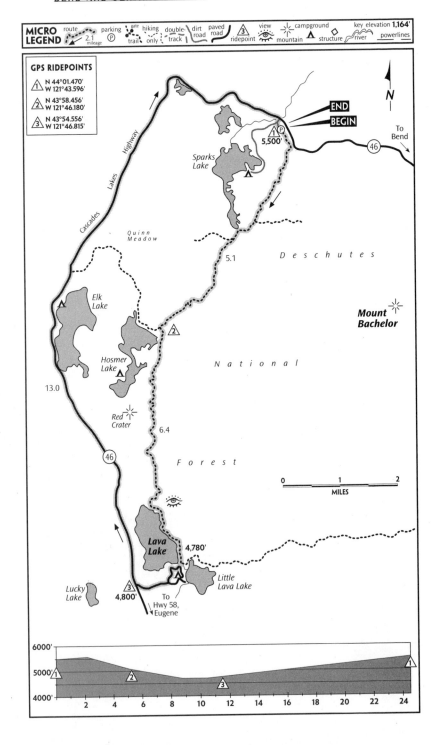

MICRO LEGEND
route 2.1 mileage | parking Ⓟ | gate trail | hiking only | double-track | dirt road | paved road | ③ ridepoint | view | campground | mountain | structure | river | powerlines | key elevation 1,164'

GPS RIDEPOINTS
△1 N 44°01.470'
   W 121°43.596'
△2 N 43°58.456'
   W 121°46.180'
△3 N 43°54.556'
   W 121°46.815'

N

END
BEGIN
5,500'
To Bend
46

Cascades Lakes Highway

Sparks Lake

Quinn Meadow

Deschutes

5.1

Elk Lake

Mount Bachelor

2

Hosmer Lake

National

13.0

Red Crater

6.4

46

Forest

0   1   2
MILES

Lava Lake
4,780'

Little Lava Lake

Lucky Lake

3
4,800'

To Hwy 58, Eugene

6000'
5000'
4000'

1   2   3   1

2   4   6   8   10   12   14   16   18   20   22   24

treaded singletrack weaves south toward Lava Lake. The trail rolls in places, zips in others, as it winds through low pines. It's a gray pumice trail and can get loose in the driest months. Sporadically located water bars and embedded rocks make the trail interesting for intermediate riders but all-out fun for advanced riders. From the south end of the loop at Lava Lake, it's a road ride to complete the route. By turning left on Trail 31 at Lava Lake and then combining a series of roads, you can easily construct an epic loop around Mount Bachelor. Check out the map.

Driving Directions

From the junction of US Highway 97 and Northwest Franklin Avenue in Bend, set your odometer to zero and head west on Franklin. Franklin becomes Northwest Riverside Boulevard. At 1.2 miles, turn right onto Northwest Tumalo Avenue. Continue straight ahead as Tumalo becomes Northwest Galveston Avenue. At 1.6 miles, turn left onto Northwest 14th Street; this soon becomes Century Drive. Proceed west on Century Drive (State Highway 46) past Mount Bachelor. At 27.3 miles, turn left toward Sparks Lake and Soda Creek Campground on graveled Forest Road 400. Immediately bear left at the fork and park on the left next to the trailhead, 27.5 miles.

The Ride

From the trailhead, take the singletrack toward South Sparks Lake. Cruise through the pine forest on a gray, rolling singletrack. After numerous twists and turns, short climbs and descents, reach a fork at **2.1** miles and bear right, heading toward Quinn Meadow. At **2.5** miles, the trail divides again: Go left. From here the trail noodles for a distance before descending toward Hosmer Lake. At **5.1** miles, reach a fork and turn left, toward Lava Lake. The trail descends quickly from the fork, then noodles again as it skirts to the east of Red Crater. Just past the **7**-mile mark, check out views of Lava Lake to the south.

From here, the trail rips downhill, slaloming verily through the pines. At **8.9** miles, reach the northeast corner of Lava Lake. Follow the trail, at times root-strewn, as it hugs the eastern shore of the lake. At **10.4** miles, reach a fork and turn right. Immediately cross a small creek to the boat launch at Lava Lake Campground. Check out the picturesque views across the lake of South Sister and Mount Bachelor. From the launch, take the main campground road to Hwy 46. At **11.5** miles, turn right on Hwy 46. The paved highway climbs gradually to the north toward South Sister. At **14.4** miles, pass by

Along the northeast shore of Lava Lake

the road to Hosmer Lake on the right. Just over a mile farther, the highway wraps around the west side of Elk Lake. Pass the turnoff to Elk Lake on the right at **17** miles. At **24.3** miles, turn right on the dirt road toward Sparks Lake. Bear left at the fork and arrive at the trailhead, **24.5** miles.

Gazetteer

Nearby camping: Soda Creek (primitive)
Nearest food, drink, services: Bend, Sunriver

35 Paulina Creek

⊛⊛⊛⊛

Distance	17.3-mile loop (11.2-mile option)
Terrain	Long moderate to tough singletrack climb, bomber doubletrack descent; 2,080-foot gain; views
Duration	3 to 4 hours
Travel	Bend—28 miles; Eugene—110 miles
Skill level	Intermediate
Season	Summer, fall
Maps	U.S. Forest Service: Fort Rock Ranger District
Restrictions	Trail is uphill-only for bikes; USFS Trail Park Pass required
More info	Newberry National Volcanic Monument, Bend–Fort Rock District, 541-388-5664, www.fs.fed.us/r6/deschutes/monument/monument.html

The Scoop

When I reached the top of this loop at Paulina Lake, I was surprised that I'd climbed more than 2,000 feet. The climb along Paulina Creek, on the Peter Skene Ogden Trail, is well graded. Since it's well traveled by hikers and equestrians, the trail is open to bicycles only for uphill riding. Not to fret: The steadiness of the grade and the smooth, hard-packed tread mitigate the pain, and the breakneck doubletrack descent makes this a great ride despite the restriction. Cut it short with the option, or combine this ride with the loop around Newberry Caldera (ride 36) for an outstanding, all-day epic.

Driving Directions

From Bend, drive about 24 miles south on US Highway 97 and turn left on Paulina East Lake Road (Forest Road 21), following the sign for Newberry Crater. Zero out your odometer here. At 2.9 miles, turn left toward Ogden Group Camp. At 3 miles, bear right toward the trailhead. At 3.2 miles, reach the gravel parking area at the trailhead.

The Ride

From the parking area, immediately cross the creek and ride up Peter Skene Ogden Trail toward Paulina Lake. The trail braids apart at **0.3** mile, reconnects, then crosses a doubletrack. Reach a T at **0.8** mile: Turn right, then immediately left on a doubletrack. A few pedal rotations farther, reach a fork and bear left. At **1** mile, the trail crosses Paulina Creek, narrows to single-track, and climbs, paralleling the creek through a pine forest. Pass a small waterfall on the right, then bend away from the creek, following the trail around the outside of the McKay Crossing Campground. At **2.8** miles, cross a dirt road and continue up on Peter Skene Ogden Trail.

The trail, which is never far from the river, climbs at an even rate. Around **3.5** miles, the trail passes through a recent burn—young sprouts among the charred pines. After passing another falls at **4.4** miles, the trail ascends more steeply. At **5.4** miles, reach a fork and bear left (right is a bailout; see "Option" below). At **6.1** miles, ride through a small campsite; follow the trail as it jogs to the left here and continues the steady climb. At **8.3** miles, pass stunning Paulina Falls. WOOF! After burning several large Toblerones' worth of calories, reach the upper trailhead at **8.6** miles. Bear right to reach the paved road, then turn right and ride over Paulina Creek as it flows out of Paulina Lake.

At the T, turn right on FR 21, which is paved, and burn ass downhill. At **8.9** miles, bear right into a parking area. Under power lines at the far side of the lot, find a rough doubletrack, FR 500, and take it. It's a bomber descent, and

Fire-blackened forest along Paulina Creek

the old, scooped-out doubletrack almost forms a half pipe. Reach a fork at **9.6** miles and stay to the right, following the power lines. At **9.8** miles, bear right, again mimicking the power lines. At **10.1** miles, stay to the left. At **11.7** miles, pass the short tie trail on the right that connects with Peter Skene Ogden Trail.

From the tie trail, continue the fast descent. When you pass through the burn around the **12.7**-mile point, follow the main road beneath the power lines. Ride straight through a four-way at **14.3** miles. When FR 500 merges with a wide gravel road, FR 2120, at **14.6** miles, bear left. Stay on FR 2120. At **16.8** miles, turn right on FR 21. Ride a short distance down this paved road and then turn right, heading toward Ogden Group Camp. Bear right at the fork, reaching the trailhead to complete the loop at **17.3** miles.

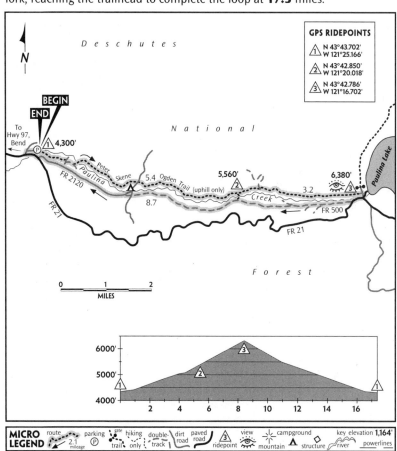

Option

For riders with less time or an insufficient supply of calories, turn right at the fork at 5.4 miles. From there, the trail drops to a bridge over Paulina Creek, then climbs to meet FR 500 at 5.6 miles (the 11.7-mile point above). Turn right on FR 500 and descend to the trailhead, 11.2 miles.

Gazetteer

Nearby camping: Paulina Lake, McKay Crossing (primitive)
Nearest food, drink, services: La Pine, Sunriver, Bend

Paulina Falls

36
Newberry Caldera
⊕⊕⊕⊕

Distance	22.4-mile loop (39.4-mile epic option)
Terrain	Difficult dirt-road climb to Paulina Peak, rangy dirt and pumice singletrack; 1,520-foot gain; views
Duration	4 to 6 hours
Travel	Bend—38 miles; Eugene—120 miles
Skill level	Advanced
Season	Late summer, fall
Maps	U.S. Forest Service: Fort Rock Ranger District
Restrictions	USFS Trail Park Pass required
More info	Newberry National Volcanic Monument, Bend-Fort Rock District, 541-388-5664, www.fs.fed.us/r6/deschutes/monument/ monument.html

The Scoop

Just south of Bend, the Paulina Mountains and Newberry Caldera (referred to as a crater by many) rise modestly out of the rolling central Oregon desert at the intersection of three fault zones, and you might not think twice about driving right past the signs that point to Newberry Crater. That would be a big mistake. The views, the remarkable geographic features, and the wonderful trail combine to make this one of the most outstanding rides I've ever done. The loop begins with a strenuous dirt-road climb up Paulina Peak, Newberry's high point at nearly 8,000 feet. From the top of the peak, you can trace with your finger the entire upcoming route around the rim of the caldera. Lakes, obsidian and lava flows, and pumice cones fill the caldera's bowl. To the west, across the wide Deschutes River valley, the Cascade Range juts up from the hot plain; to the east the hazy swells of eastern Oregon seem to go on forever (they do). The rest of the route—all singletrack, on pumice and dirt—circles the lip of the rim, climbs North Paulina Peak, and then verily launches down to the visitors center to finish.

Driving Directions

From Bend, drive about 24 miles south on US Highway 97 and turn left on Paulina East Lake Road (Forest Road 21), following the sign for Newberry

Paulina Lake from Newberry Caldera's high point, Paulina Peak

Crater. Zero out your odometer here. At 13.2 miles, turn left into the parking area opposite the visitors center.

The Ride

From the visitors center parking, ride out FR 21 toward East Lake. At **0.2** mile, turn right on FR 500 toward Paulina Peak. The road becomes gravel at **0.7** mile, and the long, grinding climb up Paulina Peak begins. Stay on the main road as you climb. Pass Trail 57 on the left at **0.9** mile and then again, on both the right and left, at **3.3** miles. You may be battling hallucinations at this point. (Note: Turn right on Trail 57 if you just can't imagine pedaling up to the top.) **WOOF!** Reach the summit of Paulina Peak at **4.3** miles. Check out the incredible 360-degree views of the Cascades, the caldera—its lakes and obsidian flows—and eastern Oregon.

The trail from the top is closed to bikes, so ride back down the dirt road. At **5.3** miles, turn left on Trail 57, rocky and loose to begin. When the trail forks at **5.4** miles, go left. Dirt and pine-needled, the trail wraps through a stand of grand fir for a distance, then emerges, now coarse and gray, into a sparse pine forest, where it shows off views of the lakes and the obsidian flows in the crater below and mimics the roll and swell of the pumiced rim. At **7.8**

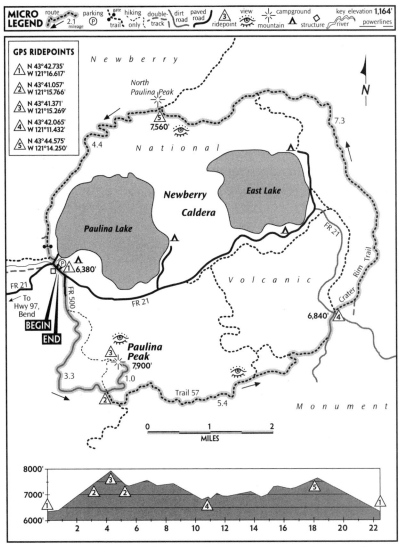

GPS RIDEPOINTS

△1 N 43°42.735' W 121°16.617'

△2 N 43°41.057' W 121°15.766'

△3 N 43°41.371' W 121°15.269'

△4 N 43°42.065' W 121°11.432'

△5 N 43°44.575' W 121°14.250'

miles, go right at the fork. After several more swells and a short noodle, the trail switchbacks through loose pumice down the outside lip of the caldera. Take care while surfing the pum through this section because pumice cuts on your face hurt.

After a fast descent, reach a fork at **9.7** miles and bear right toward FR 2127. At **10.4** miles, the trail ends in a T at the road—turn left and climb. At **10.7** miles, FR 2127 ends at FR 21. The singletrack begins again across this intersection. The trail immediately forks—go right on Crater Rim Trail, heading north now around the rim. At **11.3** miles, bear left on a wide trail. From here, the oversize trail climbs, then drops, then climbs some more, inching toward the high point on the opposite side of the caldera from Paulina Peak. Some of the pitches are very steep (or was it Paulina Peak that killed my legs' zip?). Ignore a ski trail on the right at **15.5** miles. At **16.4** miles, reach a fork and bear right, climbing through pine and mountain hemlock.

When the trail forks again, at **18** miles, bear left and follow the sign to Paulina Lake. The trail noodles across the southern toe of North Paulina Peak, then descends. Pass a wonderful viewpoint on the left at **18.6** miles. Check your brakes here because the trail verily launches down the west side of the caldera's rim, aiming south now. At **22** miles, stay left at the fork. At **22.3** miles, pass through a white gate and bear left to a paved road. Turn right on the road and cross Paulina Creek. Reach a T at a stop sign and turn left. A few pedal rotations farther, reach the visitors center parking lot, **22.4** miles, to complete the ride.

Option

Add the Paulina Creek loop (ride 35) to this ride to create an epic. Ride up Paulina Creek, grind to the top of Paulina Peak, spin counterclockwise around the rim, and then bomb down FR 500 to complete the madness. It's a 39.4-mile trip, with a 3,600-foot gain—**WOOF!**—but for those who aren't intimidated, this is one of the best rides anywhere.

Gazetteer

Nearby camping: Paulina Lake, McKay Crossing (primitive)
Nearest food, drink, services: La Pine, Sunriver, Bend

37 / Cultus Lake

◉◉◉

Distance	15.4-mile loop
Terrain	Singletrack and dirt roads, up and down, no major climbs; 400-foot gain; views
Duration	3 to 4 hours
Travel	Bend—42 miles; Eugene—100 miles
Skill level	Intermediate
Season	Late summer, fall
Maps	U.S. Forest Service: Bend Ranger District
Restrictions	USFS Trail Park Pass required
More info	Deschutes National Forest, Bend-Fort Rock District, 541-388-5664, www.fs.fed.us/r6/deschutes/

The Scoop

We scouted the ride around Cultus Lake twice. The first time, in June, when the snowpack had barely melted out, we were swarmed by mosquitoes and

Little Cultus Lake

forced to steeplechase the blowdown. Not the best time. In late August, though, with the trail cleared and the mosquito population at bay, this is a good ride. The trail wraps around the north side of Little Cultus Lake, swings past Deer Lake, then rounds the expanse of Cultus Lake. From the small resort on the east end of Cultus Lake, the route uses forest roads to create a loop. The trail rolls and heaves in spots, but there are no monster climbs to worry about. Note: If you are camped at Little Cultus Campground, you don't need a Trail Park Pass.

Driving Directions

From Bend, drive south on US Highway 97. After about 15 miles, turn right on Forest Road 40. After traveling 22 miles farther, turn left onto State Highway 46 and set your odometer to zero. At 1.3 miles, turn right on FR 4635. At 2 miles, turn left on FR 4630 toward Little Cultus Lake. FR 4630 becomes FR 4636. At 3.9 miles, bear left on FR 4636, then bear right toward Little Cultus Lake Campground. Keep the campground on your right and proceed to the day-use parking area next to the second boat launch at 5.2 miles.

The Ride

From the parking area at the second boat launch, turn left on FR 4636 and ride back along the campground. At **0.6** mile, bear left toward Deer Lake Trail, staying on FR 4636. At **1** mile, find a campsite and the start of Deer Lake Trail on the left. The trail follows the contour of the north side of Little Cultus Lake. At **2.5** miles, cross an intermittent creek. At **2.8** miles, pass a campsite on the shore of Deer Lake. Over the next half-mile, ignore several blocked-off spur trails. Cross a bridge at **3.4** miles and immediately take a right at the fork, following the bike route sign toward Cultus Lake. At **3.6** miles, pass through a stand of dead trees.

At **4.6** miles, reach a T at a doubletrack and turn left. The doubletrack affords the first through-the-trees views of Cultus Lake. Pass West Cultus Lake Campground on the right. Stay on the doubletrack, ignoring trails down into the campground. **WHOA!** At **4.9** miles, just as the doubletrack drops down to the campground, bear left onto the singletrack. At **5.4** miles, cross a log bridge and reach a T—turn right. From here, stay to the right, bypassing trails on the left that head into Three Sisters Wilderness. Ride straight through a three-way at **6.9** miles. Stay on the main trail as you pass through another campground. At **8.7** miles, reach a fork and turn left, following the sign to the trailhead.

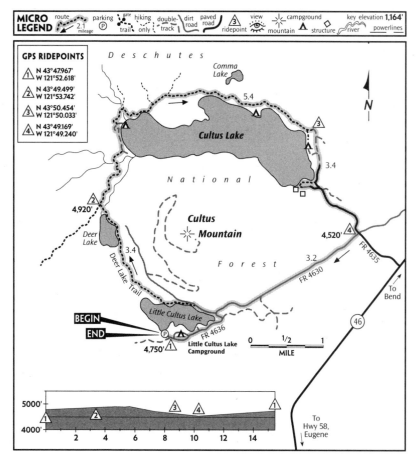

At **8.8** miles, reach the trailhead and bear right on the dirt road. Ignore a spur road on the left. At **9** miles, continue straight when you reach an improved gravel road, bypassing the campground entrance. The road becomes paved at **9.4** miles. When you reach a kiosk on the right at **9.7** miles, bear right and ride down toward the lake. Follow the trail that hugs the lakeshore. Cross a bridge after leaving the campground, then turn right, continuing along the lake. At **9.9** miles, arrive at Cultus Lake Resort and turn left onto a gravel road. Turn left again on the paved road. At **10.3** miles, reach a T and turn right onto FR 4635. At **12.2** miles, turn right onto FR 4630, which is gravel and washboarded in spots. Continue straight at **13.9** miles toward Little Cultus Lake as the road becomes FR 4636. At **14.7** miles, turn left at the fork. Bear right, then ride past the campground to the day-use area at the second boat launch, ending the ride at **15.4** miles.

Gazetteer

Nearby camping: Little Cultus Lake
Nearest food, drink, services: Sunriver, Bend

38 Lemish Lake

⊕⊕⊕

Distance	13-mile lollipop (18.6-mile option)
Terrain	Short doubletrack access to singletrack loop, some tough climbs; 840-foot gain; views
Duration	2 to 4 hours
Travel	Bend—42 miles; Eugene—100 miles
Skill level	Advanced
Season	Late summer, fall
Maps	U.S. Forest Service: Bend Ranger District
Restrictions	USFS Trail Park Pass required
More info	Deschutes National Forest, Bend-Fort Rock District, 541-388-5664, www.fs.fed.us/r6/deschutes/

The Scoop

Like most of the other high lakes southwest of Bend—Todd, Sparks, Hosmer, Lava, Cultus, and Waldo, to name a few of mountain-bike interest—the trails

Lemish Lake

around Lemish Lake can be a mosquito war zone in July and August. This is not to say don't go—it's a fine ride that passes a nice mountain lake—only to say that a long soak in the DEET tub wouldn't be a bad idea.

Driving Directions

From Bend, drive about 15 miles south on US Highway 97 and then turn right on Forest Road 40. After traveling 22 miles farther, turn left onto State Highway 46 and set your odometer to zero. At 1.3 miles, turn right on FR 4635. At 2 miles, turn left on FR 4630 toward Little Cultus Lake. FR 4630 becomes FR 4636. At 3.9 miles, bear left on FR 4636, then bear right toward Little Cultus Lake Campground. Keep the campground on your right and proceed to the day-use parking area next to the second boat ramp at 5.2 miles.

The Ride

From the parking area at the second boat ramp, pedal back to FR 4636 and turn right, riding away from the campground. At **0.2** mile, bear right at the fork. When the doubletrack divides again at **0.3** mile, stay left on FR 4636, heading toward Lemish Lake Trail. Stay on the main road, gradually ascending through a fir and pine forest. At **2** miles, turn left into a small trailhead parking area and head out Lemish Lake Trail. Although the trail is wide leaving the trailhead, it soon narrows and climbs steadily around the broad, oblong west flank of Lemish Butte. At **2.5** miles, the trail divides as it reaches Lemish Lake—turn right. After traversing the west shoreline, the trail becomes faint as it climbs through a rocky meadow.

Away from the lake, the trail ascends, steep and then level, steep and then level. After rolling over several high points around the **5**-mile mark, the trail drops to a sump at the eastern base of Charlton Butte and crosses a low bridge over the meadow. At **5.4** miles, reach a four-way and turn left, toward Clover Meadow (for a longer ride, see "Option" below). Through a dark forest, mixed with fir and pine, the trail quickly climbs to the ride's high point at **5.6** miles. From here, the trail races eastward, traversing down a ridge away from the butte.

Around **6.8** miles, ride into a bright, open stand of lodgepole pine. At **7.2** miles, cross a doubletrack. The trail widens to doubletrack and forks at **7.4** miles—take the right prong. **WHOA!** This turn is easy to miss. At **7.8** miles, reach a T at Clover Meadow and turn left, heading toward Lemish Lake. Somewhat sandy, the trail weaves through young pines. At **8.6** miles, cross a fork of Charlton Creek. Back in the mixed forest now, the trail rolls easily north. Lemish Lake is visible again around **10** miles. At **10.5** miles, reach a fork to complete the lollipop. Turn right and descend to the trailhead at **11** miles. Turn right on the road and glide back to the boat ramp at Little Cultus Lake, **13** miles.

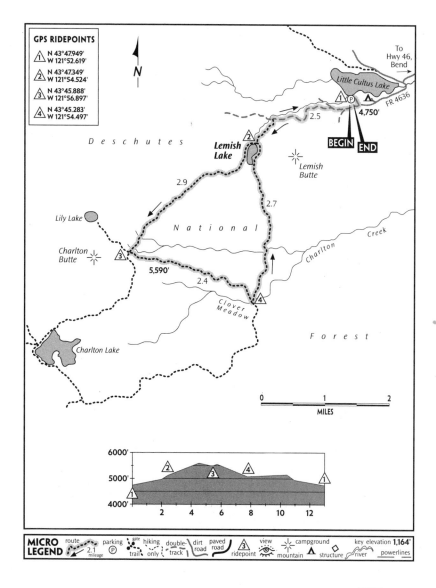

Option

From the four-way intersection at the 5.4-mile point, continue straight toward Charlton Lake. The trail climbs for about two miles and then drops to the lake. Ride around the lake counterclockwise, then at the south end climb steeply away from the lake. After the climb, stay to the left, rolling and then descending. Reach Clover Meadow at about 13.4 miles (the 7.8-mile mark above). This option adds 5.6 miles and several tough climbs on a sometimes technical trail.

Gazetteer

Nearby camping: Little Cultus Lake
Nearest food, drink, services: Sunriver, Bend

Oakridge and Eugene

Oakridge is a tiny town on State Highway 58 that you can blow through in a minute if the blue lights don't waylay you. But for all its out-of-the-way smallness, Oakridge has as much mountain-bike cachet as Bend. It's an easy day trip from Eugene and weekend from Portland. Most of the rides are either riverside traverses or steep mountain climbs followed by wild singletrack descents, and the trails vary from beginner to expert.

The McKenzie River Trail is perhaps the best-known trail in Oregon. And this long riverside trail lives up to its terrific billing (see rides 41 and 42). The waterfalls, the Blue Pool, the technical lava rock sections, and the zippy, big-tree slaloms combine to make this a riot.

Ten rides in this section follow mountain roads up and singletracks down, and every one will put a smile on your face (after the ascent makes you promise to work out more). Olallie Mountain (ride 43), King Castle (ride 44), Aubrey Mountain (ride 49), Dead Mountain (ride 50), and Larison Rock (ride 52) are on the short side but are all thrilling. Hardesty Mountain (ride 46), Buckhead Mountain (ride 51), Larison Creek (ride 53), Moon Point (ride 55), and Windy Lakes (ride 57) are longer and more difficult, but months later you'll still be dreaming about the Jedi descents. Moon Point might be the best—faster and less technical than the others.

The Waldo Lake Trail (ride 56) doesn't fit into either a riverside or mountain-climb category, but as one of the top trails in Oregon it deserves some ink. This 22-mile singletrack circumnavigates Waldo Lake—it's spectacular, challenging, and all-out fun.

Lowell, Oakridge, and Rigdon Ranger Districts were combined into one now called Middle Fork Ranger District. There's an office in Lowell and a new one being built in Oakridge along Hwy 58. While the district has done a great job of keeping their non–Wilderness Area trails open to bikes, the trails out of the Goodman Creek/Hardesty Mountain Trailhead get overused, especially in wet weather, and the Forest Service asks cyclists to ride elsewhere. Listen to that request because the next step could be a trail closure.

The Disciples of Dirt, a Eugene-based mountain bike club, leads rides, works on trails, and helps keep trails open. If you live in Eugene, become a member; if you're addicted to the rides in this area, become a member.

39

OAKRIDGE AND EUGENE
Cummins Creek
☼☼☼

Distance	10.3-mile loop
Terrain	Long, relentless paved road climb, fast singletrack descent, with some technical spots; **1,510-foot gain**; views
Duration	2 to 4 hours
Travel	Eugene—84 miles; Portland—163 miles
Skill level	Intermediate
Season	Year-round
Maps	Cummins Creek Wilderness map
Restrictions	USFS Trail Park Pass required
More info	Siuslaw National Forest, Cape Perpetua Visitors Center, 541-547-3289, www.fs.fed.us/r6/siuslaw/

The Scoop

Slightly over half this ride follows paved roads, but views of the ocean and a fun descent make up for the overdose of asphalt. The pavement is actually a

Heceta Head Lighthouse near Cummins Creek

blessing because it takes some of the bite out of the 1,500-foot climb to the trailhead. From the top, the trail follows the edge of Cummins Creek Wilderness, through old-growth stands toward the Pacific Ocean. After a steep, technical drop, the gee-whiz descent follows what used to be an old road—it's fast and fun. Although most of the trails around Cape Perpetua are closed to bicycles, the Forest Service deserves some credit for keeping this one open.

Driving Directions

From Eugene, drive west on State Highway 126. When Hwy 126 ends at the Pacific Ocean in Florence, turn right and drive north on US Highway 101. Proceed 23 miles north, then turn right and follow the sign for Cape Perpetua Visitors Center. Park in the visitors center parking lot.

The Ride

From the visitors center, ride down the entrance road to US 101 and turn right. Northbound on US 101, take the first right turn, **0.5** mile, onto Forest Road 55. From here the long climb begins. Pass the turnoff to Cape Perpetua

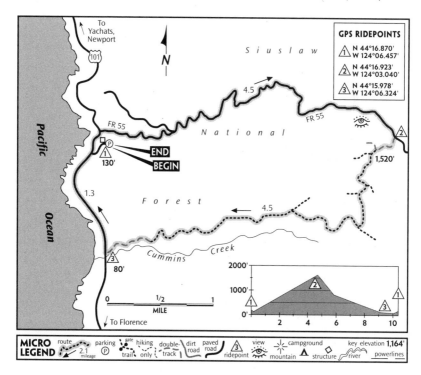

Campground on the right, and then—**1.3** miles—pass the road to Cape Perpetua Overlook (a side trip to the overlook adds 2 miles and 400 feet of climbing to the trip). FR 55 continues its steady, winding ascent. WOOF! At **4.5** miles, find a gravel parking area on the right. This is the Cooks Ridge trailhead.

From the trailhead, pedal out the wide, grassy trail to a fork at **4.7** miles. Bear left on Cummins Creek Trail and climb to the crest of the ridge. (Note: Don't turn left on either Gywnn Creek Trail or Cooks Ridge Trail.) At **5.1** miles, reach a fork and bear left. For the next one-half mile, the trail descends precipitously on a loose, rocky tread, so parts may have to be walked. Stay on the main trail, ignoring a trail on the right to a viewpoint and one on the left that's also closed to bikes. On a long bend to the right, the trail widens and levels out as it meets the terrace of an old road, **5.9** miles. This is Cummins Creek Loop Trail. Decommissioned for many years, the road is now a wide trail, with a sweet downhill grade and long sweeping turns that follow Cummins Creek along the edge of the Wilderness Area. At **7.4** miles, pass a trail on the right. At **8.7** miles, the trail ends at a dirt road. Follow the road down to US 101 at **9** miles. Turn right onto the highway and ride north to the visitors center entrance road on the right, **10.1** miles. Pedal up the hill to the parking lot to complete the ride, **10.3** miles.

Gazetteer

Nearby camping: Cape Perpetua, Carl Washburne
Nearest food, drink, services: Yachats, Florence

40 | OAKRIDGE AND EUGENE
Siltcoos Lake
⊕⊕

Distance	4-mile lollipop
Terrain	Rolling singletrack, a few short climbs, some steep; 300-foot gain
Duration	1 hour
Travel	Florence—8 miles; Eugene—69 miles
Skill level	Intermediate
Season	Spring, summer, fall
Maps	No helpful supplementary map available
Restrictions	USFS Trail Park Pass required
More info	Siuslaw National Forest, Oregon Dunes National Recreation Area, 541-271-3611, www.fs.fed.us/r6/siuslaw/

The Scoop

Located south of Florence on the Oregon coast, lovely Siltcoos Lake sits a couple of miles inland from the ocean, just across the highway from the state's

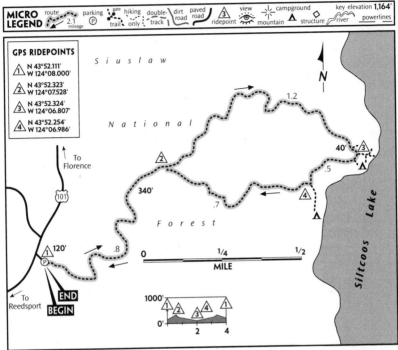

GPS RIDEPOINTS

1. N 43°52.111' W 124°08.000'
2. N 43°52.323' W 124°07.528'
3. N 43°52.324' W 124°06.807'
4. N 43°52.254' W 124°06.986'

Siuslaw

To Florence

National

101

340'

Forest

120'

.8

.7

.5

40'

1.2

Siltcoos Lake

0   1/4   1/2
MILE

1000'

0'

To Reedsport

END
BEGIN

vast sand dunes. The singletrack winds and rolls through dark forests down to a number of primitive campsites along the lake—a good place for mountain-bike camping. This is a short, easy ride, a great place to introduce beginners to singletrack. For experienced cyclists touring down the coast, this trail would present little problem, even with panniers.

Driving Directions

From Eugene, drive west on State Highway 126. When Hwy 126 ends at the Pacific Ocean in Florence, set your odometer to zero, turn left, and drive south on US Highway 101. At 8 miles, turn left onto the paved road that leads to Siltcoos Lake trailhead, less than 100 yards up the hill.

The Ride

From the parking area, take the wide, smooth dirt trail. Lined with fern, salal, and Oregon grape, the trail ascends into a dark, often fog-draped forest. It's a moderate climb, but it may be a challenge for first-timers. After topping out, the trail drops to a fork at **0.8** mile—bear left on North Route Trail. The trail surfs the landscape's waves, through cedar and spruce, toward Siltcoos Lake.

Ignore a lesser trail on the left, then immediately reach a fork at **1.9** miles. Turn left, riding past primitive campsites on the left and right, to the lake shore, **2** miles.

To return, ride back to the fork you first reached at 1.9 miles, now **2.1** miles, and bear left on South Route Trail toward US 101. Stay on the main trail. At **2.5** miles, reach a fork and turn right (a left leads to more primitive sites at South Camp). Walk up a short set of stairs, then grind up a winding climb. When you arrive at a fork, **3.2** miles, turn left and continue the ascent. Cross over the high point at **3.5** miles, and then glide down to the trailhead to complete the ride, **4** miles.

Gazetteer

Nearby camping: Carter Lake, Siltcoos Lake (primitive)
Nearest food, drink, services: Florence

41 McKenzie River

☼☼☼☼

Distance	26.5-mile one-way shuttle
Terrain	Riverside singletrack, technical in places, fast in others, no long hills; 1,770-foot loss; views
Duration	5 to 9 hours
Travel	Eugene—75 miles; Bend—75 miles; Portland—185 miles
Skill level	Advanced
Season	Summer, fall
Maps	McKenzie Ranger District map
Restrictions	USFS Trail Park Pass required
More info	Willamette National Forest, McKenzie District, 541-822-3381, www.fs.fed.us/r6/willamette/

The Scoop

This is one of the best rides anywhere, and that's not limited to Oregon. The spectacular scenery—waterfalls and blue pools, humongous cedars and blooming rhododendrons—seems perfectly balanced with the ride's challenging singletrack and all-day distance. Put off taking this incredible one-way trip until you've put in enough training miles to enjoy the entire length *and* until you've organized the two-car shuttle, because riding this as an out-and-back is not going to put as many stories in your head or as big a smile on your face. Ride a good story!

Driving Directions

From Eugene, drive just over 51 miles east on State Highway 126. Before reaching milepost 52, find the McKenzie River trailhead on the left alongside the highway. Leave a car here. Set your odometer to zero and continue east on Hwy 126. At 3.3 miles, bear left to remain on Hwy 126. At 22.2 miles, turn right on a dirt road, following the sign to the McKenzie River trailhead.

The Ride

Two trails exit from the south end of the trailhead parking area—take the one on the right that immediately crosses the creek. At **0.2** mile, cross a dirt road. At **0.9** mile, reach a fork and bear right. The trail, fast and hard-packed with some roots, bends around Clear Lake to the right. At **2.3** miles, reach a T

Tamolitch Falls flowing into the Blue Pool along the McKenzie River

at a gravelly road at Clear Lake Resort. Bear left, riding down the road and past a parking area. At **2.5** miles, bear left to regain the McKenzie River Trail.

After crossing a couple of bridges as you ride to the west of Clear Lake, reach a T at **3.6** miles and turn right toward Sahalie Falls. The trail is narrower and more technical here, a taste of what's to come. At **4.1** miles, cross a paved road and then carefully cross Hwy 126. After following the river for a short distance, bear right at a wide gravel pullout and cross over McKenzie River. From here, the trail follows the west bank of the river, descending. At **4.8** miles, pass Sahalie Falls. It's spectacular, especially during the melt-off in early summer.

When the trail divides at **5.5** miles, turn right, continuing down McKenzie River Trail toward Tamolitch Falls. The trail becomes gradually more technical, with roots and rocks and tight corners, as it meanders through a deep forest, highlighted by huge Douglas firs and cedars. It's quiet here, the roar of the river gone; freakishly, most of the McKenzie River flows underground at this point. At **9.2** miles, the river's back as it rushes into the Blue Pool at Tamolitch Falls. It's very cool here, and though it's short of the halfway mark, this is the lunch spot.

OAKRIDGE AND EUGENE

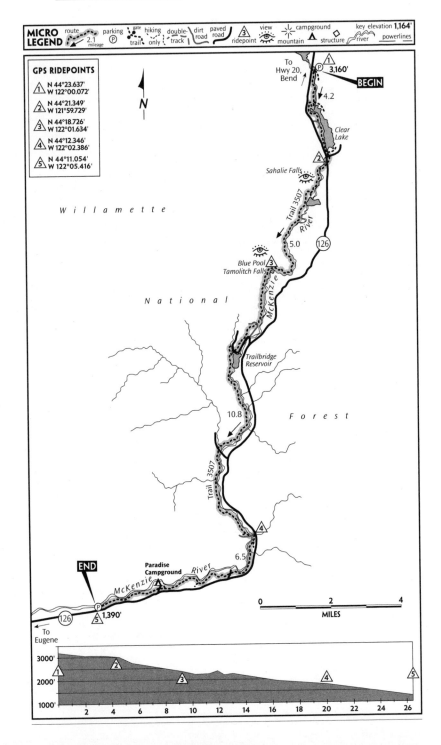

MICRO LEGEND route ~~~ 2.1 mileage △ parking Ⓟ gate • hiking trail only ⋯ double-track ~~ dirt road ~~ paved road △3 ridepoint 👁 view 🌄 mountain ⛺ campground ▲ structure ◇ river ⩘ powerlines key elevation **1,164'**

GPS RIDEPOINTS

△1 N 44°23.637' W 122°00.072'

△2 N 44°21.349' W 121°59.729'

△3 N 44°18.726' W 122°01.634'

△4 N 44°12.346' W 122°02.386'

△5 N 44°11.054' W 122°05.416'

N

To Hwy 20, Bend

Ⓟ △1 **3,160'**

BEGIN

↓4.2

Clear Lake

△2

Sahalie Falls 👁

Trail 3507

McKenzie River

5.0

126

Blue Pool 👁
Tamolitch Falls △3

W i l l a m e t t e

N a t i o n a l

Trailbridge Reservoir

10.8

F o r e s t

Trail 3507

△4

6.5

END

Paradise Campground

McKenzie River

Ⓟ △5 **1,390'**

126

To Eugene

0   2   4
MILES

3000'
△1   △2
2000'   △3   △4   △5
1000'
2   4   6   8   10   12   14   16   18   20   22   24   26

Below the Blue Pool, the trail becomes quite a bit more technical—expert-level, really—zagging through corridors of sharp pumice, up and down. But the actual trials-riding doesn't last long as you drop alongside the river. The trail upsurges and crosses two forest roads. At **12.4** miles, after a short cannonball, reach a paved road and turn right. After a few pedal strokes, the McKenzie River Trail begins again on the left and immediately begins climbing. At **13.2** miles, the trail kisses a gravel road at a yellow gate.

A few miles downriver, the riding is idyllic, winding next to the river through bunches of fern and Oregon grape, rhododendron and salal. Moss is everywhere, and the old-growth cedar and Douglas fir are just awesome. At **16.3** miles, cross over a bridge and then a paved road. From here, the trail climbs unexpectedly for a short distance, but then drops and crosses a series of bridges. Creepy-looking vine maples are part of the riverside flora now; the forest is dense with undergrowth.

At **18.3** miles, reach a gravelly doubletrack and bear left, continuing downriver. Pass through a gate at **18.6** miles, and immediately turn right to regain the singletrack. Just after a bridge crossing, **19.8** miles, bear left at the fork. At **19.9** miles, reach a T and turn left onto Forest Road 2650. A few spins of the pedals farther, reach Hwy 126. The McKenzie River Trail starts up again here on the right, now paralleling the highway for a short distance. When the trail forks at **20.2** miles, bear right, following the Trail sign. Reach a T at a dirt road, **20.9** miles, and turn left. Follow the Trail signs. At **21.4** miles, reach a fork and bear left. At **21.5** miles, again bear left at the fork, pedal down the narrow dirt trail, and cross a paved road near Belknap Hot Spring.

The singletrack continues downriver. When the trail divides at **22.5** miles, stay to the right to continue down McKenzie River Trail. Pass through a grove of giant cedars. Cross a dirt road at **23.1** miles. The trail forks at **24** miles: Bear right. A short distance farther, cross the paved entrance road to Paradise Campground. The hard-packed trail zips along here, winding through the salal and Oregon grape. At **25.1** miles, cross a dirt road. From here, the trail noodles the flats between the river and the highway. Reach the lower McKenzie River trailhead at **26.5** miles to complete the ride.

Gazetteer

Nearby camping: Paradise
Nearest food, drink, services: McKenzie Bridge, Eugene

OAKRIDGE AND EUGENE

42 | McKenzie River Short
◉◉

Distance	5-mile out-and-back
Terrain	Flat, winding, hard-packed singletrack; 170-foot gain
Duration	1 hour
Travel	Eugene—52 miles; Bend—75 miles; Portland—160 miles
Skill level	Intermediate
Season	Late spring, summer, fall
Maps	McKenzie Ranger District map
Restrictions	None
More info	Willamette National Forest, McKenzie District, 541-822-3381, www.fs.fed.us/r6/willamette/

The Scoop

The McKenzie River Trail is one of the most talked-about trails in the West, and it should be: The river is beautiful, the trail is buff, and the old growth is magic. This ride is the ultrashort version for beginners and families. From the

turnaround point at Paradise Campground, the trail continues 24 more miles upriver, and depending on your fitness you may want to continue up. For cyclists who can't put together a shuttle, you can begin at the lower trailhead and ride a long out-and-back. Whether beginner or advanced, you don't reach any obvious turnaround point until the Blue Pool at Tamolitch Falls, 17 tough miles upriver.

Driving Directions

From Eugene, drive just over 51 miles east on State Highway 126. Before reaching milepost 52, find the McKenzie River trailhead on the left alongside the highway. Park here.

The Ride

From the trailhead, pedal east on McKenzie River Trail. The trail, wide and hard-packed, noodles through the fir flats between the highway and the river. At times the trail runs along the river. At **1.4** miles, cross a dirt road. At **2.5**

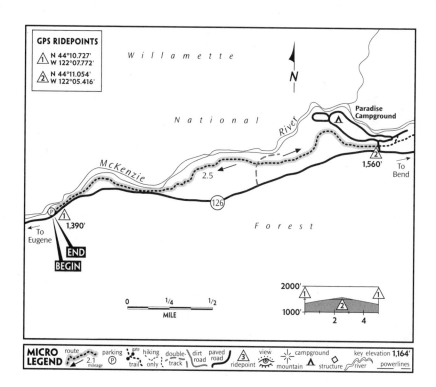

McKenzie River

miles, reach the paved entrance road to Paradise Campground. For this easy beginner ride, turn around here and pedal back to the lower trailhead, **5** miles.

Gazetteer

Nearby camping: Paradise
Nearest food, drink, services: McKenzie Bridge, Eugene

43 Olallie Mountain

☸☸☸

Distance	9.5-mile loop
Terrain	Tough paved and dirt-road climb, sweet singletrack descent; 2,390-foot gain; views
Duration	2 to 3 hours
Travel	Eugene—55 miles; Bend—80 miles; Portland—165 miles
Skill level	Advanced
Season	Summer, fall
Maps	McKenzie Ranger District map
Restrictions	USFS Trail Park Pass required
More info	Willamette National Forest, McKenzie District, 541-822-3381, www.fs.fed.us/r6/willamette/

The Scoop

Olallie Mountain is a standard forest-road climb followed by a gee-whiz single-track descent. It's fun and not too long, though the big elevation gain makes the climb seem like it will never end. Most of the ascent follows a narrow, winding paved road that's never too steep. The first dirt-road pitch is straight up, but that's it for the hard climbing. As a distraction during the climb, you'll enjoy views of the central Oregon Cascades, including Hood, Jefferson, Washington, and Three Sisters. The singletrack zips down the north slope of O'Leary Mountain on Olallie Trail. However, the trail's namesake, Olallie Mountain (*olallie* is the Chinook word for "berries"), is actually located many miles to the south of this loop. Adventurous riders may want to try both Olallie Mountain and King Castle (ride 44) for a 24-mile, 5,000-foot-gain day.

Driving Directions

From Eugene, drive about 50 miles east on State Highway 126. Just past the tiny town of McKenzie Bridge, turn right on Horse Creek Road (Forest Road 2638), and set your odometer to zero. Pass by FR 2639 on the right, then at 1.8 miles turn right onto FR 1993. At 4.7 miles, stop at the small trailhead parking pullout on the left.

The Ride

From the pullout on FR 1993, ride up the paved road. It's narrow, winding, and steep and seems to go on forever, but the paved surface provides the grip that a steep gravel road doesn't, so it's not a frustrating climb. At **3.7** miles, cross over a sharp ridge that runs northeast. On clear days, Mount Washington and Three Sisters come into view as you crest the ridge. The climb continues. At **5.1** miles, turn right onto FR 340, passing around a big green gate. The gravel road climbs steeply at first, but then the grade eases and traverses.

After a short, sweeping descent, reach a fork in the road at **5.9** miles.

There's a pullout on the right that affords excellent views of Mount Hood, Mount Jefferson, Mount Washington, and Three Sisters. When you are done soaking it in, take the left fork. Ignore a road back to the right. **WHOA!** At **6.1** miles, turn right on an unmarked and easily missed singletrack. The trail descends quickly. It's a fast, fun drop down a ridge that extends north from O'Leary Mountain. At **8.5** miles, pass an enormous rock wall on the left. In late spring and early summer, rhododendrons bloom across the hillside. At **9.5** miles, the trail dumps out onto FR 1993 at the parking area.

Gazetteer

Nearby camping: Paradise
Nearest food, drink, services: McKenzie Bridge, Eugene

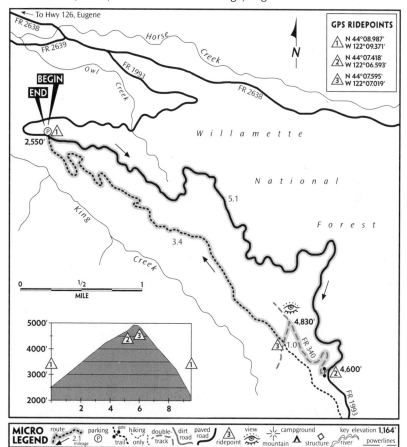

44 King Castle

✿✿✿✿

Distance	14.5-mile loop (12.5-mile option)
Terrain	Tough dirt-road and singletrack climb, epic singletrack descent; 2,370-foot gain; views
Duration	3 to 5 hours
Travel	Eugene—55 miles; Bend—80 miles; Portland—165 miles
Skill level	Advanced
Season	Summer, fall
Maps	McKenzie Ranger District map
Restrictions	USFS Trail Park Pass required
More info	Willamette National Forest, McKenzie District, 541-822-3381, www.fs.fed.us/r6/willamette/

The Scoop

This is a tougher ride than Olallie Mountain (ride 43), with a longer climb on a gravelly road and a taxing singletrack ascent to the very top. The views are

The McKenzie River valley from the north cliffs of Castle Rock

terrific, but the real reason for this ride's existence is the descent. It rocks. From the tight, steep switchbacks near the summit to the no-brakes forest traverses farther down, the descent from Castle Rock is nearly perfect. Hardcores may want to attempt King Castle and Olallie Mountain on the same day—a 24-mile, 5,000-foot-gain feat. If you do, be certain to get a photo of you and your bike at the top with Deathball Rock in the distance. Deathball Rock, huh huh, that's cool.

Driving Directions

From Eugene, drive about 50 miles east on State Highway 126. Just past the tiny town of McKenzie Bridge, turn right on Horse Creek Road (Forest Road

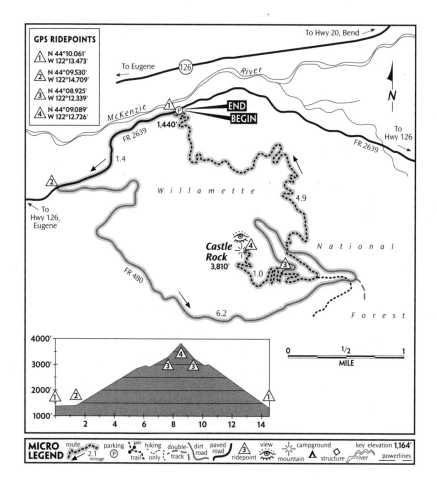

2638), and set your odometer to zero. At 1.4 miles, turn right onto King Road East (FR 2639). At 5.4 miles, turn left into King Castle trailhead and park.

The Ride

From the trailhead, ride back to FR 2639 and turn left. At **1.4** miles, turn left onto a dirt road (FR 480) and begin the serious climb. Stay on the main road as you ascend. After a couple miles, the road, gravelly in sections, spirals counterclockwise around Castle Rock, climbing in fits and starts. At **7.6** miles, the main road ends at a trailhead. The trail immediately splits—go right on Castle Rock Trail and climb toward the top of the mountain. Steep, tight switchbacks mount the southwest face of Castle Rock. **WOOF!** Reach the rocky summit at **8.6** miles and—before passing out—check out the terrific views in every direction.

When you are done picnicking at the edge of the cliffs, ride the tight switchies back toward the trailhead. At **9.6** miles, just before returning to the trailhead, reach a fork and take a hard right toward King Castle Trail and continue the fast descent. At **10.1** miles, reach a fork and bear left on King Castle Trail. The trail climbs for a short distance and then resumes the frolicking descent. At **10.7** miles, reach a T at a dirt road and turn right. Immediately turn left onto a doubletrack to continue down King Castle Trail. The doubletrack quickly narrows to a fast, hard-packed singletrack, and slingshots you around the lower north slope of Castle Rock. It's a sweet descent through a thick forest. At **14.5** miles, reach the trailhead parking to complete the loop.

Option

From the 7.6-mile point, turn left at the fork. This eliminates the one-mile climb to the top of Castle Rock (and the subsequent one-mile descent). Follow the directions from the 9.6-mile mark.

Gazetteer

Nearby camping: Paradise
Nearest food, drink, services: McKenzie Bridge, Eugene

45 Elijah Bristow State Park
⊛⊛

Distance	3.2-mile lollipop
Terrain	Wide, easy, flat dirt trail; no elevation gain
Duration	1 hour
Travel	Eugene—15 miles
Skill level	Beginner
Season	Spring, summer, fall
Maps	Elijah Bristow State Park Trail Guide
Restrictions	None
More info	Oregon State Parks, 800-551-6949, www.prd.state.or.us

The Scoop

Elijah Bristow State Park has about eight miles of multi-use trails, as well as grassy fields and picnic areas. The route described here is easy and flat—designed for families and kids—but there's lots of exploration potential beyond this route. Some of the trails at the park are rocky and more technical,

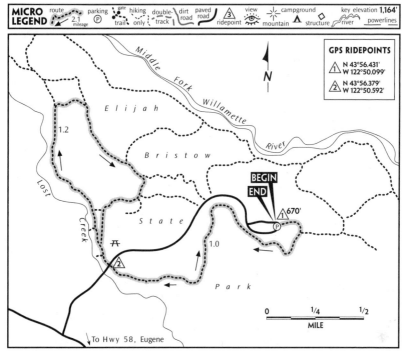

especially the trails along Middle Fork of the Willamette River. The park is heavily used by equestrians, so ride with care. Remember, when you meet horses on the trail, stop and talk to the horse and rider as they pass.

Driving Directions

From Eugene, drive south on Interstate 5. Take exit 188A and head east on State Highway 58. Drive about 10 miles east on Hwy 58, and turn left on Wheeler Road, setting your odometer to zero and following the signs for Elijah Bristow State Park. At 0.3 mile, turn right into the park. Proceed to the paved parking area at the end of the road, 1.1 miles.

The Ride

Adjacent to the paved parking area next to the bathrooms, there's a grassy dirt area for overflow parking. From the overflow parking area, take the wide dirt trail that begins near the wooden hitching post and exits into the trees. After a few pedal strokes, reach a T and turn right. The trail becomes gravelly. At **0.5** mile, when the trail runs alongside the entrance road, stay to the left.

Cross a paved trail at **0.6** mile, continuing straight ahead on the wide, gravelly trail. From here, the trail winds around the outside of a large grassy field.

At **1** mile, cross the paved entrance road, then ride straight across an open parking area to the trail. Stay to the left, but don't turn left onto one of the trails that lead to Lost Creek. The trail winds through cedar and fern, maple and blackberry. Cross a low bridge at **1.4** miles, then immediately turn right at the fork. Reach a T at **1.6** miles and turn right. From here, stay on the main trail, ignoring lesser spurs. At **1.9** miles, reach a fork and bear right. Stay to the right, passing three more doubletracks on the left. At **2.1** miles, reach a fork and bear left. At **2.2** miles, reach the paved entrance road again. Cross the paved road and retrace your tracks back around the field to the overflow parking area to complete the ride, **3.2** miles.

Gazetteer

Nearby camping: Black Canyon, Shady Dell
Nearest food, drink, services: Eugene

46 Hardesty Mountain

✿✿✿✿

Distance	19.5-mile loop
Terrain	Numbing dirt-road and singletrack climbs, zowie singletrack descent; 3,240-foot gain
Duration	4 to 6 hours
Travel	Eugene—27 miles; Bend—115 miles
Skill level	Advanced
Season	Summer, fall
Maps	Middle Fork Ranger District map
Restrictions	USFS Trail Park Pass required
More info	Willamette National Forest, Middle Fork District, 541-782-2283, www.fs.fed.us/r6/willamette/

The Scoop

The trail system that originates from the Goodman Creek/Hardesty Mountain trailhead gets a lot of use. The big parking area fills up on sunny Saturdays and Sundays with cyclists itching to head out onto Hardesty, Goodman, South Fork Willamette, and Eula Ridge Trails, and beyond. It's a great area that expands as the map unfolds, full of intermediate and advanced riding, steep climbs, and space-voyager descents. If *climb high and descend fast* is your motto, you'll love this area. However, all this trail love can lead to a trail that's overused. If you've got time, check out the great rides farther east near Oakridge. Avoid this area altogether during wet weather when any use can damage the trails. And hey, don't skid. If this area continues to get overridden, the Forest Service may close it to bikes. Note: This is a tough loop, as the trail gains and loses a lot of elevation over the first five miles before you ever even begin the 3,240-foot grunt. Pack your food and water accordingly.

Driving Directions

From Eugene, drive south on Interstate 5. Take exit 188A and head east on State Highway 58. Drive about 22 miles east on Hwy 58, and turn right into a big dirt parking area. This is the Goodman Creek/Hardesty Mountain trailhead.

Fern hallway on South Willamette Trail

The Ride

From the trailhead, ride out Hardesty Trail, a buff dirt singletrack, toward South Willamette Trail. At **0.2** mile, reach a fork—bear left and begin climbing. Ignore a lesser trail on the left at **0.3** mile. The singletrack is nice, but the climb is steep. At **0.6** mile, reach a fork and bear left on South Willamette Trail 3465. The trail begins by traversing the hillside, then quickly descends. A short climb follows the descent. At **2** miles, reach a gravel road and turn left, following the Trail sign. A short distance farther, turn right on singletrack again. After noodling through a rich forest, the trail becomes gravel, veers to the right, and starts climbing. Cross a doubletrack and continue up. Segments of the South Willamette Trail may be overgrown, so you'll need to put your head down and hog through the underbrush.

After a long climb, the trail descends quickly to a creek crossing at **4.4** miles. From here, the trail mounts a sharp ridge, and parts of the next quarter mile may have to be walked. Drop to another creek, North Creek, at **5.3** miles. After a short push out of the ravine, reach an unmarked fork and bear left. Cross South Creek a short distance farther. The trail ends at Eula Ridge trailhead, **5.7** miles, on Hwy 58. Turn right and pedal along the highway. At

6.3 miles, turn right on Patterson Mountain Road (Forest Road 5840). The paved road immediately becomes gravel and heads up. Stay on the main road as you climb. At **6.8** miles, reach a fork and bear right. At **7.7** miles, bear right and continue up the main road. The ascent is steep and relentless.

At **11.3** miles, reach a four-way at Patterson Saddle. Take a hard right turn onto FR 550 and continue the climb up toward Hardesty Mountain. At **13.1**

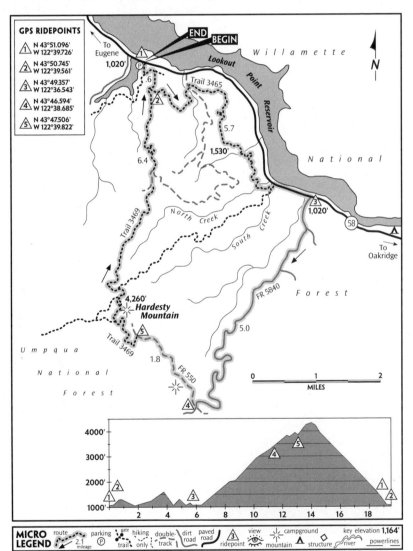

miles, take Trail 3469 on the left. The trail climbs, then traverses to a fork at **13.7** miles—take a sharp right, continuing the climb on Hardesty Trail 3469. WOOF! Finally the trail crests the western shoulder of Hardesty Mountain. It's downhill from here; the trail is narrow and, in spots, technical, and the hillside is steep. At **14** miles, reach an unmarked fork and bear left. A few pedal strokes farther, ignore a trail on the right. At **14.1** miles, reach a fork and turn left (to the right are the concrete footings that used to be the old Hardesty Mountain lookout). Around the corner, **14.2** miles, reach a fork and stay right.

From here the trail frolics down the north slope of the mountain. Steep switchbacks and fast traverses are spiced with technical sections that force short, hair-ball maneuvers. When the trail divides at **14.5** miles, go left to continue on Trail 3469. At **17.1** miles, hit a doubletrack and bear right. The singletrack begins again on the left at **17.2** miles. Switchie practice begins in earnest. Cross a doubletrack at **18.4** miles. At **18.9** miles, reach a fork and bear left. At **19.2** miles, pass by Goodman Trail on the left. Reach the trailhead at **19.5** miles to complete the loop.

Gazetteer
Nearby camping: Black Canyon, Shady Dell
Nearest food, drink, services: Oakridge

Near the top of Hardesty Mountain

47 Salmon Creek Loop

☸☸☸

Distance	7.5-mile loop
Terrain	Technical singletrack loop, not much up and down; 160-foot gain
Duration	1 to 2 hours
Travel	Eugene—42 miles; Bend—100 miles
Skill level	Advanced
Season	Spring, summer, fall
Maps	Middle Fork Ranger District map
Restrictions	USFS Trail Park Pass required
More info	Willamette National Forest, Middle Fork District, 541-782-2283, www.fs.fed.us/r6/willamette/

The Scoop

The first half of this loop, up the north side of Salmon Creek, is heavily used by walkers and runners. Numerous interconnecting trails, most of which are

Salmon Creek

wide and easy, crisscross the north side of the creek, making it a fun, if sometimes confusing, route. Once you cross the bridge over the creek at the
halfway point, though, the trail becomes narrow, technical, and less traveled,
but the route is easier to follow. Salmon Creek is lovely, and the view from the
bridge, of water running across green rock slabs though a fir and vine maple
forest, is extraordinary.

Driving Directions

From Eugene, drive south on Interstate 5. Take exit 188A and head east on
State Highway 58. Drive about 36 miles east on Hwy 58 to Oakridge. At the
stoplight at Crestview Street in Oakridge, set your odometer to zero and continue east on Hwy 58. At 1.7 miles, turn left on Fish Hatchery Road. At 3 miles,
cross Salmon Creek, then immediately—before crossing the railroad tracks
and reaching Forest Road 24 (Salmon Creek Road)—park in the dirt parking
area on the right.

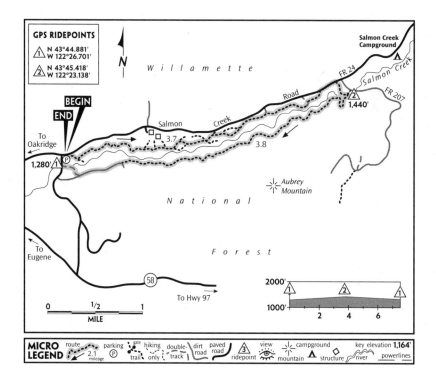

The Ride

From the dirt parking area, head out Salmon Creek Trail 4365. Stay on the main trail, ignoring spurs down to the creek. The trail is wide, rolling, and wood-chipped. At **0.9** mile, pass under a railroad trestle. From **1** mile to **1.2** miles, ignore three trails on the left that lead to the former ranger station. At **1.3** miles, reach a fork and bear left. At **1.5** miles, bear right at the fork and then immediately turn left at the T. At the **2**-mile mark, ride straight through a four-way. At **2.1** miles, stay to the right, passing two trails on the left. At **2.4** miles, ignore a trail back to the left. The way narrows here. A short distance farther, pass by a spur on the left that leads to Salmon Creek Road. Then bear right onto a doubletrack and continue along the creek.

At **2.6** miles, ignore a spur to a camp spot on the right. At **2.9** miles, stay on the main doubletrack, ignoring a spur on the left to Salmon Creek Road. At **3.2** miles, bear left (a camp spot is straight ahead). **WHOA!** Almost immediately, turn right on an easily missed singletrack—Salmon Creek Trail 4365. The trail climbs through the woods, then ends at Salmon Creek Road. Turn right and ride along this paved road to the **3.5**-mile mark, where Trail 4365 starts up again on the right. Stay on the main trail as it crosses two doubletracks. At **3.7** miles, reach a fork and take a hard right, now heading downriver. Cross the elaborately constructed wood bridge over Salmon Creek. The creek is beautiful here, and it's a good place to linger.

From the bridge, the trail is ragged and root-strewn as it follows the creek, and some riders may be forced to walk short sections. At **6.4** miles, the trail routes around the rocky base of a railroad trestle. Shoulder your bike and climb underneath the trestle to the trail beyond. At **6.5** miles, cross over a tiny diversion dam and then bear left on the doubletrack. At **6.8** miles, cross a bridge and veer right on the dirt road. **WHOA!** Reach a fork in the road at **7.1** miles, turn right on the lesser doubletrack, and head toward the creek. The doubletrack follows the creek and then ends at Fish Hatchery Road. Turn right on this paved road. Cross over Salmon Creek to reach the parking area at **7.5** miles.

Gazetteer

Nearby camping: Salmon Creek Falls, Packard Creek
Nearest food, drink, services: Oakridge

48 Salmon Creek Warrior Trail

✦✦

Distance	5.2-mile out-and-back
Terrain	Wide, nearly flat trail; **140-foot gain**
Duration	1 hour
Travel	Eugene—42 miles; Bend—100 miles
Skill level	Beginner
Season	Spring, summer, fall
Maps	Middle Fork Ranger District map
Restrictions	USFS Trail Park Pass required
More info	Willamette National Forest, Middle Fork District, 541-782-2283, www.fs.fed.us/r6/willamette/

The Scoop

Salmon Creek Trail, also known as the Warrior Cross-Country Trail because the local high school cross-country team trains here, is heavily used by runners, walkers, and cyclists. But the wide trail has good sight lines and accommodates

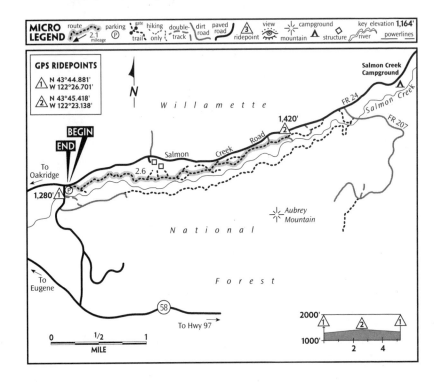

users well. This trail, easy and flat, perfect for beginners and families, winds along Salmon Creek through a pretty forest.

Driving Directions

From Eugene, drive south on Interstate 5. Take exit 188A and head east on State Highway 58. Drive about 36 miles east on Hwy 58 to Oakridge. At the stoplight at Crestview Street in Oakridge, set your odometer to zero and continue east on Hwy 58. At 1.7 miles, turn left on Fish Hatchery Road. At 3 miles, cross Salmon Creek, then immediately—before crossing the railroad tracks and reaching Forest Road 24 (Salmon Creek Road)—park in the dirt parking area on the right.

The Ride

From the dirt parking area, head out Salmon Creek Trail 4365. Stay on the main trail, ignoring spurs down to the creek. The trail is wide, rolling, and wood-chipped. At **0.9** mile, pass under a railroad trestle. From **1** mile to **1.2** miles, ignore three trails on the left that lead to the former ranger station. At

1.3 miles, reach a fork and bear left. At **1.5** miles, bear right at the fork and then immediately turn left at the T. At the **2**-mile mark, ride straight through a four-way. At **2.1** miles, stay to the right, passing two trails on the left. At **2.4** miles, ignore a trail back to the left. The way narrows here. A short distance farther, pass by a spur on the left that leads to Salmon Creek Road, then bear right onto a doubletrack and continue along the creek. At **2.6** miles, there's a spur to a camp spot on the right. From here the route is more difficult to follow, so for this ride, turn around and retrace your tracks. Return to the parking area at **5.2** miles.

Gazetteer

Nearby camping: Salmon Creek Falls, Packard Creek
Nearest food, drink, services: Oakridge

49 Aubrey Mountain

Distance	11.4-mile loop
Terrain	Tough dirt-road climb, great singletrack descent, paved roads; 1,050-foot gain
Duration	2 to 3 hours
Travel	Eugene—42 miles; Bend—100 miles
Skill level	Intermediate
Season	Late spring, summer, fall
Maps	Middle Fork Ranger District map
Restrictions	USFS Trail Park Pass required
More info	Willamette National Forest, Middle Fork District, 541-782-2283, www.fs.fed.us/r6/willamette/

The Scoop

The ride begins with a playful pedal along Salmon Creek Trail. After the four-mile warm-up, a dirt road heads up Aubrey Mountain at an insane clip—one of the steepest climbs in this book. A friend said he preferred Aubrey Mountain as a night ride so he didn't have to look at the incline ahead of him. Okay, but the climb is less than one and a half miles long. How hard can it be? The traversing and switchbacking descent will put a smile on your face and is definitely worth the mile and a half of pain. And the south slope of Aubrey Mountain affords great views of the Middle Fork of the Willamette River valley. Unless you're riding at night.

Driving Directions

From Eugene, drive south on Interstate 5. Take exit 188A and head east on State Highway 58. Drive about 36 miles east on Hwy 58 to Oakridge. At the stoplight at Crestview Street in Oakridge, set your odometer to zero and continue east on Hwy 58. At 1.7 miles, turn left on Fish Hatchery Road. At 3 miles, cross Salmon Creek, then immediately—before crossing the railroad tracks and reaching Forest Road 24 (Salmon Creek Road)—park in the dirt area on the right.

Along the south slope of Aubrey Mountain

The Ride

From the parking area, head out Salmon Creek Trail 4365. Stay on the main trail, ignoring spurs down to the creek. The trail is wide, rolling, and wood-chipped. At **0.9** mile, pass under a railroad trestle. From **1** mile to **1.2** miles, ignore three trails on the left that lead to the former ranger station. At **1.3** miles, reach a fork and bear left. At **1.5** miles, bear right at the fork and then immediately turn left at the T. At the **2**-mile mark, ride straight through a four-way. At **2.1** miles, stay to the right, passing two trails on the left. At **2.4** miles, ignore a trail back to the left. The way narrows here. A short distance farther, pass by a spur on the left that leads to Salmon Creek Road. Then bear right onto a doubletrack and continue along the creek.

At **2.6** miles, ignore a spur to a camp spot on the right. At **2.9** miles, stay on the main doubletrack, ignoring another spur on the left to Salmon Creek Road. At **3.2** miles, bear left (a camp spot is straight ahead). **WHOA!** Almost immediately, turn right on an easily missed singletrack—Salmon Creek Trail 4365. The trail climbs through the woods, then ends at Salmon Creek Road. Turn right and ride along the side of this paved road to the **3.5**-mile mark, where Trail 4365 starts up again on the right. Stay on the main trail as it

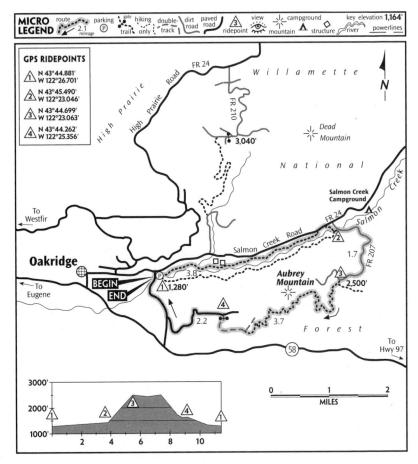

crosses two doubletracks. At **3.7** miles, reach a fork and bear left. At **3.8** miles, reach FR 207 and turn right.

FR 207 crosses over Salmon Creek and becomes gravel. At **4.1** miles, the road bends to the right and heads steeply up the eastern shoulder of Aubrey Mountain. From here the road gains elevation in huge, grueling, and unrelenting chunks. Though it's short, at over 700 feet per mile it's one of the steepest climbs in this book. At **5.2** miles, pass an unmarked singletrack on the left. At **5.5** miles, turn left onto Eugene to Crest Trail 3559. The trail immediately divides—bear right. This is a fun section, traversing in and out of the steep side-sloped folds of Aubrey Mountain on a gradual descent. At **7.5** miles, you pop out of the fir forest into an open area of low oak and maple.

At **7.6** miles, the trail reenters the fir forest and immediately begins a furious, switchbacking descent. When the trail ends at FR 022 at **8.5** miles, turn left and descend. The dirt road winds and rolls. At **9.2** miles, pass through a gate and reach a paved road. Turn left and cruise down this fast, winding descent (too bad it's pavement). Cross a set of railroad tracks at **10.2** miles. The road ends at a T at **10.5** miles—turn right. At **11.4** miles, cross over Salmon Creek and reach the dirt parking area on the right to complete the loop.

Gazetteer

Nearby camping: Salmon Creek Falls, Packard Creek
Nearest food, drink, services: Oakridge

50 Dead Mountain

✿✿✿

Distance	12.4-mile loop
Terrain	Moderate to difficult paved and dirt-road climb, singletrack descent; 1,740-foot gain
Duration	2 to 4 hours
Travel	Eugene—42 miles; Bend—100 miles
Skill level	Intermediate
Season	Late spring, summer, fall
Maps	Middle Fork Ranger District map
Restrictions	USFS Trail Park Pass required
More info	Willamette National Forest, Middle Fork District, 541-782-2283, www.fs.fed.us/r6/willamette/

The Scoop

In many ways, this ride is a cousin to Aubrey Mountain (ride 49). Both rides begin from the same trailhead, but Dead Mountain explores the north side of

Wildlife on High Prairie Road

the Salmon Creek valley, Aubrey Mountain the south. Both loops combine road climbs with ripping singletrack descents, and neither is too long. In fact, if you are in shape, a reasonable day might include both loops. Dead Mountain begins with a long, paved-road climb up and across High Prairie, followed by a shorter dirt-road ascent. From the top, the singletrack flies down the southwestern edge of the mountain. It's an exhilarating ride.

Driving Directions

From Eugene, drive south on Interstate 5. Take exit 188A and head east on State Highway 58. Drive about 36 miles east on Hwy 58 to Oakridge. At the stoplight at Crestview Street in Oakridge, set your odometer to zero and continue east on Hwy 58. At 1.7 miles, turn left on Fish Hatchery Road. At 3 miles,

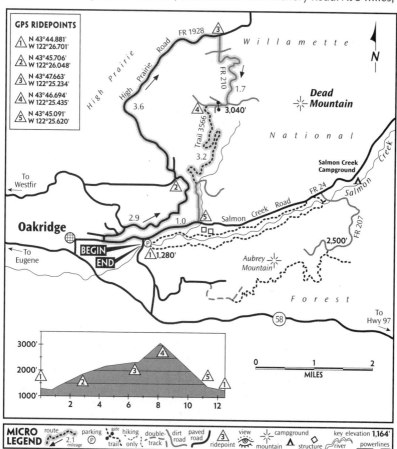

cross Salmon Creek, then immediately—before crossing the railroad tracks and reaching Forest Road 24 (Salmon Creek Road)—park in the dirt area on the right.

The Ride

From the parking area, cross the railroad tracks to Salmon Creek Road (FR 24) and turn left toward Oakridge. As you enter Oakridge, heading west, the road becomes East First Street. At **0.7** mile, turn right on Oak Street. Proceed one block up the hill and turn right on East Second Street, still climbing. A few pedal strokes farther, bear left on Westoak Road. At **1.2** miles, bear right on High Prairie Road. The paved road climbs north. At **2.9** miles, reach a fork and bear right. Bear left a short distance farther, continuing north on High Prairie Road (FR 1928). After climbing about one mile farther, follow the northwest bend in the road across the oak-scattered flats of High Prairie.

At **6.5** miles, turn right on Dead Mountain Road (FR 210), which is gravel. At **6.7** miles, ride straight through a four-way. From here, the road winds steeply up the northwest flank of Dead Mountain, through a fir forest. The climb is relentless and wearing. At **8.1** miles, reach a T and turn right on FR 190. It's here that you cross over the western ridge of Dead Mountain. At **8.2** miles, when the road divides again, bear left and ride around the gate. The road almost immediately divides again—stay to the right. WHOA! Just as you might think about gaining some speed, turn left onto Flat Creek Trail 3566.

The sweet, smooth, fern-lined singletrack slaloms down the hillside. The forest is somewhat open and light, and the trail is fast. At **10.7** miles, cross a creek and climb to FR 2404. Turn right on this gravel road and descend. FR 2404 ends at a T with Salmon Creek Road (FR 24). Turn right on Salmon Creek Road. Pass by the former ranger station on the left. At **12.4** miles, turn left and cross the railroad tracks to the parking area to complete the loop.

Gazetteer

Nearby camping: Salmon Creek Falls, Packard Creek
Nearest food, drink, services: Oakridge

51

OAKRIDGE AND EUGENE
Buckhead Mountain
⊕⊕⊕⊕

Distance	20.2-mile loop
Terrain	Long, strenuous dirt-road climb, singletrack climbs and descents; 2,970-foot gain
Duration	4 to 6 hours
Travel	Eugene—38 miles; Bend—105 miles
Skill level	Advanced
Season	Summer, fall
Maps	Middle Fork Ranger District map
Restrictions	None
More info	Willamette National Forest, Middle Fork District, 541-782-2283, www.fs.fed.us/r6/willamette/

The Scoop

The potential for pain is mind-boggling: From the town of Westfir, numerous forest roads climb toward Buckhead Mountain, on toward Sourgrass Mountain, and way up to Alpine Ridge. From the high ridgeline, Alpine Trail—fast and buff in sections, rough, technical, and challenging in others—wends its way back down to Westfir. Toss in a jaunt out the Tire Mountain Trail, and you could easily cobble together a 50-mile ride. So much for the hypothetical; for most riders, the actual will be enough of a challenge—20 miles and nearly 3,000 feet of elevation gain. After a three-mile, paved-road warm-up, the route turns up a dirt road and climbs, climbs, climbs. From the top, the singletrack dives down the ridgeline, technical in spots, overgrown in others, and makes you feel like a space shuttle pilot. The few tough ascents on the trail allow the water in your eyes to dry before the next precipitous drop.

Driving Directions

From Eugene, drive south on Interstate 5. Take exit 188A and head east on State Highway 58. After driving about 32 miles east on Hwy 58 toward Oakridge, turn left, following the signs to Westfir. Set your odometer to zero. Cross the Middle Fork of the Willamette River and reach a T at 0.5 mile—turn left on Westfir-Oakridge Road, continuing toward Westfir. Stay to the right on Westfir-Oakridge Road. At 2.3 miles, reach a four-way stop at the town of

Covered bridge in Westfir

Westfir. Park in the paved lot on the right side of this intersection, across from the covered bridge.

The Ride

From the four-way stop in Westfir, ride east, upriver, on North Fork Road (Forest Road 19). The road is paved and level. At **2.9** miles, turn left on FR 1910, which is dirt, and cross North Fork of the Middle Fork of the Willamette River. When the road divides immediately across the river, bear right on the main road, FR 1910. The climbing begins pronto and doesn't relent as it winds up the steep ridge between Dartmouth and Short Creeks, east of Buckhead Mountain. Stay on the main road as you climb, passing FR 680 on the right and several lesser roads on the left. At **8.4** miles, reach a fork and bear right, continuing on FR 1910 (FR 683 is to the left).

WOOF! At **10.8** miles, reach the top of the road section at a fork. Turn left onto FR 1911. Stay on the main road to the left. At **11.2** miles, turn left onto a singletrack, Alpine Trail 3450. The trail immediately begins a serious climb up and around a high knoll. At **11.6** miles, the way levels and traverses, crossing the ride's high point a short distance farther. Reach a fork in the trail at **12.5** miles and bear left, beginning a nearly continuous eight-mile descent. At **14.1** miles, cross a dirt road, then stay to the right of a wood structure. Reach a fork at **14.6** miles and bear left. After crossing a dirt road at **16.7** miles, the trail climbs toward Buckhead Mountain.

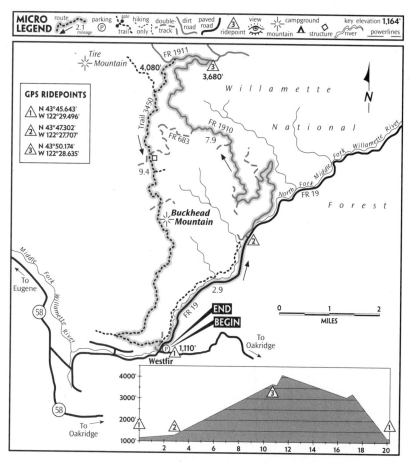

MICRO LEGEND — route, 2.1 mileage, parking Ⓟ, gate, hiking trail, double-track, dirt road, paved road, 3 ridepoint, view, campground, mountain, structure, river, powerlines, key elevation 1,164'

GPS RIDEPOINTS

⚠️1 N 43°45.643'
W 122°29.496'

⚠️2 N 43°47.302'
W 122°27.707'

⚠️3 N 43°50.174'
W 122°28.635'

Tire Mountain 4,080'

FR 1911

3 3,680'

Willamette

Trail 3450

FR 683

FR 1910 7.9

9.4

National

North Fork Middle Fork Willamette River

FR 19

Forest

Buckhead Mountain

2

Middle Fork Willamette River

To Eugene

58

2.9

FR 19

END
BEGIN

To Oakridge

0   1   2
MILES

Ⓟ 1,110'
Westfir

58

To Oakridge

4000'
3000'
2000'
1000'

3

2

2   4   6   8   10   12   14   16   18   20

At **17.1** miles, the trail levels and, for a short distance, traverses the west flank of the mountain. From here, the trail romps and corkscrews down the ridge that extends south from Buckhead Mountain. After a couple of hair-ball sections and several road crossings, reach a T at **18.9** miles and turn left, traversing east. At **19.8** miles, the trail ends at a road. Pass around the gate and bear right. Ride under the railroad tracks. Cross the North Fork of the Middle Fork of the Willamette via a covered bridge, and arrive in Westfir to complete the loop, **20.2** miles.

Gazetteer

Nearby camping: Salmon Creek Falls, Packard Creek
Nearest food, drink, services: Oakridge

52

OAKRIDGE AND EUGENE
Larison Rock
⊕⊕⊕

Distance	10.2-mile loop
Terrain	Tough paved-road climb, steep singletrack descent; 2,060-foot gain
Duration	2 to 3 hours
Travel	Eugene—43 miles; Bend—100 miles
Skill level	Intermediate
Season	Summer, fall
Maps	Middle Fork Ranger District map
Restrictions	USFS Trail Park Pass required
More info	Willamette National Forest, Middle Fork District, 541-782-2283, www.fs.fed.us/r6/willamette/

The Scoop

A favorite of Oakridge locals, this ride begins with a steep climb up a paved road and finishes with a rocket descent down the precipitous north slope of Larison Rock. The trail's signature is a 12-inch tread disappearing around a

blind corner on a steep Oregon grape- and rhododendron-covered hillside. It's fun and—unless you take a flier—usually over all too quickly. Like many of the steep trails in the Middle Fork Ranger District, this one can get beat up during wet weather. Avoid this trail from late fall through the spring when the trail might be susceptible to damage.

Driving Directions

From Eugene, drive south on Interstate 5. Take exit 188A and head east on State Highway 58. Drive about 36 miles east on Hwy 58 to Oakridge. At the stoplight at Crestview Street in Oakridge, set your odometer to zero and continue east on Hwy 58. At 1.9 miles, turn right on Kitson Springs Road (Forest Road 23) toward Hills Creek Dam. At 2.4 miles, turn right on FR 21. At 2.7

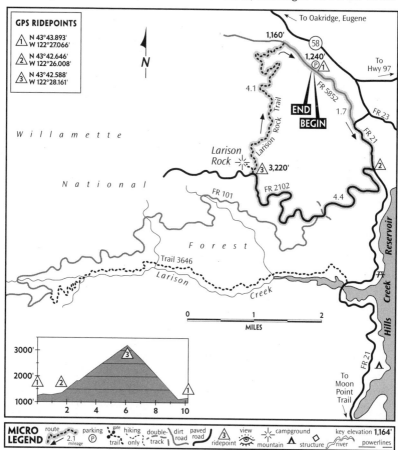

miles, immediately after crossing Middle Fork of the Willamette River, turn right on FR 5852. At 3.8 miles, turn right into the large gravel parking area.

The Ride

From the parking area, turn left on FR 5852 and pedal back to FR 21. Reach the T with FR 21 at **1** mile and turn right. At **1.7** miles, turn right on Larison Rock Road (FR 2102), which is paved, and immediately begin climbing. It's a steep, four-mile climb. Stay on the main road. WOOF! After burning several Ben & Jerry's pints' worth of calories, turn right on Larison Rock Trail at **6.1** miles. The trail immediately forks—go right and descend. (The left prong climbs to the top of Larison Rock.) This is an exciting descent: The trail down is sweet, smooth, and fast, through an understory of salal, Oregon grape, fern, and rhododendron. Tight switchbacks, a narrow tread, and several ragged, hair-ball sections of trail keep it interesting. At **9.5** miles, when the trail ends at a dirt road, turn right. Reach the parking area on the left at **10.2** miles to complete the ride.

Gazetteer

Nearby camping: Packard Creek, Sand Prairie
Nearest food, drink, services: Oakridge

53

Larison Creek

⊕⊕⊕⊕

Distance	19-mile loop
Terrain	Paved and dirt-road climbing with steep pitches, technical singletrack descent; 1,540-foot gain; views
Duration	3 to 6 hours
Travel	Eugene—45 miles; Bend—98 miles
Skill level	Expert
Season	Summer, fall
Maps	Middle Fork Ranger District map
Restrictions	USFS Trail Park Pass required
More info	Willamette National Forest, Middle Fork District, 541-782-2283, www.fs.fed.us/r6/willamette/

The Scoop

Put on your adventurer's cap for this one. After a pleasant paved warm-up and a steep, but also paved, climb, this loop follows a quiet dirt road that

Mossy, grotto-like Larison Creek Trail

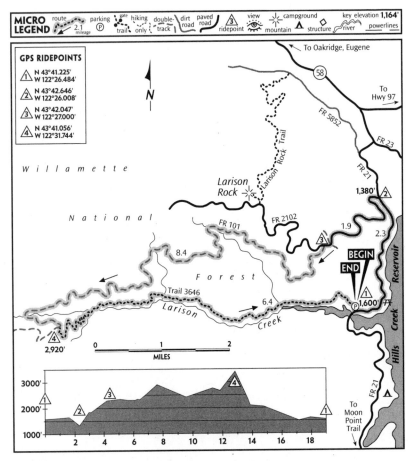

MICRO LEGEND — route — 2.1 mileage — parking ℗ — gate — hiking trail — double-track only — dirt road — paved road — ③ ridepoint — view — ✳ mountain — campground — ⚐ structure — ◇ river — powerlines — key elevation **1,164'**

GPS RIDEPOINTS
⚠1 N 43°41.225' W 122°26.484'
⚠2 N 43°42.646' W 122°26.008'
⚠3 N 43°42.047' W 122°27.000'
⚠4 N 43°41.056' W 122°31.744'

To Oakridge, Eugene

To Hwy 97

Willamette

National

Forest

Larison Rock

Larison Rock Trail

FR 5852

FR 23

FR 21

1,380'

FR 2102

FR 101

1.9

2.3

③

BEGIN END

8.4

Trail 3646

Larison Creek

6.4

1,600'

Reservoir

Hills Creek

2,920'

0   1   2
MILES

3000'
2000'
1000'
2   4   6   8   10   12   14   16   18

To Moon Point Trail

FR 21

circuitously climbs to the upper reaches of Larison Creek. The upper section of Larison Creek Trail—technical, root-strewn, overgrown, and steep—is not well maintained. But if you are an expert rider and can get past the sadistic blackberry vines, the stubborn manzanita branches, and the ragged trail, this is a good one.

Driving Directions

From Eugene, drive south on Interstate 5. Take exit 188A and head east on State Highway 58. Drive about 36 miles east on Hwy 58 to Oakridge. At the stoplight at Crestview Street in Oakridge, set your odometer to zero and continue east on Hwy 58. At 1.9 miles, turn right on Kitson Springs Road (Forest Road 23) toward Hills Creek Dam. At 2.4 miles, turn right on FR 21. Stay on FR

21. At 3.5 miles, pass by FR 2102 on the right. At 5.8 miles, turn right into a dirt parking area at the trailhead.

The Ride

From the trailhead parking area, ride to FR 21 and turn left, heading north. The paved road follows the winding shoreline of Hills Creek Reservoir. Pass by the dam at **1.9** miles and descend. At **2.3** miles, turn left onto Larison Rock Road (FR 2102), also paved, and begin a steep climb. Stay on the main road that snakes to a fork at **4.2** miles, and turn left on FR 2102-101. The road may be closed to motor vehicles due to washouts, but it continues to be passable on a bike. A quiet one-laner, the road traverses high above Larison Creek and generally heads west.

After nearly five miles of rolling up and down, into creek drainages and then back out, descend quickly to a wide pullout at **9.4** miles, where views of Larison Creek valley and Diamond Peak spread out. From here, continue down the road—doubletrack now—for a pitch through a diverse forest of cedar and fir, maple and oak. The doubletrack heads up again, drops to cross over Larison Creek at **11.9** miles, and climbs up the south side of the valley. Just after crossing over the ridge, **12.6** miles, turn left onto Larison Creek Trail 3646. As it passes through an old clearcut, the trail's top half-mile needs brushing—big-time. Long sleeves are recommended as protection against manzanita and blackberry that clamor for your skin.

Just after the **13**-mile point, the trail slides into the woods, and it's the technical switchbacks rather than the sadistic overgrowth that make the descent a challenge. At **13.7** miles, pass through a series of vertical, ultratight switchies into the grotto of Larison Creek. The next few miles are narrow, rocky, and root-strewn—technical but consistently ridable. Moss, fern, salal, and Oregon grape flourish in the shade of fir, cedar, and vine maple. Around the **17**-mile mark, the trail becomes wider and smoother. Pass through a primitive camp area at **17.4** miles. From here, the trail rolls beside a long arm of Hills Creek Reservoir. At **19** miles, reach the trailhead parking area to complete the loop.

Gazetteer

Nearby camping: Packard Creek, Sand Prairie
Nearest food, drink, services: Oakridge

54 Middle Fork Willamette

Distance	20-mile loop
Terrain	Easy paved-road climb, tricky singletrack descent; 460-foot gain
Duration	3 to 5 hours
Travel	Eugene—60 miles; Bend—115 miles
Skill level	Advanced
Season	Late spring, summer, fall
Maps	Middle Fork Ranger District map
Restrictions	None
More info	Willamette National Forest, Middle Fork District, 541-782-2283, www.fs.fed.us/r6/willamette/

The Scoop

Middle Fork Willamette Trail runs nearly thirty miles, winding northwest from the blunt end of the long Middle Fork valley near Timpanogas Lake down to Sand Prairie Campground at Hills Creek Reservoir. It's a riverside trail—no long climbs—that is sometimes hard-packed and fast, sometimes ragged and technical, and sometimes overgrown and difficult to follow—and the ten-mile segment described here is all of that. Periodically the river washes away parts of the trail, and new sections are built in their place. This olio of trails can cause confusion, so be patient and take the newer trail if you are unsure. A paved forest road links both ends of this Middle Fork segment to form the twenty-mile loop. Other ride formats are possible, such as an out-and-back or a two-car shuttle on this or other sections of the trail. The Middle Fork makes a good Sunday ride after a Moon Point (ride 55) Saturday.

Driving Directions

From Eugene, drive south on Interstate 5. Take exit 188A and head east on State Highway 58. Drive about 36 miles east on Hwy 58 to Oakridge. At the stoplight at Crestview Street in Oakridge, set your odometer to zero and continue east on Hwy 58. At 1.9 miles, turn right on Kitson Springs Road (Forest Road 23) toward Hills Creek Dam. At 2.4 miles, turn right on FR 21. Stay on FR 21. At 14.6 miles, pass Sand Prairie Campground on the right. At milepost 17, pass Youngs Flat on the right—a good place to park if you're only here for the

Another creek crossing on the Middle Fork Willamette Trail

day. At milepost 18, at 21.3 miles, turn into Secret Campground on the right and park. (Note: Don't park in a camp spot if you are not camping.)

The Ride

From the dirt-road entrance to Secret Campground, turn right on FR 21. Ride up the paved forest road, gradually climbing. At **2.5** miles, turn right on FR 2134 and cross over Middle Fork of the Willamette River. The road divides at **2.6** miles—bear right on FR 2133, which is gravel, and follow the sign for Middle Fork Trail. At **3.3** miles, turn right onto Middle Fork Trail 3609. Just after a short bridge, **3.6** miles, the trail braids apart—bear left. When the trail braids back together at **3.9** miles, stay left. The trail climbs in a few spots, but for the most part it winds and zips, following the river downward. A few sections are technical, with roots and rocks and sketchy side slopes.

At **7.5** miles, ignore a camp spot and a spur road on the left. At **7.7** miles, the trail seems to end at a paved road, FR 2127. Turn right and cross over the river. At **7.8** miles, reach FR 21 and turn left. A few spins of the pedals farther, turn left to return to Trail 3609. At **8.8** miles, turn left at a dirt road, glide to the river, and then turn right onto the trail again. At **8.9** miles, reach a fork and bear right. At **9.4** miles, ignore a lesser trail back on the left. The trail

OAKRIDGE AND EUGENE

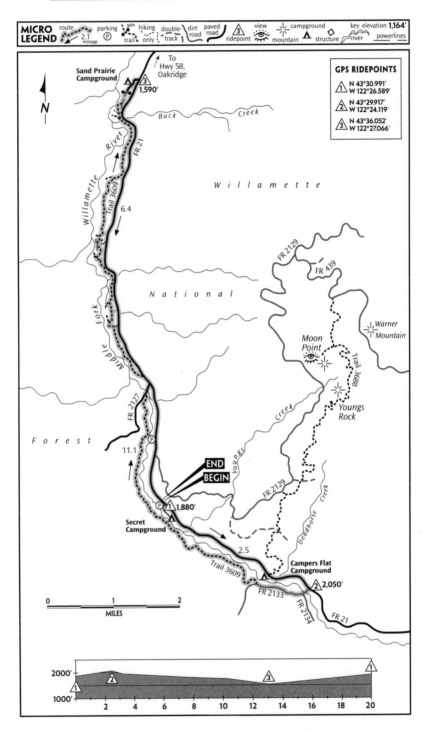

MICRO LEGEND route 2.1 mileage | parking P | gate · hiking trail only | double-track | dirt road | paved road | ⟨3⟩ ridepoint | view | campground | mountain | ⟨A⟩ structure | river | powerlines | key elevation **1,164'**

Sand Prairie Campground
⟨3⟩ 1,590'

To Hwy 58, Oakridge

N

Buck Creek

GPS RIDEPOINTS
⟨1⟩ N 43°30.991'
W 122°26.589'
⟨2⟩ N 43°29.917'
W 122°24.119'
⟨3⟩ N 43°36.052'
W 122°27.066'

W i l l a m e t t e

FR 21

Trail 3609

6.4

FR 2129

FR 439

N a t i o n a l

Moon Point

Warner Mountain

Trail 3688

Youngs Rock

W i l l a m e t t e

Middle Fork

FR 2127

11.1

F o r e s t

P

END
BEGIN

P ⟨1⟩ 1,880'

Secret Campground

Youngs Creek

FR 2129

Deadhorse Creek

2.5

Campers Flat Campground
⟨2⟩ 2,050'

Trail 3609

FR 2133

FR 2134

FR 21

0   1   2
MILES

2000' ⟨2⟩   ⟨3⟩   ⟨1⟩
1000' ⟨1⟩
      2   4   6   8   10   12   14   16   18   20

kisses FR 21 a short distance farther, then passes through a camp spot—bear right and then left to continue on the trail.

When the trail divides at **10.2** miles, bear right on the Horse Trail. At **10.5** miles, reach a dirt road and turn right. **WHOA!** This is a confusing area without much signage for help. Pass a dirt road on the right and then immediately turn right onto an obscured and unmarked trail. Almost immediately the trail forks—bear left. At **10.7** miles, reach another fork and bear right. At **11.7** miles, ignore a trail back on the left. The trail kisses FR 21 a couple of times a short distance farther. Cross over a bridge at **12.7** miles, then reach a fork and bear right. Quickly cross a road and bear left to continue on the trail. When the trail pops out onto a gravel road at **13.1** miles, go left. Ride to the left of the gate, scooting along the river. At **13.3** miles, the trail ends at the paved road at Sand Prairie Campground. Stay to the left on the main campground road. At **13.6** miles, reach FR 21 at the entrance to the campground and turn right. Ride south on FR 21 to Secret Campground on the right, **20** miles, to complete the loop.

Gazetteer
Nearby camping: Secret (primitive), Sand Prairie
Nearest food, drink, services: Oakridge

55

OAKRIDGE AND EUGENE
Moon Point
⊛⊛⊛⊛

Distance	19.1-mile loop (33.9-mile option)
Terrain	Long, strenuous dirt-road climb, epic singletrack descent; 3,500-foot gain; views
Duration	3 to 6 hours
Travel	Eugene—60 miles; Bend—115 miles
Skill level	Advanced
Season	Summer, fall
Maps	Middle Fork Ranger District map
Restrictions	None
More info	Willamette National Forest, Middle Fork District, 541-782-2283, www.fs.fed.us/r6/willamette/

The Scoop

Long a favorite of Eugene mountain bikers, this climb around Moon Point and Youngs Rock is a classic dirt-road climb and singletrack descent. Be sure to allow for some time at Moon Point—the view is indeed vertigo inducing. The descent is incredible, arguably the best in the Eugene and Oakridge area—it's less technical than Hardesty Mountain (ride 46), Buckhead Mountain (ride 51), and Larison Creek (ride 53) and longer than Olallie Mountain (ride 43), King Castle (ride 44), Aubrey or Dead Mountain (ride 49 or 50), and Larison Rock (ride 52). A few sections are technical, even hair-ball, but no-brakes and ridable switchies are the rule. One of my friends went through four inner tubes on this loop. Hot rims? Tiny thorns? Sharp rocks? Defective tubes? A cheap pump? Operator error? Who the hell knows. We had a great ride despite it.

Driving Directions

From Eugene, drive south on Interstate 5. Take exit 188A and head east on State Highway 58. Drive about 36 miles east on Hwy 58 to Oakridge. At the stoplight at Crestview Street in Oakridge, set your odometer to zero and continue east on Hwy 58. At 1.9 miles, turn right on Kitson Springs Road (Forest Road 23) toward Hills Creek Dam. At 2.4 miles, turn right on FR 21. Stay on FR 21. At 14.6 miles, pass Sand Prairie Campground on the right. At milepost 17, pass Youngs Flat on the right—a good place to park if you're only here for the

Lots of theories, not many answers

day. At milepost 18, at 21.3 miles, turn into Secret Campground on the right and park. (Note: Don't park in a camp spot if you are not camping.)

The Ride

From the entrance to Secret Campground, turn left and ride north on FR 21. At **0.7** mile, turn right on FR 2129. (If you begin from the parking area at Youngs Flat, ride south on FR 21 for just over one-quarter mile and turn left on FR 2129.) This gravelly road immediately begins a steep ascent, winding haphazardly toward Youngs Rock and Moon Point. Stay on the main road. It's a demanding climb and, with little shade, can be quite hot. The road wraps its way beneath Youngs Rock and then Moon Point, the two most prominent features of Warner Mountain, and then circles around behind Moon Point. WOOF! At **7** miles, the road finally flattens out. The way is easier from here, though there are still 700 feet to climb. At **8.8** miles, reach a fork and turn right on FR 439 toward Warner Mountain Lookout. At **10** miles, bear right to continue up the main road. At **10.3** miles, turn right onto Moon Point Trail 3688.

The trail, narrow and overgrown in spots, ascends slightly. When the trail divides at **11.1** miles, bear right to Moon Point. The ridable section of the trail ends at **11.5** miles. Lay your bike down and walk down to Moon Point.

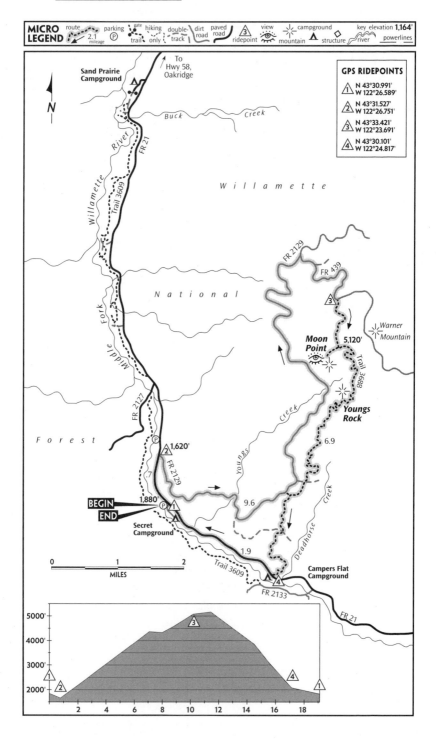

MICRO LEGEND — route 2.1 mileage, parking Ⓟ, gate · hiking trail only :, double-track, dirt road, paved road, ③ ridepoint, view 👁 mountain, campground, structure ◇, river, key elevation **1,164'**, powerlines

GPS RIDEPOINTS

△1 N 43°30.991' W 122°26.589'
△2 N 43°31.527' W 122°26.751'
△3 N 43°33.421' W 122°23.691'
△4 N 43°30.101' W 122°24.817'

Sand Prairie Campground

To Hwy 58, Oakridge

N

Buck Creek

Willamette River

FR 21

Trail 3609

Middle Fork

Willamette

National

FR 2127

FR 2129

FR 2129

FR 439

③

Warner Mountain

Moon Point 5,120'

Trail 3688

Youngs Rock

Youngs Creek

6.9

Forest

Ⓟ

△2 1,620'

.7

FR 2129

BEGIN END 1,880' Ⓟ △1

Secret Campground

9.6

Deadhorse Creek

1.9

Trail 3609

△4

FR 2133

Campers Flat Campground

FR 21

0   1   2
MILES

5000'
4000'
3000'
2000'

△3

△2 △1 △4 △1

2   4   6   8   10   12   14   16   18

Near the top of Moon Point

When you are done checking out the spectacular views from the jagged rocks, turn around and ride back to the previous fork, now **11.9** miles, and turn right. From here, the trail takes turns switchbacking and traversing down through light forests and open ridges toward Youngs Rock. This is an awesome descent. Pass around the south face of Youngs Rock on a scree slope. The fast, corkscrewing descent continues. Cross a dirt road at **15.3** miles. At **15.6** miles, reach a fork and bear left toward Campers Flat Campground. At **16.2** miles, cross a dirt road and begin a short, no-brakes roller coaster. The trail ends at FR 21 at **17.2** miles. Turn right on the paved road and ride back to Secret Campground to complete the ride, **19.1** miles.

Option

Combine this ride with ride 54, Middle Fork Willamette, for a 33.9-mile epic. It's probably best to begin this ride from Sand Prairie Campground, about halfway through ride 54. Pedal up FR 21, turn left on FR 2129, and follow the Moon Point directions to the 17.2-mile point. From there, turn left on FR 21, pedal south about one-half mile, and turn right on FR 2134. Follow the ride description for Middle Fork Willamette beginning from the 2.5-mile point.

Gazetteer

Nearby camping: Secret (primitive), Sand Prairie
Nearest food, drink, services: Oakridge

56 Waldo Lake

✿✿✿✿

Distance	21.4-mile loop
Terrain	Singletrack loop, sometimes challenging, around beautiful mountain lake; 340-foot gain; views
Duration	4 to 6 hours
Travel	Eugene—70 miles; Bend—60 miles
Skill level	Advanced
Season	Late summer, fall
Maps	Middle Fork Ranger District map
Restrictions	USFS Trail Park Pass required
More info	Willamette National Forest, Middle Fork District, 541-782-2283, www.fs.fed.us/r6/willamette/

The Scoop

Along with Newberry Caldera (ride 36), McKenzie River (rides 41 and 42), Surveyors Ridge and Surveyors Epic (rides 3 and 4), Waldo Lake is one of the classic Oregon mountain-bike trails. For the incredible scenery, the remoteness, and the challenge, it's a must-do for every serious mountain biker. The route—entirely singletrack—circles Waldo Lake, one of the largest in the central Oregon Cascades. The trail, which borders Waldo Lake Wilderness for nearly half the route, is hard-packed, zippy, and fast in spots, jagged, technical, and steep in others. By the halfway point you may think that the ride will never end, but the second half of the ride is easier than the first, as long as you follow the directions below and travel clockwise. The 340-foot elevation gain belies all the ups and downs along the way—the cumulative gain is actually more than 1,500 feet.

Driving Directions

From Eugene, drive south on Interstate 5. Take exit 188A and head east on State Highway 58 toward Oakridge. About 24 miles east of Oakridge, still on Hwy 58, turn left on Forest Road 5897 and set your odometer to zero. At 7 miles, turn left on FR 5896 toward Shadow Bay Campground. Stay on the paved road. At 8.7 miles, bear left toward the boat ramp. At 9.1 miles, turn right and park in the large gravel parking area just above the lake.

Small inlet on the north shore of Waldo Lake

From Bend, drive about 15 miles south on US Highway 97 and then turn right on FR 40. After traveling 22 miles farther, turn left onto State Highway 46. Drive about 7.5 miles south and turn right on FR 4290. This road is quite rough. Proceed slowly 9 miles west on FR 4290, then turn left on FR 5897. Go about 4 miles south on FR 5897, turn right on FR 5896 toward Shadow Bay Campground, and set your odometer to zero. Stay on the paved road. At 1.7 miles, bear left toward the boat ramp. At 2.1 miles, turn right and park in the large gravel parking area just above the lake.

The Ride

Don't take the trail that begins from the gravel parking area. Instead, ride back to the road and bear right down to the boat ramp. From the edge of Waldo Lake at the boat ramp, take Lakeshore Trail on the left. After a few hundred yards, ignore a trail on the left. Stay on the main trail. At **0.5** mile, reach a fork and go right on Waldo Lake Trail 3590. The trail wraps clockwise around the lake. Bear left to pass South Waldo Shelter, then go right at the fork at **1.7** miles. When you reach another fork at **2.3** miles, bear right again. From here, the trail becomes more technical, narrow, and steep, as it runs north along the west side of the lake.

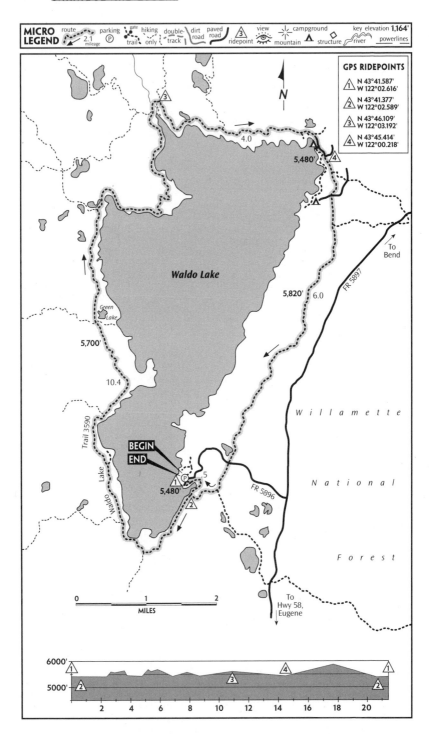

MICRO LEGEND

route · 2.1 mileage · parking ⓟ · gate · hiking trail only · double-track · dirt road · paved road · △3 ridepoint · view · mountain · campground · structure · river · key elevation 1,164' · powerlines

GPS RIDEPOINTS

△1 N 43°41.587' W 122°02.616'
△2 N 43°41.377' W 122°02.589'
△3 N 43°46.109' W 122°03.192'
△4 N 43°45.414' W 122°00.218'

N

△3

4.0

5,480'

△4

To Bend

FR 5897

Waldo Lake

5,820' 6.0

Green Lake

W i l l a m e t t e

5,700'

10.4

Trail 3590

Waldo Lake

BEGIN END

△1 ⓟ .5

5,480'

△2

FR 5896

N a t i o n a l

F o r e s t

To Hwy 58, Eugene

0   1   2
MILES

6000' △1   △4   △1
5000' △2   △3   △2

2 4 6 8 10 12 14 16 18 20

At **3.7** miles, reach a fork and bear left. (The right prong makes an interesting side trip to Klovdahl Headgate, about one-quarter mile.) At **4.2** miles, reach a fork and bear right, following the lakeshore. The trail, which is rough in spots, rises and falls in sharp spikes, then climbs away from the lake around **4.8** miles. Ride straight through a four-way at **6.1** miles, continuing on Waldo Lake Trail. From here, the trail becomes more ridable. At **7.8** miles, bear right at the fork, following the shoreline. The trail creeps along the rocks above the lake for a distance, crosses a point, then continues along the edge of the lake.

At **10.9** miles, bear right at the fork and cross North Fork of the Middle Fork of the Willamette River. Ignore a trail on the right that leads to a picnic spot next to the lake. The trail immediately divides again—go right. After a few rolls in the terrain, enter a recent catastrophic burn. The ashy gray trail is dusty but fast, and the tall, gray rampikes are quite eerie. Just after reentering the woods, reach a fork at **14.1** miles and bear left. At **14.2** miles, bear left at a second fork. When the trail divides again at **14.3** miles, go right. The trail ends at a parking area at North Waldo Campground. Pedal along the campground road, passing the boat launch on the right at **14.5** miles. Stay to the right on the paved road, ignoring several trails on the right. At **14.9** miles, just as the road veers to the left, find Waldo Lake Trail 3590 on the right and take it. After a few pedal strokes, the trail forks—go left. When the trail divides again at **15.1** miles, bear right to stay on Trail 3590.

Cross the paved road to Islet Campground at **15.6** miles. From here, climb up the hard-packed trail toward the loop's easily gained high point at **17.7** miles. The trail traverses and then descends. Cross a paved road at **20** miles. When the trail forks at **20.4** miles, bear right. At **20.9** miles, take a sharp right (unless you want to take another loop around the lake). At **21.3** miles, reach a fork and bear right. At the top of the hill, cross the road to the parking area to complete the loop, **21.4** miles.

Gazetteer

Nearby camping: Shadow Bay, Gold Lake
Nearest food, drink, services: Oakridge

57

OAKRIDGE AND EUGENE
Windy Lakes

Distance	21.2-mile loop (15.1-mile option)
Terrain	Moderate dirt-road and singletrack climbs, fast singletrack descent; 1,300-foot gain; views
Duration	3 to 5 hours
Travel	Eugene—80 miles; Bend—70 miles
Skill level	Intermediate
Season	Late summer, fall
Maps	Crescent Ranger District map
Restrictions	USFS Trail Park Pass required
More info	Deschutes National Forest, Crescent Ranger District, 541-433-2234, www.fs.fed.us/r6/deschutes/

The Scoop

The Windy Lakes loop is lousy with mosquitoes and high mountain lakes, meaning there's a lot of both. Unfortunately, there are more mosquitoes than lakes, so be prepared. A long way for most riders to travel, this is a great intermediate mountain-bike ride, and the lakes are really the highlight. After a relatively easy dirt-road climb, a well-graded singletrack climbs and descends through the high, lake-pocked expanse between Summit and Crescent Lakes. Lots of pines grow up here, but the volcanic-gray soil reflects hot and bright in midsummer and the trail is loose and sandy in sections.

Driving Directions

From Eugene, drive south on Interstate 5. Take exit 188A and head east on State Highway 58 toward Oakridge. After about 37 miles, pass through Oakridge and continue east on Hwy 58. Proceed 35 miles farther to Crescent Lake Junction and turn right on Forest Road 60. Set your odometer to zero. At 2.3 miles, turn right to remain on FR 60. At 7.4 miles, turn left on FR 290 to Tandy Bay. Park at the turnaround by the lake.

From Bend, drive south on US Highway 97 to the town of Crescent. At Crescent, turn right and take FR 61 to Hwy 58. Turn right and head north on Hwy 58. Just over 3 miles farther, reach Crescent Lake Junction and turn left onto FR 60. Zero out your odometer here. At 2.3 miles, turn right to remain on FR

Summit Lake

60. At 7.4 miles, turn left on FR 290 to Tandy Bay. Park at the turnaround by the lake.

The Ride

From the dirt turnaround at Tandy Bay, ride FR 290 back out to FR 60 and turn left. Ride this paved road to a fork at **0.4** mile and take a hard right onto FR 6010. This sand-colored dirt road immediately heads up. Pass Metolius-Windigo Trail on the right and left as you climb. Around **1.5** miles, check out the sporadic views of Diamond Peak (and adjacent Diamond Rockpile). The road, which winds through a pure stand of lodgepole pines, climbs in fits and starts, but it's never too steep. At **4.2** miles, bypass Meek Lake Trail on the left and Snell Lake Trail, into Diamond Peak Wilderness, on the right. Continue west on FR 6010.

At **5.7** miles, turn left into a trailhead parking area on the shore of Summit Lake. From here, take Summit Lake Trail toward Windy Lakes, heading south. The trail is easy and level here as it bends clockwise around the lake. After a short way, though, the trail veers southeast, away from the lake, and begins a steady climb into a mixed fir and pine forest. Beginning around the **7.9**-mile point, ride by a series of small lakes on the right and left. Descend

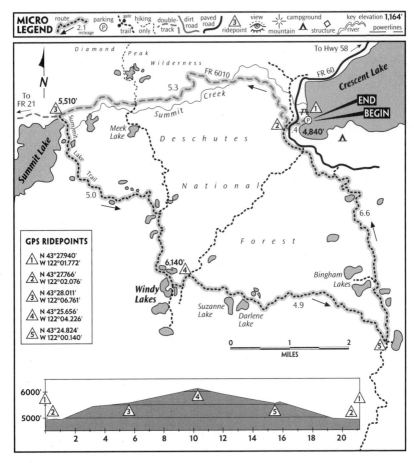

for a pitch to a fork at **9** miles—turn right, continuing toward Windy Lakes. The trail, pine-needled and firm, immediately resumes the ascent. Pass more small lakes, then at **10.2** miles, reach North Windy Lake. A few spins of the pedals farther, the trail rounds the north end of East Windy Lake. Reach a T at **10.6** miles and turn left. At **10.7** miles, reach another T and again turn left, following the sign toward Oldenberg Lake. When the trail forks at **10.9** miles, bear right and begin a fast descent.

After a ripping traverse, noodle past Suzanne Lake and then Darlene Lake before cruising down the trail—no brakes—toward Oldenberg Lake. From Darlene Lake, the trail is dusty and ashy, and the forest is a pure stand of lodgepole pines. Pass Diamond Peak Viewpoint at **13.7** miles. At **15.6** miles, reach a sandy four-way and turn left (Oldenberg Lake is straight ahead). After

North Windy Lake

a short climb descend to a fork at **16.6** miles. Stay to the right, following the sign toward the trailhead. The wide trail is sandy in sections, so the descent is fast in places, slower and surflike in others. Ride in control because the trail is heavily used by equestrians.

Pass a lake on the left at **18.5** miles. At **19.4** miles, reach an unmarked fork and bear left on Metolius-Windigo Horse Trail. At **20.1** miles, pass a trail on the right and then one on the left—continue on Metolius-Windigo Horse Trail. At **20.7** miles, reach FR 6010 and turn right. At **20.8** miles, FR 6010 ends at FR 60—turn left on this paved road. At **21.1** miles, turn right on FR 230 to Tandy Bay. Reach the picnic area at the lake at **21.2** miles to complete the loop.

Option

Feeling ready to bonk? Here's how to shave a little more than 6 miles from this loop: At the fork at 10.9 miles, bear left (rather than right). The descent is a riot. When you reach the Metolius-Windigo Horse Trail, turn left and follow the directions above from the 20.1-mile point.

Gazetteer

Nearby camping: Crescent Lake, Spring
Nearest food, drink, services: Crescent Lake Junction, La Pine

58 Row River

Distance	11-mile out-and-back (25.8-mile option)
Terrain	Wide, paved rail-trail, easy and level; **170-foot gain**
Duration	1 to 2 hours
Travel	Eugene—21 miles; Portland—130 miles
Skill level	Beginner
Season	Year-round
Maps	BLM Row River Trail map
Restrictions	None
More info	US Bureau of Land Management, Eugene District, 541-683-6600, www.edo.or.blm.gov/rec/row_trail/

The Scoop

In 1994 the US Bureau of Land Management acquired this abandoned railroad grade set along Row River. Since then the BLM has paved nearly thirteen miles of the old grade for recreational use. The trail now has a number of

Dorena Lake

trailheads and picnic areas, many on Dorena Lake, a reservoir along Row River. The trail is wide, flat, and paved, perfect for families.

Driving Directions

From Eugene, drive about 18 miles south on Interstate 5. Take exit 174 toward Dorena Lake. At the end of the interstate ramp, set your odometer to zero and turn left on Row River Road. At 0.9 mile, turn right on Currin Conn, then quickly turn left on Mosby Creek Road. At 3.1 miles, turn left on Layng Road. Immediately turn left again into the paved parking area at Row River Trail's Mosby Creek trailhead.

The Ride

Row River Trail heads northeast from the trailhead. The trail immediately crosses Mosby Creek. At **0.7** mile, follow the trail across Layng Road. At **1.5** miles, the trail passes over Row River and then crosses Row River Road. Cross the road again at **3** miles, climbing slightly. At **3.6** miles, Dorena Lake is visible on the right. Pass Dorena Dam picnic area here. At **4.2** miles, ride by Row

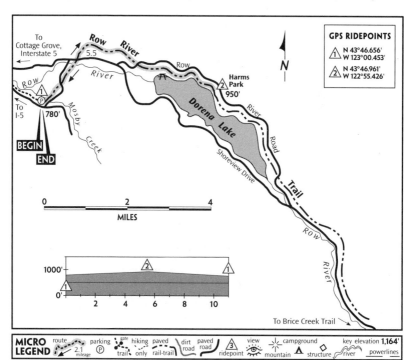

Point, one of the trail's seven access spots. At **5.5** miles, reach Harms Park. This Lane County park has picnic tables that overlook the lake. There are toilets here but no water, so plan your picnic accordingly. Turn around here and glide back to Mosby Creek trailhead, **11** miles.

Option

Row River Trail continues 7.4 miles farther east from Harms Park. If you start at Mosby Creek trailhead, ride to the trail's end, and return, the total trip clocks in at 25.8 miles.

Gazetteer

Nearby camping: Rujada, Cedar Creek (primitive)
Nearest food, drink, services: Cottage Grove

59 | OAKRIDGE AND EUGENE
Brice Creek
✿✿✿

Distance	10.4-mile loop
Terrain	Easy paved-road climb, somewhat technical singletrack descent; 450-foot gain
Duration	1 to 3 hours
Travel	Eugene—41 miles; Portland—150 miles
Skill level	Advanced
Season	Late spring, summer, fall
Maps	USGS 7.5 minute: Rose Hill
Restrictions	None
More info	Umpqua National Forest, Cottage Grove District, 541-942-5591, www.fs.fed.us/r6/umpqua/

The Scoop

Here's the ride for those who just don't like those long, grinding climbs so much. The creekside trail is technical in spots and climbs in short spurts, but

Swimming holes along Brice Creek

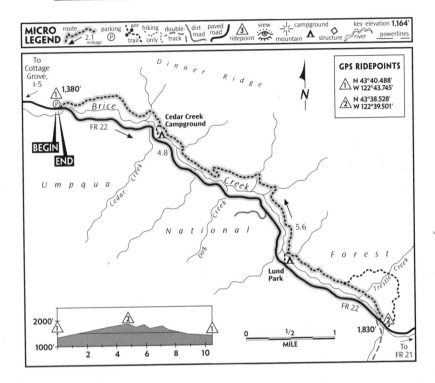

there's no multithousand-foot ascent (or subsequent attempt to cough up a lung). An easy paved-road climb leads to the upper end of the singletrack. Some riders may prefer to ride out and back on the trail rather than ride out the paved road to create a loop. Your choice. Either way, the creek, with its pools and flows and mesmerizing canyon geology, makes this a short but beautiful trip.

Driving Directions

From Eugene, drive about 18 miles south on Interstate 5. Take exit 174 toward Dorena Lake. At the end of the interstate ramp, set your odometer to zero and turn left on Row River Road. At 4.3 miles, continue straight on Shoreview Drive (Row River Road turns to the left). But at 11.3 miles, stay to the right as Shoreview merges with and becomes Row River Road. Proceed east on Row River Road. At 19.4 miles, bear right onto Brice Creek Road, which becomes Forest Road 22. At 22.8 miles, park on the left at the narrow gravel strip at Brice Creek Trail's West Trailhead.

The Ride

From West Trailhead, pedal up FR 22. The paved road ascends at an easy rate as it follows the creek. Pass Cedar Creek Campground on the left at **1.2** miles. When the road forks at **2.8** miles, bear left and continue alongside Brice Creek. The deep valley and forest of cedar, fir, and maple shade the narrow road. Pass Lund Park on the left at **3.6** miles. Reach a fork at **4.8** miles—bear left and cross a bridge over Brice Creek. Immediately across the bridge, turn left on Brice Creek Trail 1403. The singletrack traverses the bank above the creek, rising and falling with the steep folds of the hillside. At **5.5** miles, reach a fork and stay to the left. Climb and then descend to a fork at **6.2** miles—bear right, riding toward West Trailhead. (To the left you'll find a bridge across the river to Lund Park.)

The tread is rocky in spots, root-strewn in others. Salal and Oregon grape, various ferns, and mosses combine to form a rich understory. At **6.3** miles, ignore a trail to a camp spot on the left. From here, the trail, ragged, technical, and exposed in sections, stays close to the creek, which flows from pool to pool down the narrow, rocky canyon. It's a picturesque setting (and the swimming's good too). At **8.9** miles, reach a fork and bear right. At **10.4** miles, reach the West Trailhead to complete the loop.

Gazetteer

Nearby camping: Rujada, Cedar Creek (primitive)
Nearest food, drink, services: Cottage Grove

Portland and Salem

Trapped within the concrete gridwork of Portland? Unless you plan to put in some miles on the Leif Erikson Trail at Forest Park (ride 65), cartwheel down some of the fire lanes there, or spin out Springwater Corridor to play on the trails at Powell Butte (ride 66), you'll need to throw your bike on the rack and start driving. The good news is that you don't have to burn through too much gas to reach a bunch of trailheads, and the variety of the trails you discover might surprise you, from root-strewn routes in the lowlands to rocky zip-fests in Mount Hood's fir forests.

Head west to Tillamook State Forest to find lots of zippy, lunging trails near the summit of the coast range. While you're sampling the singletrack at Tillamook Burn (ride 61) and Gales Creek (ride 60), keep an eye open for new trails that the good folks who manage the state forest have been working on. Think your quads are too big for the Tillamook? Try Standard Grade (ride 62), which offers up one of the most brutal climbs anywhere.

Want to bring the family? There are a number of mellower rides that are also close in. Check out Banks-Vernonia Trail (ride 64) or go carve some fun turns out at Hagg Lake (ride 63).

Heading eastward, you quickly ascend into the evergreen mountains near Mount Hood. Here you'll find numerous options, from short, easier routes like the Crosstown Trail (ride 68) and Timothy Lake (ride 71) to expert and sometimes insane riding at Ski Bowl (ride 70) and Flag Mountain (ride 67).

But if you steer east on State Highway 224, you'll head toward some of the most alluring trails in this section of *Kissing the Trail*. Nothing will cure the blues like a good romp down Dry Ridge's 4,000-foot descent (ride 72). And tackling the rock jungle gym on the scenic trail to Red Lake (ride 74) is frustrating on some days, exhilarating on the others.

The Portland United Mountain Pedalers (PUMP) and Salem's Merry Cranksters manage to get a fair amount of trail work accomplished between rides. PUMP is one of the primary reasons that the trail around Hagg Lake was reopened. The Cranksters, meanwhile, keep adding to that maze of trails near Molalla River (see rides 75 and 76), and more are coming. If you do much riding in the northwestern corner of Oregon, or even in Southwest Washington, sign up with one of these clubs.

60

PORTLAND AND SALEM
Gales Creek
☻☻☻

Distance	8.4-mile lollipop
Terrain	Tough singletrack and dirt-road climb, singletrack descent; 1,010-foot gain
Duration	1 to 3 hours
Travel	Portland—39 miles
Skill level	Advanced
Season	Spring, summer, fall
Maps	Tillamook State Forest Recreation Resources
Restrictions	None
More info	Tillamook State Forest, Forest Grove District, 503-357-2191, www.odf.state.or.us/

The Scoop

The first two miles—a singletrack climb, steep in short sections and littered with roots—might require a push here or there. The rest of the ride is a cobble of

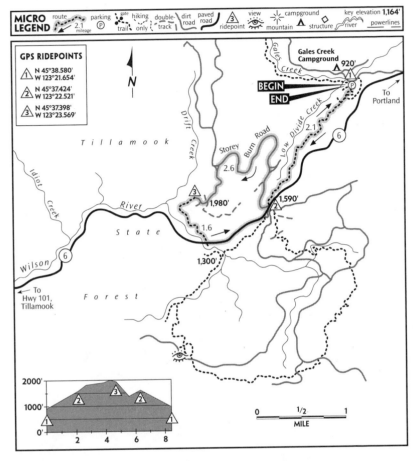

dirt roads and new singletrack. There are lots of great trails in this area, and the land managers are busy creating more miles that will be open to mountain bikes. Check out the continuation of Gales Creek Trail, a freshie completed in spring 2000 that heads north from Gales Creek Campground all the way to Belcamp Road. You might want to combine this ride with Tillamook Burn (ride 61). Note: Gales Creek Campground is closed and the road gated between November and mid-May. If you ride this trail when the campground is closed, park at the entrance along State Highway 6—don't block the gate—and ride down to the second day-use parking area to begin. This will add about one and a half miles to the lollipop.

Driving Directions

From Portland, drive about 20 miles west on US Highway 26 to its junction with State Highway 6. Take Hwy 6 westbound. Pass milepost 36 and set your odometer to zero. At 0.9 mile, turn right on a gravel road toward Gales Creek Campground. At 1.6 miles, park in the second day-use area on the left. (The campground is closed during the winter and spring; see note above.)

The Ride

There are numerous trails out of Gales Creek Campground, so be sure to begin from the second day-use parking area on the left. Three trails exit from this parking area—take the one farthest to the left. At **0.1** mile, bypass two trails on the left. Ignore another trail on the left at **0.2** mile. At **0.6** mile, reach another unmarked fork, but this time stay to the left. From here the trail, technical and root-strewn in places, climbs up the lush valley along Low Divide Creek. It's a tough climb, and some sections may have to be walked. At **2.1** miles, Gales Creek Trail ends at the east end of a large gravel pullout along Hwy 6. At the west end of the gravel pullout, a dirt road heads up to the right. This is Storey Burn Road—take it.

The first bend in the road is steep, but the grade eases after a short distance. At **2.7** miles, ignore a dirt road on the left. At **2.8** miles, pass by two dirt roads on the right. From here, the road traverses, gaining little elevation. At **3.9** miles, reach a fork and bear left on the lesser road. Pass by a gravel parking area on the right and continue up and around the hillside. At a three-prong fork, **4.4** miles, take the center road. The road ends at a turnaround at **4.7** miles. WHOA! A singletrack really does begin just beyond the end of the road, though you may have to scramble down to it.

The singletrack descends at a fast rate as it wraps around the hillside to the left. At **5.5** miles, the trail peters out under a highway trestle, the Graham Bridge. Bear left and scramble up the ragged trail to Hwy 6. Carefully cross the highway, turn left, and ride east, climbing toward the summit. At **6.3** miles, reach the summit. Cross the highway to the large gravel pullout on the left. Gales Creek Trail begins on the east end of the pullout. Take the trail and descend back to Gales Creek Campground, **8.4** miles.

Gazetteer

Nearby camping: Gales Creek
Nearest food, drink, services: Forest Grove, Portland

61 Tillamook Burn

✦✦✦

Distance	7.9-mile loop (12.3-mile option)
Terrain	Winding singletrack, lots of ups and downs, a few steep; 600-foot gain
Duration	1 to 3 hours
Travel	Portland—45 miles
Skill level	Intermediate
Season	Spring, summer, fall
Maps	Tillamook State Forest Recreation Resources
Restrictions	None
More info	Tillamook State Forest, Forest Grove District, 503-357-2191, www.odf.state.or.us/

The Scoop

This singletrack loop, known both as the Historic Hiking Trail and Nels Rogers/Gravelle Brothers Trail, straddles the crest of the Coast Range in Tillamook State Forest near the summit of State Highway 6. Though the trail crosses a multitude of dirt roads and random trails, the route is well signed by name and also with brown carbonate bike signs. The ride's elevation gain checks in at the easy end of moderate—just 600 feet—but the trail climbs and drops incessantly and is almost never level. Of course that's why mountain bikers like to ride here—it's fun. For a longer ride, combine this with Gales Creek (ride 60).

Driving Directions

From Portland, drive about 20 miles west on US Highway 26 to its junction with Hwy 6. Take Hwy 6 westbound. Pass milepost 36 and set your odometer to zero. At 0.9 mile, pass by the gravel road to Gales Creek Campground on the right. At 3.7 miles, reach the summit and turn left on Beaver Dam Road toward Rogers Camp trailhead. At 3.8 miles, turn left at the T. At 3.9 miles, reach Rogers Camp trailhead and park in the dirt lot.

The Ride

From Rogers Camp trailhead, take the steep, narrow dirt road that heads up to the south, away from Hwy 6. At **0.1** mile, turn right onto a singletrack. The

tough climb continues: steep with just enough roots to keep you focused. The trail levels, passes straight through a four-way, then climbs again. Reach a high point at **0.5** mile. From here, the trail twists and corkscrews—more roots—down to a dirt-road crossing at **1** mile. Splash across a creek at **1.2** miles and bear left. At **1.6** miles, pass straight through another four-way. Beyond this point, the trail crosses numerous roads, both dirt and gravel. Follow the brown carbonate signs that point the way.

Climb to another high point at **3.1** miles, then descend the fast, hard-packed trail. It's a fun romp. Reach a gravel road at **3.4** miles and turn right. After about fifty yards, turn left to regain the trail and continue the fast descent. After another short climb, through fir trees with a salal and Oregon grape understory, cross a gravel road. The trail, rocky and root-strewn here, drops and weaves, then crosses another road. WHOA! Reach a four-way at **5.4** miles and take a hard right turn. (The trail on the left leads to University Falls.) The trail drops and climbs and drops again, then cruises down to a bridge—marked Piranha Crossing—over Elliott Creek at **6.1** miles. Bear right and cross the bridge.

The route follows an old roadbed, descending to a low point at **6.9** miles. Turn right and ride across a series of bridges. From here, the wide trail climbs away from the creek at a hectic rate. WOOF! As you reach Hwy 6 at **7.6** miles, bear right and ride around the Oregon Department of Transportation gravel shed. At **7.7** miles, turn right on Beaver Dam Road toward Rogers Camp trailhead. Turn left at the T, and return to the trailhead at **7.9** miles.

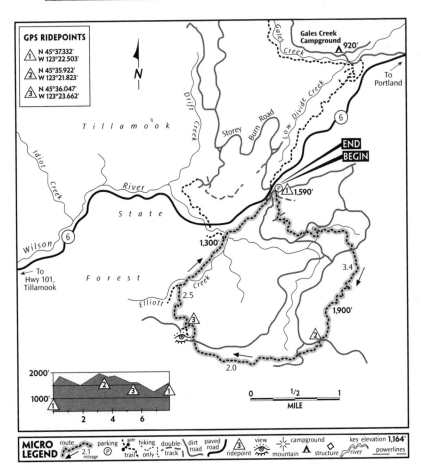

Option

Not quite long enough for you? Start the ride at Gales Creek Campground and follow the directions for Gales Creek (ride 60). At the 2.1-mile point, cross Hwy 6 and ride up to Rogers Camp trailhead, 2.3 miles, then follow this loop. At Beaver Dam Road, just before the end of the loop, cross Hwy 6 instead of riding up to Rogers Camp trailhead. From the large gravel pullout on the north side of the highway, take Gales Creek Trail back to the campground. This creates a 12.3-mile lollipop.

Gazetteer

Nearby camping: Gales Creek
Nearest food, drink, services: Forest Grove, Portland

PORTLAND AND SALEM

62 Standard Grade

✽✽✽✽

Distance	23.8-mile loop
Terrain	Absurdly steep, rocky road climb, lots of pushing, dirt- and paved-road descents; 2,320-foot gain
Duration	4 to 6 hours
Travel	Portland—45 miles
Skill level	Advanced
Season	Spring, summer, fall
Maps	Tillamook State Forest Recreation Resources
Restrictions	None
More info	Tillamook State Forest, Forest Grove District, 503-357-2191, www.odf.state.or.us/

The Scoop

Want a challenge and a great workout? You've got it. Standard Grade and Badger Lake (ride 14) are the only difficult rides in this book that don't head

Views to the west from Standard Grade Road

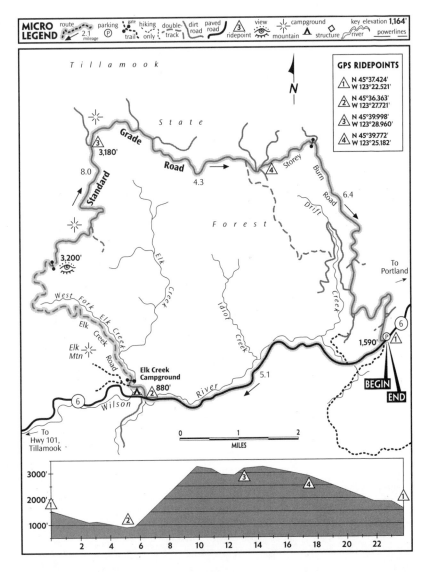

MICRO LEGEND: route 2.1 mileage · parking Ⓟ · gate · hiking trail only · double-track · dirt road · paved road · 3 ridepoint · view mountain · campground · structure · river · key elevation **1,164'** · powerlines

GPS RIDEPOINTS

1 N 45°37.424' W 123°22.521'

2 N 45°36.363' W 123°27.721'

3 N 45°39.998' W 123°28.960'

4 N 45°39.772' W 123°25.182'

Tillamook State Forest

N

Grade Road

Standard

3 3,180'

8.0

4.3

4 Storey

Burn Road

Drift

6.4

3,200'

West Fork Elk Creek

Elk Creek

Elk Creek Road

Elk Mtn

Elk Creek Campground

2 880'

Idiot Creek

Creek

5.1

River

6 Wilson

To Hwy 101, Tillamook

To Portland

1,590' Ⓟ 6 1

BEGIN

END

0   1   2
MILES

3000'
2000'
1000'

2   4   6   8   10   12   14   16   18   20   22

out onto singletrack. However, the dirt-road climb up to Standard Grade will hurt you, I promise. It's easily the toughest four-mile segment in this book. This big, fat loop tracks both dirt and paved roads and affords a few long views of Mount Hood, but Standard Grade isn't as much about views or lack of dirt trails as it is about plumbing the depths of your brain's wildest hallucinations and testing your legs' quiver point.

Driving Directions

From Portland, drive about 20 miles west on US Highway 26 to its junction with State Highway 6. Take Hwy 6 westbound. Pass milepost 36 and set your odometer to zero. At 0.9 mile, pass by the gravel road to Gales Creek Campground on the right. At 3.7 miles, reach the summit and park in the wide gravel pullout on the right.

The Ride

From the wide gravel pullout, ride west on Hwy 6. The ride begins at the summit of the Coast Range, so the highway descends at a fast rate as it follows the course of the Wilson River. During all but the warmest months, start out with a windbreaker because the fast paved-road descent, combined with the deep, shaded valley, can leave you chilled. Stay on the highway. At **5.1** miles, turn right on Elk Creek Road. At **5.5** miles, pass a parking area on the left, then cross over Elk Creek. Continue up the road, ignoring a trail on the left and then riding around a rusted cable that blocks the road to motorized use.

From here, the road heads straight up, following West Fork of Elk Creek as it rounds the east side of Elk Mountain. Climbing 550 feet per mile, the road is absurdly steep. However, loose drainage berms and a minefield of death-cookies pose the real challenge, so plan on a four-mile hike-a-bike. This climb will make you feel like a test rat, prove the inadequacy of Cliff Shots, and evoke curses aimed at this book, as well as the inventors of the mountain bike. It's tough. Needless to say, that windbreaker is history.

WOOF! With hallucinations crescendoing, ignore a faint road on the right and then pass around an old gate at **9.7** miles. At **9.9** miles, there's a wide turnout that affords long views of Mount Hood, Mount Jefferson, and Mount Adams. This is the ride's high point. From here, the road—Standard Grade Road—bends left and traverses along the top of the ridge, rolling easily. Ignore a private road on the right at **11.9** miles. When the road divides at **13.1** miles, bear right and ride east on Standard Grade Road. At **14.3** miles, pass Kenny Creek Road on the left. At **14.5** miles, reach a fork and bear right, staying on the main road.

At **16.6** miles, the road forks—go left, then bypass a lesser road on the right a short distance farther. At **17.4** miles, pass a road on the left, followed by one on the right. Immediately reach a fork and stay right onto Storey Burn Road. The road descends around the top of a clearcut, then climbs to a yellow gate. Ignore the road back to the left at the gate. From here, Storey Burn Road descends at a fast rate, and it's fun. Watch out for vehicles on the road. Stay on the main road as you drop, passing numerous lesser roads on the right and left. At **21.4** miles, after ignoring a lesser road on the left, reach a fork and bear left. At **21.9** miles, pass by two lesser roads on the right. When the road divides at **23** miles, bear right. Ignore a road on the right at **23.2** miles. Reach the gravel pullout along Hwy 6 to complete the loop, **23.8** miles.

Gazetteer

Nearby camping: Gales Creek
Nearest food, drink, services: Forest Grove, Portland

63

PORTLAND AND SALEM
Hagg Lake
⊕⊕⊕

Distance	14.1-mile loop
Terrain	Short ups and downs on singletrack around the lake; 100-foot gain
Duration	2 to 3 hours
Travel	Portland—36 miles
Skill level	Intermediate
Season	Spring, summer, fall
Maps	Henry Hagg Lake information brochure
Restrictions	Entrance fee required; Closed November through April
More info	Washington County Parks, 503-359-5732, www.co.washington.or.us/ deptmts/sup_serv/fac_mgt/parks/haggmap.htm

The Scoop

Hagg Lake makes a great mountain-bike access story. The trail was closed to bikes for a number of years, but thanks to trail and advocacy work by the Portland United Mountain Pedalers (PUMP) and a small group of local Hagg Lake cyclists, the trail is now open for mountain-bike business. Don't ride this loop in wet weather, or it may be closed again. The trail undulates its way around the lake, climbing and dropping, winding and zipping in equal parts. There are numerous secondary spur trails along the way, making it fairly easy to get off the main route. Still, you can't really get lost. One rider even told me that he takes a slightly different route around the lake every time out. Superpopular with the fishing and boating crowd, Hagg Lake can be packed on summer weekends, so plan accordingly.

Driving Directions

From Portland, take US Highway 26 westbound for about 20 miles. Bear left on State Highway 6 and proceed about 2.5 miles. Turn left on State Hwy 47, now heading south toward Forest Grove. Drive about 7 more miles, then stay on Hwy 47 as it zigzags south through Forest Grove. Just over 2 miles south of Forest Grove, turn right on Southwest Scoggins Valley Road toward Hagg Lake, and set your odometer to zero. Pass through the toll booth. At 3.5 miles, turn

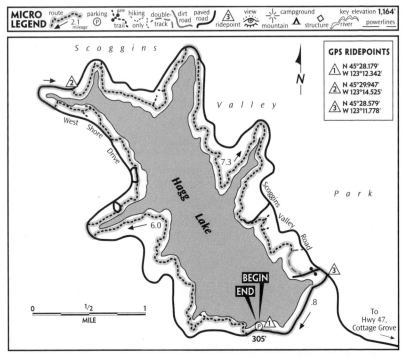

left on Southwest West Shore Drive. Cross over the top of the earthen dam; then, at 4.3 miles, park at the large gravel parking area on the right.

The Ride

From the parking area, take the paved road away from the dam. About a hundred yards beyond the parking area, turn right onto the singletrack. Stay on the main trail as it zips and rolls counterclockwise around the lake. At **0.4** mile, pass straight through a four-way. At **0.7** mile, reach a fork and go left. At **0.9** mile, stay to the left again at the fork. Ride straight through a four-way at **1.1** miles. After a mile of sharp climbs and descents, pass through a confusing section of trail at **2.1** miles—stay on the main trail, keeping the picnic tables on the right. At **3.3** miles, the trail ends at a T with the paved circumference road—turn right. At **3.4** miles, the trail begins again on the right.

Stay to the right as you ride through a small picnic area at **3.7** miles. Pedal across a large paved parking area at **4** miles. At the far end of the paved lot, the dirt trail starts up again. At **4.6** miles, reach a T and turn left, climbing. The trail almost immediately divides—turn right. Just before reaching the paved circumference road, **4.9** miles, turn right. At **5.2** miles, the trail kisses

Getting ready for trail work at Hagg Lake

the paved road on the left. Reach a T with the road at **5.4** miles and turn right. The paved road descends and then climbs. At **6** miles, find a gravel pullout on the right. The trail begins again at the edge of this pullout. At **6.4** miles, turn right just before reaching the paved road. After about fifty yards, reach a T and again turn right.

At **7.2** miles, bear right at the fork and then ignore a trail back on the left. When you reach a T at the circumference road again, **8** miles, turn right. At **8.2** miles, bear right to retake the singletrack. Over the next mile and a half, stay to the right at each of four intersections. At **10.6** miles, pop out at a parking area along the paved road—bear right, then immediately go right again to continue on the singletrack. At **11** miles, reach a fork and go left, climbing. At **11.9** miles, the trail ends at a paved boat ramp. From here, curve around to the left, then turn right onto the singletrack. Reach a T at **12.1** miles and turn right. Turn right at a second T a short distance farther. At **12.5** miles, ride straight through a four-way. When you arrive at a wide gravel path at **12.9** miles, go right and descend. The trail ends for good at a paved spur road at **13.1** miles. Turn left and climb past the gate. At **13.3** miles, reach the main road around the lake and descend. Take the next right. Follow the road as it crosses the dam at the southeast end of Hagg Lake. At **14.1** miles, reach the large gravel parking area on the right to complete the ride.

Gazetteer

Nearby camping: Gales Creek, Champoeg State Park
Nearest food, drink, services: Forest Grove

64 Banks-Vernonia Trail

Distance	28-mile out-and-back (shorter options)
Terrain	Gravel and paved rail-trail, a few gradual hills; 580-foot gain
Duration	2 to 6 hours
Travel	Portland—27 miles
Skill level	Beginner
Season	Year-round
Maps	Oregon State Parks: Banks-Vernonia Trail Guide
Restrictions	None
More info	Oregon State Parks, 800-551-6949, www.prd.state.or.us

The Scoop

Managed by Oregon State Parks, the Banks-Vernonia State Trail is the proto-typical rail-trail: wide, easy grades, and long sweeping turns. The trail begins in the town of Banks, south of US Highway 26, and meanders all the way

north to Vernonia, covering twenty miles one-way. But since the first seven miles from Banks are more difficult to follow, the description below begins the ride just north of the hamlet of Buxton at the Buxton trailhead. This ride is intended for families, so disregard the twenty-eight-mile length and turn around when intuition says you should.

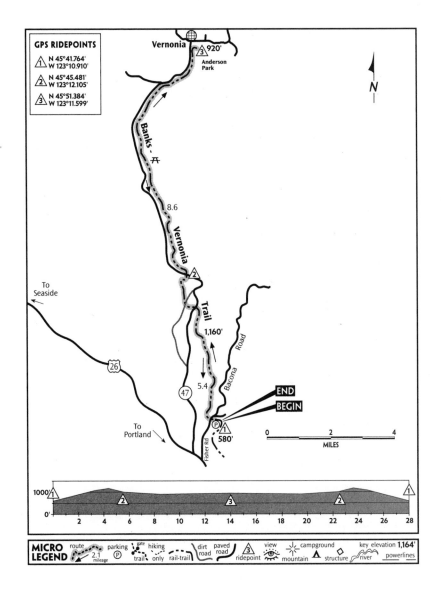

Driving Directions

From Portland, drive about 26 miles west on US 26. Just past Manning, turn right on Fisher Road toward Buxton, and set your odometer to zero. As you pass through Buxton, bear right on Bacona Road. At 1.4 miles, turn right to the trailhead for Banks-Vernonia Linear Trail. At 1.5 miles, park in the Buxton trailhead parking area on the right.

The Ride

Facing the paved trail, which is at the back of the parking area, turn right and pedal northwest. Almost immediately the trail becomes gravel and then crosses Bacona Road. From here, the trail heads north, gradually ascending through slow, arching railroad turns. Most of the trail is hard-packed gravel and easily ridable; however, in some sections the gravel is quite loose and results in slow, awkward riding. At **3.2** miles, cross a gravel road. After an easy climb, reach the ride's high point at **3.5** miles. From the crest, the trail descends at a fast rate, dropping to State Highway 47 at **4.4** miles. After carefully crossing the highway, take the trail up a steep, open hillside. This section may require a short walk. As you bear left at **4.6** miles, the trail is level and ridable again.

At **6.9** miles, the trail becomes paved and the riding easy. Pass by Beaver Creek trailhead, a nice picnic spot, at **8.1** miles. Cross a road at **8.4** miles. From here, the trail closely follows Hwy 47 along Beaver Creek. It's a nice, gradual descent into Vernonia. At **14** miles, reach the north end of the trail at Anderson Park, along the Nehalem River in Vernonia (also a nice picnic spot). Turn around here and ride back to Buxton trailhead, **28** miles.

Option

Twenty-eight miles sounds pretty intimidating, especially for beginning cyclists. You can always turn around and pedal back to Buxton trailhead. Decide the amount of time you want to be out riding and then turn around after you've been out about 40 percent of the total time (the second half of a ride often takes longer).

Gazetteer

Nearby camping: Gales Creek, Champoeg State Park
Nearest food, drink, services: Vernonia, Forest Grove

65

Forest Park

Distance	22-mile out-and-back
Terrain	Wide dirt and gravel trail; 410-foot gain
Duration	2 to 4 hours
Travel	Portland—2 miles
Skill level	Beginner
Season	Year-round
Maps	Portland Parks and Recreation: Forest Park
Restrictions	None
More info	Portland Parks and Recreation, 503-823-2223, www.ci.portland.or.us/parks/Parks/ForestPark.htm

The Scoop

Forest Park is the largest city-bound wilderness park in the United States. Trails, fire lanes, and old roads crisscross the vast area that's bordered by the Willamette River to the northeast and Skyline Boulevard at the top of the

Spinning out the miles on Leif Erikson Drive

ridge to the southwest. Bikes are prohibited from the trails in the park, but the fire lanes and dirt roads are open and make for good riding. The ride along Leif Erikson Drive, a gated dirt road, is the one moderately graded mountain-bike route in the park. It's great for beginners and families, but given the lack of mountain-bike opportunities close to Portland, many inter-mediate and advanced riders get their workouts on the Leif. The park's loose,

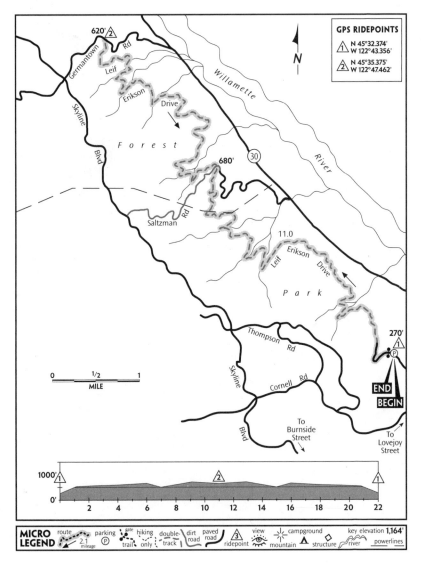

rocky fire lanes also attract many riders, and the stories of cartwheeling endos are legend.

Driving Directions

From Northwest 25th Avenue and Northwest Thurman Street in Portland, set your odometer to zero and proceed northeast on Thurman. At 1.2 miles, Thurman ends at a green gate. Park here.

The Ride

From Thurman Gate, Leif Erikson Drive heads into the thick deciduous forest, known to most Portlanders as Forest Park. Leif Erikson, an old road turned trail, winds in and out of the folds of the steep, northeast slopes of the Tualatin Mountains. The grades are easy despite the steepness of the hillside, and the hard-packed gravel tread provides good purchase and makes for easy pedaling. Numerous trails (closed to bikes) and fire lanes (open to bikes) take off from the main road. At **6** miles, when Leif Erikson crosses Saltzman Road, ride straight through the four-way intersection. Leif Erickson narrows here, and the way is more intimate. At **11** miles, reach a trailhead along Germantown Road. Turn around here and pedal back to the Thurman Gate, **22** miles.

Gazetteer

Nearby camping: Gales Creek, Champoeg State Park
Nearest food, drink, services: Portland

66 Powell Butte

✿✿✿

Distance	5.3-mile loop
Terrain	Singletrack climbs and descents, paved start and finish; 400-foot gain
Duration	1 to 2 hours
Travel	Portland—10 miles
Skill level	Intermediate
Season	Year-round
Maps	Portland Parks and Recreation: Powell Butte
Restrictions	None
More info	Portland Parks and Recreation, 503-823-2223, www.ci.portland.or.us/parks/Parks/ForestPark.htm

The Scoop

Powell Butte rises up out of the east Portland flats, between the Columbia and Willamette Rivers, to the whopping height of 612 feet. How bad can the

Slaloming down from the top of Powell Butte

hill climbs be? Numerous hiking, equestrian, and bicycling trails spread out across the 570 acres, and though there's a limited amount of sweet single-track, it's a worthwhile place to crack a sweat and feel the flow of a dirt trail. Many Portlanders use the Springwater Corridor, a paved rail-trail, to access the butte. From Springwater's Johnson Creek Boulevard trailhead at Southeast Johnson Creek Boulevard and Southeast 45th Avenue, it's an easy six-mile spin out to Powell Butte.

Driving Directions

From Portland, head east on Southeast Powell Boulevard (US Highway 26). About 2 miles after passing under Interstate 205, turn right on Southeast 136th Avenue and set your odometer to zero. At 1.2 miles, pull over and park on the right, adjacent to Springwater Corridor, a paved trail.

The Ride

From the parking spot, ride east on Springwater Corridor. After a short paved warm-up, **0.5** mile, turn left on a singletrack toward Powell Butte Nature

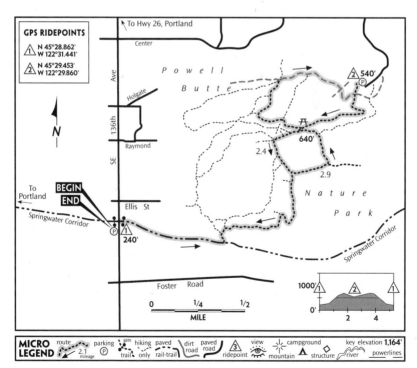

Park. At **0.6** mile, reach a fork and turn right on Pioneer Orchard Trail. Almost immediately, ignore a trail on the left. The Pioneer Orchard Trail climbs through a forest of fir, alder, and bigleaf maple. Ignore another trail on the left at **1** mile. Continue climbing.

At **1.2** miles, the grade eases and the trail pops out of the forest. When the trail divides at **1.4** miles, bear right on Orchard Loop Trail. At **1.5** miles, bear to the left and ride across a flat area near the top of the butte; the trail here is nondescript. At **1.6** miles, bear left again and pedal along the spine of the butte. Check out the views of Mount St. Helens, Mount Adams, and Mount Hood. At **1.9** miles, take a hard right turn onto a paved trail. WHOA! Almost immediately, take a hard left onto a narrow singletrack and descend.

At **2.1** miles, bear to the right, merging with Goldfinch Trail, and then bear left onto the lesser track. Reach a T and turn right. The way forks again almost immediately: Turn right. At **2.4** miles, reach a five-way and turn right, riding down a wide, gravelly trail. Ride straight through a four-way. At **2.9** miles, bear left and ride down to a trailhead. From the trailhead, pedal up the paved Mountain View Trail that switchbacks toward the top of the butte again. When the pavement ends at the top, **3.6** miles, bear right onto Orchard Loop Trail again. At **3.7** miles, reach a four-way and turn left. Ignore two trails on the right as you descend. At **3.9** miles, reach a fork and bear right, heading back into the forest on Pioneer Orchard Trail. Follow your tracks back to Springwater Corridor and turn right. Reach Southeast 136th Avenue at **5.3** miles to complete the loop.

Gazetteer

Nearby camping: Ainsworth State Park
Nearest food, drink, services: Portland

Flag Mountain

⊕⊕⊕⊕

Distance	6.7-mile loop
Terrain	Steep singletrack climbs and descents, lots of pushing; 820-foot gain
Duration	1 to 3 hours
Travel	Portland—47 miles; Bend—107 miles
Skill level	Expert
Season	Summer, fall
Maps	Green Trails: Government Camp
Restrictions	None
More info	Mount Hood National Forest, Zigzag District, 503-622-7674, www.fs.fed.us/r6/mthood/

The Scoop

Expert riders might enjoy this as the second ride of the day, or hit it during a late afternoon drive to somewhere else. The Flag Mountain loop is just too short and too steep to be a real destination trail. But the climb—Woof!— and the descent—Yikes!—are certainly a challenge. The route begins from

Mount Hood from Flag Mountain

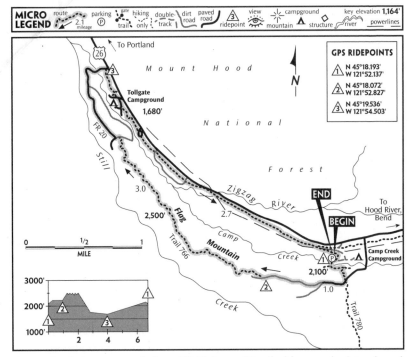

route ··· parking ⓟ gate hiking double- dirt paved ③ view ·ᵢ· campground key elevation **1,164'**
2.1 mileage trail only track road road ridepoint mountain ▲ structure ◇ river powerlines

To Portland

Mount Hood

GPS RIDEPOINTS

△1 N 45°18.193'
W 121°52.137'

△2 N 45°18.072'
W 121°52.827'

△3 N 45°19.536'
W 121°54.503'

Tollgate
Campground
1,680'

National

FR 20

Still

Forest

3.0

Zigzag River

END

2,500'

Flag

2.7

Camp

Mountain

Trail 766

Creek

BEGIN

To
Hood River,
Bend

Camp Creek
Campground

0   1/2   1
MILE

2,100'

1.0

2

Creek

Trail 780

3000'
2000'
1000'
2   4   6

Camp Creek Campground along US Highway 26, climbing on singletrack and roads to Flag Mountain Trail. Once on the unmarked trail, you'll do a lot of walking unless you weigh 100 pounds and it's all in your quads. The narrow tread—through salal and Oregon grape—and the intimate forest take some of the pain out of the grunt. From the top of the narrow, fin-shaped mountain, the trail, which is nearly vertical, offers up face-plant options on every switchback.

Driving Directions

From Portland, drive east on US 26. After about 43 miles, pass through the town of Zigzag. Just past milepost 47, turn right on Forest Road 150 toward Camp Creek Campground. At the campground kiosk, turn right. A quarter mile from the highway, reach a small day-use parking area on the right, signed Still Creek Trail No. 780.

The Ride

From the day-use parking area, cross the bridge over Camp Creek on Still Creek Trail 780. The trail forks on the opposite side of the bridge—turn left.

At **0.1** mile, take the right fork and begin a short but steep climb. Reach a paved road at **0.3** mile and turn right. When the road divides at **0.5** mile, bear right. Now gravel, the road descends and then climbs. WHOA! At **1** mile, take an unmarked and easily missed singletrack on the right. The narrow trail immediately heads straight up at a discouraging rate. It's a hike-a-bike to the **1.3**-mile point. From here—on the eastern fin of Flag Mountain—the trail flutters up and down the edge of the long, narrow mountain, dropping and ascending at a hectic rate. At **2.1** miles, pass a rocky viewpoint: Mount Hood and the Zigzag River valley.

Just after a cliff on the left, the trail drops precipitously, and you'll need to get your butt over the back wheel or it's endo time. Pass by some cabins at **2.9** miles. Just around the corner, the trail ends at a dirt road—turn left. Thirty yards farther, turn right onto FR 20, paved. Stay on the paved road as it winds past cabins and descends to a bridge over Zigzag River. At **4** miles, just before reaching US 26, turn right onto an unmarked singletrack. At **4.2** miles, ignore a trail on the left and then immediately ignore one on the right. A few pedal strokes farther, reach a paved road and turn left. At **4.3** miles, reach the entrance road to Tollgate Campground and turn right, paralleling US 26. The paved road into the campground forks at **4.4** miles—bear left and immediately take the singletrack on the left. Pedal east on the trail, still paralleling the highway, and ignore several trails on the right that access the campground.

At **4.5** miles, pass through a paved parking area at the historic Tollgate. Continue straight on Pioneer Bridle Trail. Cross a dirt road at **4.6** miles. The trail becomes a doubletrack here. Stay to the left and you'll soon pick up the trail again. Cross dirt roads at **4.9** and **5.2** miles. The trail runs alongside the highway for a short stretch. Just after crossing the Zigzag River on a wood bridge, the trail eases to the right, following power lines, and the highway is no longer visible though it's still audible. After crossing another road, **5.6** miles, the trail is a wide, rocky rough-and-tumble. Cross another road at **6.5** miles. At **6.6** miles, reach a five-way intersection under power lines: Take the singletrack just to the right of the power lines. Reach a fork at **6.7** miles and turn right. Drop down a narrow trail to the parking area immediately below to complete the ride.

Gazetteer

Nearby camping: Camp Creek, Still Creek
Nearest food, drink, services: Zigzag, Government Camp

68 PORTLAND AND SALEM
Crosstown Trail
◉◉

Distance	5.8-mile out-and-back
Terrain	Wide singletrack, easy grades; 340-foot gain
Duration	1 to 2 hours
Travel	Portland—54 miles; Bend—100 miles
Skill level	Beginner
Season	Summer, fall
Maps	Green Trails: Government Camp, Mount Hood
Restrictions	None
More info	Mount Hood National Forest, Zigzag District, 503-622-7674, www.fs.fed.us/r6/mthood/

The Scoop

The name says it all—this is an easy (but definitely not boring) trail intended for beginners and families, a great introduction to singletrack. From Summit Ski Area at Government Camp, climb a short distance under the chairlift before the frolicking traverse begins. The trail is wide, smooth, and hard-packed, but there's plenty of zip and sway to keep your interest. It's heavily traveled, so watch out for other users.

Driving Directions

From Portland, drive east on US Highway 26. Just after milepost 52, pass Ski Bowl West on the right. At milepost 54, turn left onto Government Camp Loop at the village of Government Camp. Immediately bear right into the large paved parking lot at the foot of Summit Ski Area.

The Ride

From the large parking area in front of Summit Ski Area, ride toward the base of the chairlift. Follow the brown carbonate hiker/biker signs that mark the trail. Climb for a short distance under the chairlift. At **0.2** mile, the trail switchbacks to the left and traverses into a pine forest. Ride straight through the four-way at **0.3** mile. Stay on Crosstown Trail. Wide and nontechnical, the trail rolls and swells easily. At **0.9** mile, go straight at the four-way to stay on Crosstown Trail. Proceed straight through another four-way a short distance farther.

At **1.5** miles, reach a T and turn right, heading toward Glacier View Sno-Park. The trail, zippy and fast, gradually descends from a pure pine forest into a mixed pine and fir forest. When the trail divides at **2.5** miles, bear left. After a couple more turns in the trail, pass by a fen on the right. Reach a fork at **2.8** miles and veer left to stay on the main trail. At **2.9** miles, the trail kisses a paved road near Glacier View Sno-Park. Crosstown Trail ends here; Pioneer Bridle Trail, a more challenging trail, picks up and continues west. For this ride, turn around here and retrace your route. Remember: The elevation gain on the return trip will make the going somewhat slower, but it's not too tough. Return to Summit Ski Area at **5.8** miles.

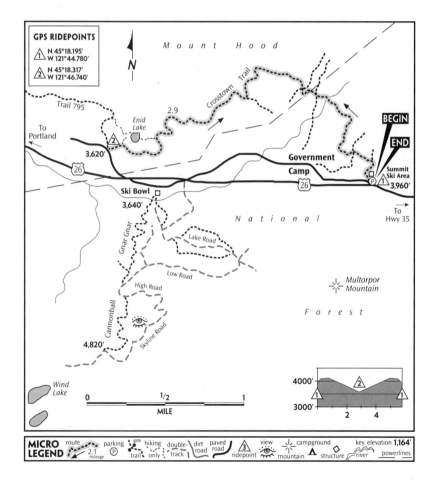

Gazetteer

Nearby camping: Still Creek, Camp Creek
Nearest food, drink, services: Government Camp, Zigzag

69 Still Creek

✿✿✿✿

Distance	19.5-mile loop
Terrain	Singletrack descent, dirt-road climb; 1,860-foot gain
Duration	3 to 5 hours
Travel	Portland—54 miles; Bend—100 miles
Skill level	Intermediate
Season	Summer, fall
Maps	Green Trails: Government Camp, Mount Hood
Restrictions	None
More info	Mount Hood National Forest, Zigzag District, 503-622-7674, www.fs.fed.us/r6/mthood/

The Scoop

I met a seventy-plus-year-old hiker on the Crosstown Trail who told me she walked the trail every day. Needless to say, take the heavily traveled Crosstown Trail segment of this ride at an easy pace. The Pioneer Bridle Trail, which picks up where the Crosstown Trail ends, offers more of a technical challenge, with lots of loose rocks and a few unexpectedly steep grades. After crossing US Highway 26 and skirting Camp Creek Campground, hop on Still Creek Trail, a sweet traverse that's easily my favorite stretch of the ride. When the trail ends at Still Creek Road, it's a long dirt-road climb back to the beginning. While it's not a spectacular loop, it's a fine ride with enough difficulty and distance to satiate most intermediate-plus riders.

Driving Directions

From Portland, drive east on US Highway 26. Just after milepost 52, pass Ski Bowl West on the right. At milepost 54, turn left onto Government Camp Loop at the village of Government Camp. Immediately bear right into the large paved parking lot at the foot of Summit Ski Area.

The Ride

From the large parking area in front of Summit Ski Area, ride toward the base of the chairlift. Follow the brown carbonate hiker/biker signs that mark the trail. Climb for a short distance under the chairlift. At **0.2** mile, the trail switchbacks to the left and traverses into a pine forest. Ride straight through

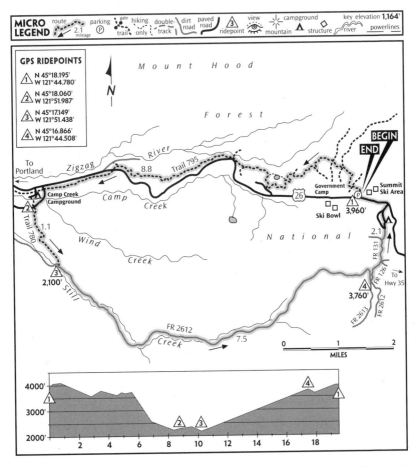

the four-way at **0.3** mile. Stay on Crosstown Trail, which winds easily. At **0.9** mile, go straight at the four-way to stay on Crosstown Trail. Proceed straight through another four-way a short distance farther.

At **1.5** miles, reach a T and turn right, heading toward Glacier View Sno-Park. The trail, zippy and fast, gradually descends from a pure pine forest into a mixed pine and fir forest. When the trail divides at **2.5** miles, bear left. After a couple more turns in the trail, pass by a fen on the right. Reach a fork at **2.8** miles and veer left to stay on the main trail. At **2.9** miles, the trail kisses a paved road near Glacier View Sno-Park—bear right onto Pioneer Bridle Trail and continue west. The trail is still wide, but the ups and downs are steeper and the riding is more technical, at times even hair-ball. Ignore the trail to Enid Lake on the right. At **3.7** miles, go right at the fork. The trail runs

Tunnel on the Pioneer Bridle Trail

right along US 26 for a stretch, then forks at **4.3** miles. Bear left and descend quickly to a short tunnel.

After a series of upsurges and steep, rocky drops, reach a fork at **6.9** miles and bear left, heading toward the highway. Carefully cross US 26 to the trail opposite. At **7** miles, the trail jogs right as it crosses a road. From here, Pioneer Bridle Trail is a rocky doubletrack. At **8.3** miles, reach a paved road, Forest Road 2632, and turn left. Stay on the paved road to **8.8** miles, then turn left on Still Creek Trail 780. The nearly perfect trail climbs into a lovely forest, then cuts a level southeast traverse on the steep lower slope of Tom Dick and Harry Mountain. At **9.9** miles, the trail drops sharply and then ends at Still Creek Road (FR 2612), the ride's low point. Turn left on the road and begin climbing.

The road ascends at a healthy, though not strenuous, rate. Watch for vehicles as you climb. After crossing Still Creek several times and burning a six-pack full of calories, reach a four-way at **17.4** miles and take a sharp left turn on FR 2612-126. At **17.8** miles, reach a T and turn left on FR 131. When the road divides at **18.1** miles, bear right. At **18.2** miles, turn right on FR 2650, paved, and pedal through Still Creek Campground. Climb to a fork at **18.7** miles, bear right, and climb further to US 26. When you arrive at the highway

Any questions?

at **18.9** miles, turn left and ride carefully west. At **19.5** miles, reach Summit Ski Area on the right to complete the loop.

Gazetteer

Nearby camping: Still Creek, Camp Creek
Nearest food, drink, services: Government Camp, Zigzag

70

Ski Bowl

⊕⊕⊕

Distance	5.3-mile loop
Terrain	Tough dirt-road climb followed by steep, rocky, loose descent; 1,160-foot gain; views
Duration	1 to 2 hours
Travel	Portland—53 miles; Bend—100 miles
Skill level	Expert
Season	Summer, fall
Maps	Green Trails: Government Camp
Restrictions	Ski Bowl Trail-Use permit
More info	Mount Hood National Forest, Zigzag District, 503-622-7674, www.fs.fed.us/r6/mthood/

The Scoop

Get ready for bikes with lots of front and rear travel—*boing, boing*—and riders with lots of padded, reinforced, and otherwise bulletproof gear—K-rash. The riding at Ski Bowl is all about full suspension and attitude, and the steep, death-cookie-covered trails—Cannonball? Gnar Gnar!—meet the challenge. Many riders come to Ski Bowl to ride the chairlifts up and bomb down the ski runs, dirt roads, and rocky trails. If you suit up and have the right downhill bike, it's a blast. The route described here makes you earn that pell-mell descent—a tough dirt-road climb followed by a rocky descent. You'll get a good workout and avoid the cost of a lift ticket.

Driving Directions

From Portland, drive east on US Highway 26 for about 50 miles. One-half mile past milepost 52, turn right at Mount Hood Ski Bowl West. Park in the large paved lot.

The Ride

From the parking area, ride down toward the chairlift and then bear left and climb. The gravelly road is steep and loose. At **0.4** mile, reach a T and turn left on Lake Road. Immediately ignore a spur on the left, staying on the main road. As you ascend, pass by South Trail on the right and North Trail on the left. At **1** mile, bypass the same two trails again. Almost immediately, reach a four-way intersection and take a hard right on Low Road. Ignore Horse Trail on the left as you spin up the dirt road in a low gear, gaining elevation in fits and starts. At a fork, **1.7** miles, stay to the left.

At **2** miles, stay on the road as you cross over Gnar Gnar Trail. The road switchbacks up to the left and becomes High Road. Pass the historic warming hut on the left and continue up the main road, ignoring lesser spurs on the right. At **2.4** miles, the road begins a series of steep, difficult switchbacks, and its name changes to Skyline Road. As you attain the top of the ridgeline

Sign your will here

at **2.7** miles, the climb eases. Reach a notch in the ridge, **3.3** miles, that a a perfect view of south Mount Hood. About a hundred feet farther along , road, turn right on Cannonball Trail. Sign your will before descending.

After a jarring, hair-ball descent, Cannonball Trail ends at High Road, **4** miles—turn left and descend. At **4.2** miles, turn left onto Gnar Gnar Trail. Reach a fork at **4.4** miles and bear right to remain on Gnar Gnar Trail. The trail ends at **5.1** miles. Turn left and coast down to the base of the ski area, **5.3** miles, to complete the loop.

Gazetteer

Nearby camping: Still Creek, Camp Creek
Nearest food, drink, services: Government Camp, Zigzag

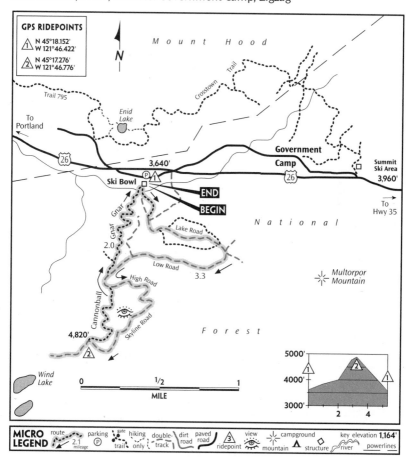

nothy Lake

Distance	8.2-mile out-and-back (15-mile option)
Terrain	Wide, flat trail; 70-foot gain; views
Duration	1 to 2 hours
Travel	Portland—79 miles; Bend—100 miles
Skill level	Beginner
Season	Summer, fall
Maps	Green Trails: High Rock
Restrictions	None
More info	Mount Hood National Forest, Zigzag District, 503-622-7674, www.fs.fed.us/r6/mthood/

The Scoop

I designed this ride for beginning mountain bikers. The trail is hard-packed and level but still somewhat zippy, and first-time singletrackers will love it. Intermediate and advanced riders will probably choose the longer option

Mount Hood across Timothy Lake

that circles the lake. Either way, Timothy Lake is a lovely place, with long views of the surrounding Cascades across the water. On summer weekends the lake can be packed with fishermen, the campgrounds full of kids, and the trails crowded. Plan ahead and ride carefully.

Driving Directions

From Portland, drive about 56 miles east on US Highway 26. Just after passing Ski Bowl, Summit, and Timberline Ski Areas, pass by State Highway 35 on the left. Continue ten more miles east on US 26. Just past milepost 66, turn right on Forest Road 42 (Skyline Road) toward Timothy Lake, and set your odometer to zero. At 8.7 miles, turn right on FR 57 and continue toward Timothy Lake. Pass four campgrounds on the right, then bear right to cross the short

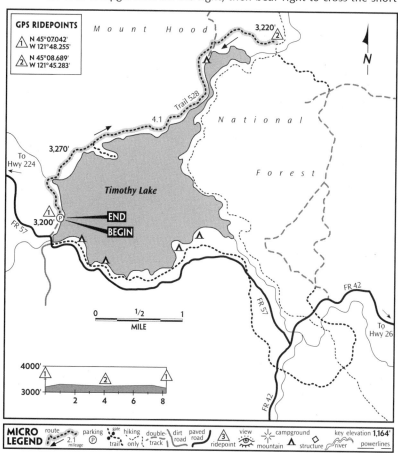

dam at 12.4 miles. Immediately beyond the dam, turn right on a dirt road. Bear to the right and then left, then park at the trailhead, 12.8 miles.

The Ride

Timothy Lake Trail 528 takes off from the trailhead at the lakeshore. The trail, wide and smooth, rolls easily through a grand-fir forest and affords numerous views of the lake. At **1** mile, reach a fork and bear left (the short spur to the right out to Meditation Point is a great addition). The wide, level trail has a surprising amount of zip, and it'll bring a smile to even expert cyclists. At **2.7** miles, ignore a lesser trail on the right. Beginning at **2.9** miles, ride past a campground on the right. Cross the campground road at **3.2** miles and continue on Trail 528. Ignore another trail on the right at **3.5** miles. After some more noodling through a nice forest, reach a T with the Pacific Crest Trail at **4.1** miles. Turn around here and retrace your route back to the trailhead, **8.2** miles.

Option

The Pacific Crest Trail runs north and south along the east side of Timothy Lake, and since bikes are prohibited from the PCT, there has been no way to circle the lake by bike. However, recent trailwork has made a loop around the lake possible. From the 4.1-mile point above, turn right on the Pacific Crest Trail, cross the bridge, and immediately bear left on Trail 537. Follow Trail 537, which utilizes new singletrack in some sections and old roadbeds in others, toward Joe Graham Horse Camp at FR 42. As the trail crosses FR 42, bear left and follow Trail 522. Trail 522 crosses the PCT and becomes Trail 534. Stay on Trail 534 as it recrosses FR 42, passes the historic ranger station, and crosses FR 57. From here, Trail 534 passes by (and through) four campgrounds and finally ends at FR 57 next to the dam at the west end of Timothy Lake. Turn right on FR 57 and cross the short dam. Immediately across the dam, turn right on the dirt road and pedal back to the trailhead. The entire intermediate loop clocks in at about 15 miles.

Gazetteer

Nearby camping: Pine Point, Hoodview
Nearest food, drink, services: Government Camp

72 Dry Ridge

☼☼☼☼

Distance	19.3-mile one-way shuttle (37.9-mile epic option)
Terrain	Strenuous dirt-road and singletrack climbing and hike-a-biking, epic descent; 4,000-foot loss
Duration	4 to 7 hours
Travel	Portland—62 miles
Skill level	Expert
Season	Summer, fall
Maps	Green Trails: High Rock, Fish Creek Mountain
Restrictions	None
More info	Mount Hood National Forest, Clackamas River District, 503-630-8700, www.fs.fed.us/r6/mthood/

The Scoop

A cursory glance at the ride stats above caused the BMXer to salivate, the single-speed cyclist's head to spin, the weekend warrior's legs to stop aching.

Lake Serene from the top of Trail 517

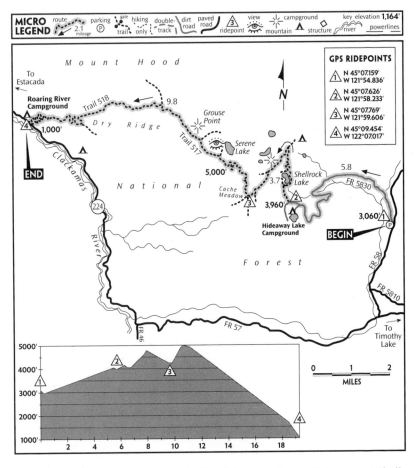

A 4,000-foot descent! No such luck. The ride up to Grouse Point—past Shell-rock Lake and Cache Meadows—and then down Dry Ridge ends up being much more difficult than the nineteen miles and freaking, eye-popping descent would indicate. The route climbs about 2,000 feet on dirt road and singletrack, several miles of which are a probable hike-a-bike. The views aren't much, though the forest is beautiful, and the descent isn't buffed out—it's ragged, sometimes overgrown, and technical—but you don't turn down a nine-mile, 4,000-foot descent, whatever the conditions. If you really want to ratchet up the calorie burn, try the epic loop option. Just be certain to bring along enough water and plenty of sweet doughy things.

Driving Directions

From Portland, drive southeast on State Highway 224 (Clackamas Highway). About 17.5 miles past Estacada, leave a car at Roaring River Campground on the left. Continue southeast on Hwy 224. About 26 miles past Estacada, turn left on Forest Road 57, and set your odometer to zero. At 7.3 miles, turn left on FR 58. At 10.3 miles, reach the junction of FR 58 and FR 5830, which is on the left. Park in the gravel pullout at this junction.

The Ride

From the junction of FR 58 and FR 5830, take FR 5830 and start pedaling. After a very short descent to cross a Shellrock Creek tributary, the road heads west and climbs toward Frazier Mountain. The gravelly road, which is exposed to the sun most of the way, ascends at a steady rate. After about **3.5** miles, the road bends to the left, crosses the creek, and switchbacks up toward Hideaway Lake. At **5.4** miles, pass the entrance to Hideaway Campground on the left. Stay on the main road to a crest, then descend to find Shellrock Lake Trail 700 on the right at **5.8** miles.

The rocky trail climbs through a clearcut, then traverses into a fir forest. After a short descent, reach a fork at **6.3** miles and turn right. Wind counterclockwise around the east side of Shellrock Lake. The trail is indistinct in spots as it passes through several campsites. Keep going around the lake to a fork at **6.6** miles and bear right toward Frazier Turnaround. From here, it's a hike-a-bike as the rocky, root-strewn trail climbs away from the lake. If the mosquitoes are out, this can be a frustrating segment of trail. WOOF! Reach a T at **7.5** miles and turn left on Trail 517 toward Cache Meadow. The trail, wide and rocky but more ridable, edges around the east face of Frazier Mountain.

At **8.1** miles, you'll gather some momentum (at last!) as the wide trail heads downhill. WHOA! At **8.3** miles, reach an easily missed fork and turn left on Grouse Point Trail 517. The singletrack corkscrews down toward the mosquito quag of Cache Meadow. It's a fast, somewhat technical descent that's over all too quickly. When the trail divides at **9.2** miles, go right. After passing a shelter, reach a four-way at **9.5** miles and turn right, continuing on Trail 517. The trail wends along the east side of Cache Meadow before heading up the steep bank toward Grouse Point. This climb is another probable hike-a-bike—the trail is steep and technical. WOOF! At **10.4** miles, the trail crests the route's high point and noodles along the top of the ridge.

At **10.6** miles, the trail divides. The short spur to the right leads to a viewpoint: Check out the view down to Lake Serene. Go back and take the left prong. Be sure to take a good break—a forearm massage wouldn't hurt either—because it's here that the romping nine-mile, 4,000-foot descent begins. Reach a fork at **11.4** miles and go left toward FR 4611. The trail, overgrown in places, loose and rocky in others, cuts a steep traverse down the wide ridge. At **13.5** miles, reach a fork and bear left on Dry Ridge Trail 518 toward Roaring River Campground. The trail whips westward, dropping at a rapid rate. *Wheee!* Your tear ducts will open up—even with glasses—and your ears will begin to pop.

Hit the first switchback at **15.7** miles. The trail forks on a scree slope at **16.1** miles—turn right and head toward Hwy 224. From here, the trail is quite technical, narrow and steep, ragged and rocky, as it drops off the precipitous western prow of Dry Ridge, and short segments may need to be walked. **WHOA!** The narrow tread switchbacks and hugs the fern-covered slope. At **19.1** miles, reach a four-way, turn left, and walk down to Roaring River Campground. Take the campground road out to Hwy 224 to complete the ride, **19.3** miles.

Option

Only one car to work with? Begin the ride at Roaring River Campground to create an epic loop. From the campground, pedal south on Hwy 224. After about 8.3 miles, turn left on FR 57. At 15.6 miles, turn left on FR 58. At 18.6 miles, all of which have been paved, turn left on FR 5830 and then follow the directions above. The full loop clocks in at 37.9 miles.

Gazetteer

Nearby camping: Roaring River, Fish Creek
Nearest food, drink, services: Estacada

73

Clackamas Riverside

✹✹✹

Distance	8.2-mile out-and-back
Terrain	Winding riverside singletrack; 130-foot gain
Duration	2 to 3 hours
Travel	Portland—52 miles
Skill level	Intermediate
Season	Summer, fall
Maps	Green Trails: Fish Creek Mountain
Restrictions	USFS Trail Park Pass required
More info	Mount Hood National Forest, Clackamas River District, 503-630-8700, www.fs.fed.us/r6/mthood/

The Scoop

Clackamas Riverside Trail 723 is a beautiful singletrack along the east side of the river through pockets of old growth. Downriver from Trail 723, the eight-mile-long Clackamas River Trail 715 was recently closed to mountain bikes. There are already too few trails open to mountain bikes—especially on the west side of the mountains—to lose eight-mile stretches very often. But some of the same pressures that closed that trail—primarily overcrowding—are in play on this one as well. Ride gently and be a courteous trail user.

Driving Directions

From Portland, drive southeast on State Highway 224 (Clackamas Highway). About 26 miles past Estacada, Hwy 224 becomes Forest Road 46 as you pass Ripplebrook Campground on the left. Cross Oak Grove Fork of Clackamas River and bear right on FR 46; then immediately turn right into Rainbow Campground. Park here.

The Ride

The Riverside Trail 723 begins from the far end of the campground loop road. After winding along Oak Grove Fork of the Clackamas River, the trail meets the main channel of Clackamas River and heads south. There are a few narrow bridges and wood walkways. Reach a fork, **2.5** miles, and bear right. Reach another set of stairs at **4.1** miles. Riverside Campground is located just

An August afternoon on the Clackamas Riverside Trail

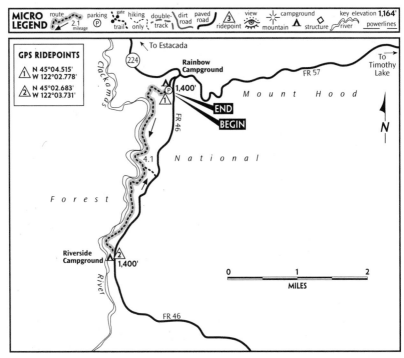

MICRO LEGEND | route 2.1 mileage | parking Ⓟ | gate hiking trail only | double-track | dirt road | paved road | ③ ridepoint | view mountain | campground structure | key elevation **1,164'** river powerlines

GPS RIDEPOINTS

⚠1 N 45°04.515'
W 122°02.778'

⚠2 N 45°02.683'
W 122°03.731'

To Estacada

224

Rainbow Campground

1,400'

END

BEGIN

FR 57

To Timothy Lake

M o u n t   H o o d

N a t i o n a l

4.1

FR 46

F o r e s t

Riverside Campground
1,400'

River

FR 46

N

0   1   2
MILES

beyond the stairs. Turn around here and pedal back to Rainbow Campground, **8.2** miles.

Gazetteer

Nearby camping: Rainbow, Riverside
Nearest food, drink, services: Estacada

74 Red Lake

❀❀❀❀

Distance	15.5-mile loop (12.5-mile option)
Terrain	Gravel-road climb, technical singletrack climbs and descents, lots of pushing; **820-foot gain**; views
Duration	4 to 6 hours
Travel	Portland—84 miles; Salem—84 miles
Skill level	Expert
Season	Summer, fall
Maps	Green Trails: Breitenbush
Restrictions	None
More info	Mount Hood National Forest, Clackamas River District, 503-630-8700, www.fs.fed.us/r6/mthood/

The Scoop

Olallie is the Chinook word for "berries," but when I started out from Olallie Meadows, I was surrounded by a lot more mosquitoes than berries, by factors of a million, at least. This is a great loop for advanced to expert riders, past many sweet mountain lakes and through a beautiful pine forest. But the trail demands a high skill level, so be ready for several miles of hike-a-bike. The uneven, rock-strewn trail climbs and drops and climbs, and even the descents are slow. You can't ever really open it up.

Driving Directions

From Portland, drive southeast on State Highway 224 (Clackamas Highway). About 26 miles past Estacada, Hwy 224 becomes Forest Road 46 as you pass Rainbow Campground. Stay on FR 46 toward Olallie Lake Scenic Area. About 22 miles past Rainbow Campground on FR 46, turn left on FR 4690 and set your odometer to zero. Stay on FR 4690, ignoring several roads on either side. At 8.3 miles, turn right on FR 4220. At 9.9 miles, bear right and park at the entrance to Olallie Meadow Campground.

From Salem, drive east on Hwy 22 toward Detroit. Just after crossing Breitenbush River, turn left on FR 46. Proceed about 24 miles northeast on FR 46, then turn right on FR 4690 and set your odometer to zero. Stay on FR 4690, ignoring several roads on either side. At 8.3 miles, turn right on FR 4220. At

Wall Lake with Potato Butte beyond

9.9 miles, bear right and park at the entrance to Olallie Meadow Campground.

The Ride

From the entrance to Olallie Meadows Campground, pedal up FR 4220 toward Olallie Lake. The gravel on the road is sometimes loose, making traction difficult, but the grade isn't too steep. Stay on the main road as you climb. Pass under some power lines at **1.3** miles. Bypass the entrance to Lower Lake Campground on the right at **3.1** miles. Reach a fork in the road at Olallie Lake, **3.9** miles, and bear right to remain on FR 4220. Mount Jefferson peeks up over the ridge across the lake. At **4.2** miles, turn right onto Red Lake Trail 719. Brushed granite boulders, scattered over the landscape, white and gray, mute the greens of low mountain hemlock and pine, and the trail climbs awkwardly through these big rocks. At **4.9** miles, reach a fork and go right. The trail skirts by a series of ponds, then passes a lake at **5.2** miles. At **5.3** miles, reach a T and turn right. Ride straight through a four-way at **5.5** miles. The climb ends a short distance farther as the trail cascades through a mogul run of granite.

The trail eases into a flat, pine-forested swale between Twin Peaks, Double Peaks, and Potato Butte; at **6.7** miles, it forks. Bear left, continuing out Red Lake Trail 719. (Note: From here, the route spurs out to Red Lake and then returns to this intersection, a three-mile out-and-back that you can skip by turning right on Trail 706 and picking up the directions below beginning at the 9.7-mile mark.) The narrow trail, a jungle gym of rocks and roots, passes

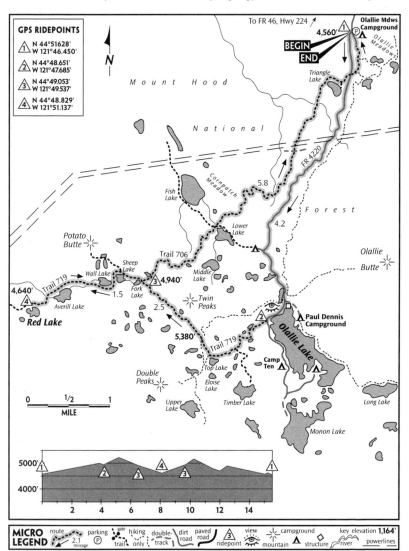

four lakes on the way to Red Lake. At **7** miles, reach a fork and bear left. Stay on the main trail. At **8.2** miles, reach Red Lake, a great place for a picnic. Turn around here and take trail 719 back to the junction with Trail 706, which you reach at **9.7** miles.

At the trail junction at **9.7** miles, turn left and ride northeast on Trail 706 toward Lower Lake. After a few tire rotations, pass a lake on the left. Unless you are both technically skilled and very fit, the next four miles require a fair amount of pushing. **WOOF!** Crest a high point at **10.3** miles and begin a technical descent punctuated by huge rocks. Reach a four-way at Lower Lake, **11.6** miles, and continue straight ahead toward Triangle Lake. (Note: You can bail out here by turning right and riding to Lower Campground and then down FR 4220. This shaves two miles and a fair amount of hike-a-bike from the ride.) Cross an easy ridge and drop to Cornpatch Meadow at **12** miles. The hike-a-bike continues as you ascend another ridge.

The trail, ragged in sections, climbs and falls in sharp, irregular spikes. At **13.5** miles, cross a dirt road and then pass under a set of power lines. The trail is faint here and difficult to follow; meanwhile, the ups and downs continue to force the occasional push. There's a horse camp at Triangle Lake, so watch out for equestrians. The trail swings around the north side of Triangle Lake at **14.6** miles. At **14.8** miles, reach a fork and bear left. Cross FR 4220 at **14.9** miles, continuing down Trail 706 on the opposite side. The trail immediately divides—go left. At **15.1** miles, when the trail divides again, bear left. Arrive at the south end of Olallie Meadows Campground a short distance farther. Pedal north and reach FR 4220 at **15.5** miles to compass the loop.

Gazetteer

Nearby camping: Paul Dennis, Camp Ten
Nearest food, drink, services: Detroit, Estacada

75 Molalla Rim

⊕⊕⊕

Distance	6.9-mile lollipop
Terrain	Dirt-road and singletrack climbing and descending, some steep sections; 760-foot gain
Duration	1 to 2 hours
Travel	Portland—37 miles; Salem—40 miles
Skill level	Intermediate
Season	Spring, summer, fall
Maps	Molalla River Trails: Loop Trails
Restrictions	Closed November through April
More info	Bureau of Land Management, Salem District, 503-375-5646, www.or.blm.gov/salem/html/rec/mollalla.htm

The Scoop

The Molalla River Recreation Area, owned and managed by the BLM, makes a great trail-use story. Molalla River Watch (an environmental group), a couple of mountain-bike clubs (Salem's Merry Cranksters and Portland's PUMP), and others have worked together with the BLM to create an outstanding shared-use trail system. These groups have been involved in the planning and construction of many of the trails, which range from easy roadbeds to steep, nasty singletrack. About twenty miles of trails crisscross the area and more are slated. This process of trail building and increasing trail use has had the collateral benefit of deterring (though not eliminating) trailhead theft and illegal dumping along the river. The route described below uses Rim Trail and Huckleberry Trail to circle the Loop Trails area at Molalla, but with the criss-crossing maze of great trails here, exploration is the real fun.

Driving Directions

From Portland, drive south to Oregon City. From Oregon City, drive a little more than 12 miles south on State Highway 213, turn left on South Molalla Road, and set your odometer to zero. After 3 miles, reach a stoplight in the town of Molalla and turn left on East Main Street (Hwy 211). At 3.6 miles, turn right on South Mathias Road, heading south toward Feyrer Park. At 3.9 miles, bear left on South Feyrer Park Road and continue to follow the signs toward Feyrer Park. At 5.6 miles, pass Feyrer Park, cross Molalla River, and reach a

T—turn right on South Dickey Prairie Road. At 11.2 miles, turn right on Molalla Forest Road, following the Molalla Recreation Corridor sign. At 14.8 miles, turn right into the Hardy Creek trailhead parking area.

From Salem, drive northeast on Hwy 213 toward Molalla. Turn right on Hwy 211 and drive through the town of Molalla. On the eastern outskirts of town, turn right on South Mathias Road toward Feyrer Park and set your odometer to zero. At 0.3 mile, bear left on South Feyrer Park Road and continue to follow the signs toward Feyrer Park. At 2 miles, pass Feyrer Park, cross Molalla River, and reach a T—turn right on South Dickey Prairie Road. At 7.6 miles, turn right on Molalla Forest Road, following the Molalla Recreation Corridor sign. At 11.2 miles, turn right into the Hardy Creek trailhead parking area.

The Ride

The wide trail, which begins next to the BLM kiosk, hogs through a thicket of blackberry before climbing steeply up the hillside. At **0.3** mile, reach a T and turn right. When the trail divides at **0.4** mile, bear left on Rim Trail and keep climbing. Immediately bypass a singletrack on the left and continue up the main trail. Around **0.5** mile, the trail narrows to singletrack and heads south. The trail is hard-packed and smooth, and it ascends the wide ridge—a mixed

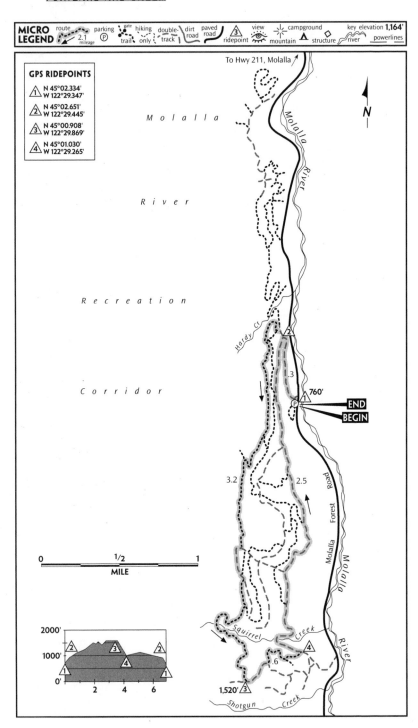

MICRO LEGEND

route 2.1 mileage | parking ℗ | gate | hiking trail only | double-track | dirt road | paved road | △ 3 ridepoint | view | mountain | campground | structure | river | powerlines | key elevation **1,164'**

GPS RIDEPOINTS

△1 N 45°02.334' W 122°29.347'

△2 N 45°02.651' W 122°29.445'

△3 N 45°00.908' W 122°29.869'

△4 N 45°01.030' W 122°29.265'

To Hwy 211, Molalla

Molalla

River

Recreation

Corridor

Molalla River

Hardy Cr

2

3

760'

P 1

END

BEGIN

3.2

2.5

Molalla Forest Road

Molalla River

0   1/2   1
MILE

Squirrel Creek

4

6

1,520' 3

Shotgun Creek

2000'
1000'
0'

2   4   6

forest to the east, pastureland to the west—in fits and starts. At **0.7** m.
to the right at a fork. When the trail forks at **1.4** miles, bear right to rei.
on Rim Trail. Ignore a trail on the right at **1.6** miles.

At **2.1** miles, reach a T and turn right, climbing up a wide trail. Bypass
Bear Woods Trail on the on the left at **2.3** miles. Almost immediately, turn
right on a singletrack, following the Rim Trail sign. At **2.5** miles, reach a fork
and bear right. The trail drops sharply, then climbs again through a recent
clearcut. The route here, with a rocky, loose, erratic tread, is hardscrabble and
may require a few short pushes. At **3.5** miles, reach a fork and go left on Bob-
cat Trail, a wide trail that descends eastward. **WHOA!** At **3.7** miles, turn left
on Squirrel Creek Trail, which is easily missed. From here, the trail corkscrews
steeply down the side of the ridge. At **3.8** miles, turn left to remain on the
singletrack. When the trail dumps out at a dirt road, turn left. The road,
known as Huckleberry Trail, traverses north. Pass Annie's Cabin on the right.
Pass by numerous trails on the left. At **5.8** miles, after a series of easy undulations, the road descends at a fast rate. At **6.6** miles, reach a fork and turn
right. Descend to the trailhead to complete the ride, **6.9** miles.

Gazetteer

Nearby camping: Feyrer Park
Nearest food, drink, services: Molalla

lalla North

...nce	5.7-mile figure eight
Terrain	Wide and narrow trails, some loose and steep, with some pushing; 350-foot gain
Duration	1 to 2 hours
Travel	Portland—37 miles; Salem—40 miles
Skill level	Advanced
Season	Spring, summer, fall
Maps	Molalla River Trails: North End Trails
Restrictions	Closed November through April
More info	Bureau of Land Management, Salem District, 503-375-5646, www.or.blm.gov/salem/html/rec/mollalla.htm

The Scoop

The trails accessible from Hardy Creek trailhead along the Molalla River are divided into three areas: South End Trails, Loop Trails, and North End Trails. South End Trails are still being assessed, planned, and constructed, while the Loop Trails, like Rim Trail (ride 75, Molalla Rim), are fun, heavily used, and ridable by most intermediates. Meanwhile, the trails in the north end are generally more advanced, rocky and technical in places, and traversed less frequently. This route tours the North End Trails, and includes Macbeth Loop, an intimate, twisting singletrack that's one of my favorites at Molalla. But, with about twenty miles of trails for all ability levels, the high exploration potential is really the highlight of the trail system here. Big thanks should go to Molalla River Watch, the Merry Cranksters, and Portland United Mountain Pedalers for the vision, stewardship, and hard work they've put into the trails, as well as to the BLM for being open to an expansion and enhancement of the system. Note: Despite a marked decrease in car prowls, vehicles parked at this trailhead—as at many trailheads—still get broken into occasionally.

Driving Directions

From Portland, drive south to Oregon City. From Oregon City, drive a little more than 12 miles south on State Highway 213, turn left on South Molalla Road, and set your odometer to zero. After 3 miles, reach a stoplight in the town of Molalla and turn left on East Main Street (State Hwy 211). At 3.6

Bridge over Hardy Creek

miles, turn right on South Mathias Road, heading south toward Feyrer Park. At 3.9 miles, bear left on South Feyrer Park Road and continue to follow the signs toward Feyrer Park. At 5.6 miles, pass Feyrer Park, cross Molalla River, and reach a T—turn right on South Dickey Prairie Road. At 11.2 miles, turn right on Molalla Forest Road, following the sign for the Molalla Recreation Corridor. At 14.8 miles, turn right into the Hardy Creek trailhead parking area.

From Salem, drive northeast on Hwy 213 toward Molalla. Turn right on Hwy 211 and drive through the town of Molalla. On the eastern outskirts of town, turn right on South Mathias Road toward Feyrer Park and set your odometer to zero. At 0.3 mile, bear left on South Feyrer Park Road and continue to follow the signs toward Feyrer Park. At 2 miles, pass Feyrer Park, cross Molalla River, and reach a T—turn right on South Dickey Prairie Road. At 7.6 miles, turn right on Molalla Forest Road, following the sign for the Molalla Recreation Corridor. At 11.2 miles, turn right into the Hardy Creek trailhead parking area.

The Ride

The trail begins near the BLM kiosk. After cutting through a thicket of black-berry, the wide, rocky trail climbs steeply up the hillside. At **0.3** mile, reach a

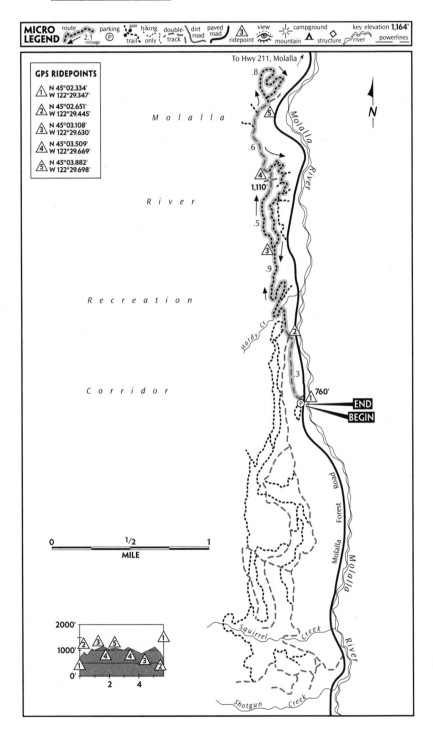

MICRO LEGEND — route 2.1 mileage · parking Ⓟ · gate · hiking trail · double-track · dirt road · paved road · △3 ridepoint · view · mountain · campground · ▲ structure · ◇ · river · key elevation 1,164' · powerlines

GPS RIDEPOINTS

△1 N 45°02.334'
   W 122°29.347'
△2 N 45°02.651'
   W 122°29.445'
△3 N 45°03.108'
   W 122°29.630'
△4 N 45°03.509'
   W 122°29.669'
△5 N 45°03.882'
   W 122°29.698'

To Hwy 211, Molalla

.8

Molalla

△5

.6

△4
1,110'

River

.5

△3

.9

Recreation

Hardy Cr.

△2

.3

Corridor

760' △

Ⓟ END
   BEGIN

N

0   1/2   1
MILE

Molalla Forest Road

Molalla River

Squirrel Creek

Shotgun Creek

2000'
△2 △3 △5
1000' △4 △3
△1   △4 △3 △2
0'
   2   4

T and turn right. When the trail divides at **0.4** mile, bear right on Looney's Trail. After a short level stretch, the trail narrows and switchbacks down to cross over Hardy Creek. The trail climbs steeply out of the drainage and crosses a recent clearcut. Reach a fork at **0.7** mile and bear left. The trail is loose and rocky, and the section between the creek and the wide trail along the top of the clearcut at **0.9** mile will be a hike-a-bike for most. At **1.2** miles, reach a fork and bear left. At **1.3** miles, bear left onto Amanda's Trail and ride back into the woods.

At **1.6** miles, ride straight through a four-way. Ignore Mark's Trail on the right at **1.7** miles, continuing straight on Amanda's Trail. From here, stay on the main trail, ignoring two trails on the left as you gently descend. At **2.3** miles, reach a fork and turn left on Macbeth Loop. After a few spins of the pedals, reach a faint, unmarked fork and bear left. The trail, fun and winding, alternates between short climbs and descents and slow noodling through the forest. At **3** miles, reach the same faint, unmarked fork and bear left (although I'd recommend a couple more circuits around Macbeth Loop). Reach a T a short glide farther and turn right, ascending on a wide trail.

During the easy climb, ignore two trails on the right. At **3.6** miles, turn left on Mark's Trail and begin a twisting descent. When the trail forks at **3.9** miles, go right. Reach a T at **4** miles and turn left. Reach another T at **4.1** miles and turn right. A short distance farther, reach a four-way and turn right on AmeriCorps Alley Trail. From here, the trail winds steeply up the clearcut hillside, and short sections may have to be walked. During the ascent, the trail becomes Clifford's Crossing Trail. At **4.5** miles, reach Amanda's Trail and bear left. At **4.8** miles, bear left again and descend—ignoring a lesser trail on the left—back to Hardy Creek. Cross the creek at **5.2** miles and climb south. After bypassing a trail on the right, turn left at **5.4** miles and descend. Reach the trailhead at **5.7** miles to complete the figure eight.

Gazetteer

Nearby camping: Feyrer Park
Nearest food, drink, services: Molalla

77 Dimple Hill

⊕⊕⊕

Distance	8.2-mile out-and-back
Terrain	Wide and narrow trails, some tough climbing; **980-foot gain**
Duration	1 to 3 hours
Travel	Portland—80 miles; Salem—35 miles
Skill level	Intermediate
Season	Spring, summer, fall
Maps	McDonald Dunn Forest Multiple-Use Road and Trail Map
Restrictions	Closed November through mid-April
More info	Oregon State University, McDonald Dunn Research Forest, 541-737-4452, www.cof.orst.edu/resfor/rec/purpose.sht

The Scoop

McDonald Dunn Research Forest, owned by Oregon State University and managed by its forestry department, spreads north from the paved edges of Corvallis. Being so close to town, the forest's trail system is usually busy with runners, walkers, equestrians, picnickers, and mountain bikers, many of whom start out right from home. Despite the maze of trails and roads—making the area ripe for exploration—the system is often crowded, so ride carefully. This route, an out-and-back to the top of Dimple Hill, features a healthy singletrack climb followed by a rocking descent on Dan's Trail. It'll get your adrenaline flowing. The lower section of this trail is closed in the winter, but the upper segment of Dan's Trail stays open year-round. Don't ride off-trail: Sensitive research projects can be damaged, costing lots of money, screwing up important data, and possibly wrecking someone's Ph.D. chances. In addition to the information number listed above, the forest maintains a recorded hotline: 541-737-4434.

Driving Directions

From Portland or Salem, drive south on Interstate 5 to exit 234B (about sixty-five miles south of Portland and twenty south of Salem). Zero out your odometer as the end of the interstate ramp becomes Pacific Boulevard Southeast. At 1 mile, Pacific Boulevard becomes US Highway 20 westbound toward Corvallis. At 2.1 miles, exit to the right, following US 20. At 10.8 miles, turn right on Conifer Boulevard. At 12.2 miles, turn left on State Highway 99

Slingshot down Dimple Hill

West (Pacific Highway West). At 12.5 miles, turn right on Walnut Boulevard. At 13.6 miles, turn right on Northwest Highland Drive. At 14.5 miles, turn left on Lester Avenue. At 15.4 miles, reach the trailhead at the end of the road.

The Ride

Several trails exit from the parking area at the end of the road—take the one on the right beyond the yellow gate. The trail, a narrow old road, immediately forks: Bear right and begin climbing. Pass by a singletrack on the left and then on the right as you ascend. At **0.5** mile, the wide trail levels somewhat and climbs more gently. Ignore two faint trails on the left. The way bends to the right, bypassing two more faint trails on the left, and affords views of Corvallis. Continue up and around to the right on the main trail. Just past a bench on the right at **0.8** mile, reach a fork and bear right onto a narrow trail.

The singletrack descends quickly. Reach a four-way at **1** mile and turn right. After a few spins of the pedals, reach a fork and bear right on Dan's Trail. Ignore a trail back to the left at **1.1** miles. At **1.2** miles, as you pass under a set of power lines, ignore another trail on the left. From here, the trail, covered with roots but still fast, descends vigorously, corkscrewing down

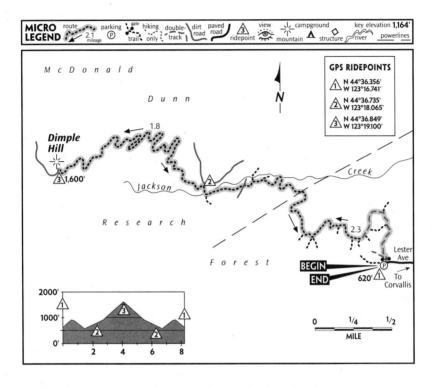

the hillside. At **1.6** miles, ignore a faint trail back on the right. A couple pedal strokes farther, reach a fork and bear left toward Dimple Hill. Cross a gravel road and continue along Dan's Trail. At **2.1** miles, ignore a lesser trail on the left and then drop to a bridge. At **2.3** miles, the trail kisses a dirt road—bear left on the singletrack and stick it into a low gear.

At **2.8** miles, pass straight through a four-way. The hard-packed trail switchbacks up the hillside through fir, bigleaf maple, and oak. It's a tough climb without much of a break, but it's all ridable. WOOF! At **4.1** miles, reach the top of Dimple Hill. The trail ends here at a gravel road. Turn around and retrace your route. The first segment—a rocket down the south slope of Dimple Hill—is fun, but remember to watch for walkers, runners, and other cyclists on the trail. Return to the parking area at **8.2** miles.

Gazetteer

Nearby camping: Big Elk (primitive), Willamette City Park
Nearest food, drink, services: Corvallis